MASTERS OF NOTHING

MATTHEW HANCOCK & NADHIM ZAHAWI

MASTERS
OF
NOTHING

HUMAN NATURE, BIG FINANCE AND THE
FIGHT FOR THE SOUL OF CAPITALISM

Biteback Publishing

Published in Great Britain in 2013 by
Biteback Publishing Ltd
Westminster Tower
3 Albert Embankment
London SE1 7SP
Revised edition copyright © Matthew Hancock and Nadhim Zahawi 2013

First published in Great Britain in 2011.

Matthew Hancock and Nadhim Zahawi have asserted their rights under the
Copyright, Designs and Patents Act 1988 to be identified as the author of this work.

ISBN 978-1-84954-456-6

10 9 8 7 6 5 4 3 2 1

A CIP catalogue record for this book is available from the British Library.

Set in Garamond

Printed and bound in Great Britain by
CPI Group (UK) Ltd, Croydon CR0 4YY

To Martha, my inspiration
To Lana, Doody, Fali and Mia

CONTENTS

ACKNOWLEDGMENTS

We both owe our thanks to our staff at the House of Commons. We could not have written the book without our team of researchers, William Hensher, Jennifer Donnellan, Simon Smethurst-McIntyre and Luke Maynard, who worked on this book on top of their day-to-day responsibilities, and Helen Thomas, who gave up her own time. We are, as ever, grateful to Helyn Dudley and Marie Sallergard, who kept our lives in order while we wrote it. We are very grateful to Nick Boles, Janan Ganesh, Michael Hart, Peter Kellner, Adam Levinson, Jesse Norman, Stephan Shakespeare and Nick Walmsley, who read and commented on early drafts, whose comments improved the book immeasurably and who kept us going. We are grateful to Iain Dale, Sam Carter and our editor Lewis Carpenter at Biteback Publishing, who were a pleasure to work with and taught us how publishing works.

We conducted a wide range of interviews, including with some who prefer to remain anonymous. All were fascinating, many were passionate and some deliciously indiscreet. Among others, we are very grateful to: Henry Angest, Mark Bathgate, Meyrick Chapman, Greg Hands MP, Stephen King, Sir Andrew Large, Ruth Lea, Vincent Reinhart, Seamus Smith and Lord Turner.

YouGov helped us explore aspects of human behavior by carrying out interviews and polls and we are especially grateful to Carole Stone, Stephan Shakespeare, Douglas Rivers and Joe Twyman. Sponsorship to fund the research was provided by

Johan Christofferson and Killik & Co, and we are specifically grateful to the partners at Killik & Co. Finally, we are both grateful to our wives and families, who put up with us when we added months spent writing a book to our already busy lives.

AUTHOR BIOGRAPHIES

Matthew Hancock is an economist and politician. He has been the Member of Parliament for West Suffolk since 2010 and is Minister for Skills in the UK Government's Departments of Business and of Education. Before entering Parliament he worked for his small family company, as an economist at the Bank of England, and as Chief of Staff to the now Chancellor of the Exchequer George Osborne. He once held the world record for the most northerly game of cricket ever played.

Nadhim Zahawi is an entrepreneur and politician. He has been the Member of Parliament for Stratford-on-Avon since 2010 and sits on the Business, Innovation and Skills Select Committee. Prior to entering Parliament he founded the market research and polling organization YouGov, taking it public in 2005 and continuing as chief executive until his selection as a parliamentary candidate. He is also a non-executive director of FTSE 250 business SThree Plc. He is a keen horse rider and was once a useful show jumper many decades ago.

INTRODUCTION

This book is about how people behave.

Not how we think we behave, or how we'd like to behave, but how we really do.

It is a story of how failure to understand how we really behave helped cause one of the biggest crises in the history of capitalism. It's a story of the extraordinary extremes of human behavior we witnessed from the so-called Masters of the Universe, of their greed, recklessness, and irrationality. Of how that failure to understand behavior led to policy mistakes that magnified the crisis. And of how the crisis will happen again unless we achieve this understanding.

In short, this is a book that looks at the world as it is, not as we would wish it to be, and tries to draw lessons from what we see.

Some time ago, economists started to make the assumption that people were always rational. Treating everyone as pure *Homo economicus* was a useful abbreviation of reality which allowed economists to model the complex world we live and work in. It helped explain things and at first yielded new insights. But over time, this assumption was used not just to explain the world, but to run it. The idea of unqualified human rationality came to govern the decisions of banks, businesses and policymakers alike.

But we are not always rational. We all know that from every day of our lives. We may be rational some of the time, but when did someone last behave irrationally towards you? Was it this morning, or yesterday? Or perhaps last week? When did you last snap at someone without good reason? Today in the rush hour? From road rage to falling in love, we are surrounded by irrational behavior. As new polling for this book reveals, people are often irrational. We buy things we do not need and cannot afford, we fly off the handle at the smallest provocation, and we get carried away by fads and superstitions. Our hearts and our heads are often in conflict. Our decisions are usually influenced by both.

Try as we might, individuals' actions cannot be accurately modeled. The world's most powerful supercomputer has yet to surpass the neural processing power of a mouse. Modeling a single human brain is difficult enough, modeling group behavior is harder still. And we should be grateful we can't model everything accurately. Wouldn't life be dull?

These facts of life matter. Rules that were written with paragons of rationality in mind had unintended consequences which overwhelmed the financial system. A combination of perverse rational incentives and raw human impulses led to group behavior which was self-reinforcing and self-destructive. Yet the growing storm went unnoticed by the authorities, because of their belief in the system they had created.

To stop another crash of this scale happening again, we need to understand how people really behave, and apply those lessons to how we run our economy.

For all the extraordinary development in our understanding of how the natural world works, and for all the amazing new technology that enriches our lives, we know precious little about how and why human beings behave as we do. Worse, we apply almost nothing of what we do know to critical questions about how we manage our economy.

Pioneering thinkers and centuries of effort have advanced the frontiers of scientific knowledge beyond the wildest dreams of our ancestors. The scientific method of controlled experimentation and rigorous observation has made modernity possible, helping to create a world of widespread comfort, where more people live than ever before.

But when it comes to an empirical understanding of human behavior, of the balance between rationality and irrationality, nature versus nurture, our thinking has advanced more sluggishly, and the break with the past is harder to discern. It's all there in Aristotle: the battle between the rational and irrational; our need to develop self-control; the danger of wayward emotions; the pull of physical desires on the mind. The ancient descriptions of behavior are as telling today as when they were written over two thousand years ago.

Of course individual fields have developed, but until very recently there was little attempt to undertake systematic, quantitative research which might bring these fields together. Basic empirical questions, about group behavior, or the extent to which we are driven by logic or greed, our loss aversion, or reciprocity had moved on little.

Fortunately after such an intellectual drought, our understanding of how we behave has recently made rapid strides. Fascinating new studies are starting to bring together the links between how we think – neuroscience and psychology – how our bodies react to how we think – physiology – and how those thoughts lead us to organize ourselves as groups – sociology, politics, and economics. Rich seams of collaboration are opening up.

This new research is being applied to policy too. Paying people to recycle is significantly more effective than fining them if they don't. Simply changing the way letters from the taxman are written increases tax yield enormously.

These new steps are important, but alone are not enough. For policies themselves are part of the system we all live in. So while it is necessary to base policy on observations of how we behave, it is not sufficient. We must also understand the dynamics: how people will react to policy, both alone and in groups. In some of the most important areas of policy, like managing the economy, this is very hard to know. But it is safer to base policy on an awareness of how little we know than on a false assumption that we know far more. The implications are profound.

In the real world of our jobs, our savings and our homes, the financial crisis that started in 2007 has dealt an almighty shock to how we thought the economy worked. For too long, policymaking made assumptions about how people *ought* to behave, without stopping to observe how we actually *do*. Assumption was mistaken for observation; description confused with prescription.

Entire schools of economic theory and policy were founded on this mistake. So it was taken as a given that if people took on debt it must have been because they could afford it. If banks made loans, it must be because they had accurately assessed the likelihood that the borrower would pay back. And governments believed that a narrow focus on inflation-targeting had solved the age-old problem of how to manage the broader economy. Theories and policies that used flawed assumptions of all-pervasive rationality contributed to the creation and bursting of one of the largest economic bubbles in history.

This book attempts to bring recent insights into human behavior to bear on one of the great debates of our times. With real stories and the emerging academic evidence we try to explain human behavior. Drawing on a rich and growing field of research from a wide variety of disciplines, we find lessons for how we can try to run our economy in future.

New polling was undertaken for this book to shed light on the question of how rational people think they are, and on how they would behave. The very first part of that polling brings out the colorful way in which we humans see ourselves.

Forty-eight percent of people claim they are always rational. But only 32 percent claim their friends are always rational.[1]

Yet we are confident that just because behavior is often irrational does not mean that it is surprising. After all, history shows that in economic life, ups and downs, cycles and bubbles are inevitable. These are not the fault of capitalism. The free market economy has emphatically proven to be the best way to sustain and enrich well-being, but for markets to be free, and to retain widespread trust and support, they require a strong framework.

In the recent past, we have learned the hard way what happens if that framework is wrong, if we assume people are always rational, that groups of people are rational too, and that if anything does go wrong, a rational government can step in to sort it out.

This attitude gained ascendency at a time when the soft, cultural constraints on behavior were being questioned. Long gone are the days captured in Walt Disney's *Mary Poppins*, when the boss punched through Mr Banks's bowler hat as a symbol of shame after his son caused a run on the bank. In the latter half of the twentieth century rigid social hierarchies were rightly challenged, to the advantage of many who had been excluded, and the unspoken rules that dominated society withered away. In their place came the thrilling combination of amazing new technology and rapid globalization, as two billion people – a third of the world's population – joined the global economy for the first time.

The bubble that led to the crash helped ferment an intoxicating tale about how the rise of the East had improved the world's prospects, while technical advance allowed our newly globalized economies to be managed more effectively than ever before.

1 YouGov general population survey, conducted 28–31 January 2013

People everywhere bought into the story, because in many ways it was true.

The sequence of events is well documented. The rise of the East had a benign effect on all our lives. With so many people trying to compete in the global market, empowered by a new ability to communicate, they drove down the cost of goods and services in the West. The success of these newly connected societies led to a rapidly rising entrepreneurial middle class, who saved a high proportion of their income. They needed somewhere safe to put their new savings, and after the shock of the Asian crisis of 1998 they invested it in the West, largely through their governments. These events should have been a triple bonanza for the West: cheaper goods, new markets, and plenty of cash-rich investors.

At the same time, the promise of the dot-com bubble had burst. In the face of recession and the shock of 9/11, interest rates were sharply cut and the Fed pumped money into the US economy. The rapid drop in the cost of everyday items, like televisions, computers and cars, meant that inflation as measured stayed low.

So what was the problem?

Normally all this cheap money would have been translated into business investment. But businesses had already invested too much in the dot-com fiasco. Instead, the easy supply of money and artificially low cost of credit combined to create a vast debt bubble, above all in the housing market. We all enjoyed it. Low interest rates in Europe and America enabled consumers to buy houses, driving up house prices and allowing us all to feel we were getting richer. Borrowing against the rising price of your house (mortgage equity withdrawal), became all the rage. In the so-called subprime sector, rising house prices provided many with the home equity they needed to refinance old loans, deferring the day of reckoning. More credit card offers than you could ever use flew in through the door. In the UK, the Royal Bank of Scotland sent an application for a credit card with a £10,000 limit and the chance to buy air miles to one Monty Slater. Monty Slater was a dog.

This uncontrolled expansion of debt might have been containable but for the fact that the banks that supplied the credit were affected by a combination of powerful new technology and a radical new attitude from regulators. The good news story gave everyone – banks, consumers, and the authorities – a justification for believing the hype, and this justification was buttressed by a moral imperative. In the US, Republican and Democrat administrations alike had long declared their ambition to transform the 'tired, the poor, the huddled masses' into proud American homeowners. The subprime mortgage sector promised to make the American Dream a bricks-and-mortar reality for millions. Anyone arguing that it was all unsustainable had to confront both the economic good news and a powerful moral consensus about the benefits of homeownership.

In finance, new technology instilled financiers with the confidence that they had found a brand new way to lend more at a lower risk. By packaging up loans into bundles and renaming the debts in smart new language, like alchemists, they thought they had converted risky loans into risk-free assets. Because they sold most of the loans on, they cared little about the quality of the loans, only the quantity. The new technology gave financiers a false belief that they could handle the lending, and a culture of growth without restraint meant they pushed ever expanding boundaries.

Armed with a good news story about the rise of the East and the diffusion of risk, we were told the cycle of boom and bust had been abolished. Many believed it. Arguing against this new paradigm was unpleasant, costly, and ineffective. Responding to small crises of the past, like the collapse of Barings in the UK and the Savings and Loans institutions in America, regulators hid behind the apparent objectivity of rules and models. Many of these rules and models assumed that humans behave rationally and the good times would never end.

But psychology tells us that much of human behavior is in fact irrational, and history tells us the good times always end.

To understand why behavior matters, it is telling to look at the financial crash from the perspective of those who saw it coming. There weren't many. But there were some who spoke out. Their problem was that no one wanted to listen.

They can testify that anyone who stood in the way of the dream was brushed aside. Like fools in the corner, they were ignored. The louder they shouted, the more deafening the silence. Economists like Raghuram Rajan and Nouriel Roubini spoke out on their worries, but to no avail. Several leading financiers tried to make the case: the billionaire hedge fund manager Jim Chanos, as well as Sir Andrew Large, then Deputy Governor of the Bank of England. They and others like them were consistently ignored.

It is astonishing that even as events tested prevailing assumptions and found them wanting, no one listened. From the collapse of the giant hedge fund Long Term Capital Management, to the default of Russia in 1998, and the dot-com crash, a series of bubbles should have raised questions. As each collapse happened, governments stepped in to clear up the mess, not stopping to consider the underlying problems that caused each crisis. Of course, the urge to prevent economic misery was understandable, but the failure to recognize and deal with the underlying problems was mistaken.

So the almighty debt bubble grew, and all the more quickly because it was effectively sanctioned by governments. In the US Alan Greenspan, the Chairman of the Federal Reserve, the man in charge of US monetary policy from 1987 to 2006, had a simple approach to economic management: he would not act against a growing bubble but would instead deal with the consequences when it burst. The growth and bursting of each bubble all strengthened his belief in this approach. In each case, by cutting interest rates quickly and flooding the system with liquidity the Western economy recovered.

Greenspan even went so far as to tell the world that he would rescue the economy from any crisis. Such a promise built up the boom still further. In the UK, Finance Minister turned Prime Minister Gordon Brown made exactly the same mistake, telling Parliament he had abolished boom and bust and encouraging companies, banks, and households to borrow yet more. This implicit government support meant that instead of dealing with the underlying problems, the bubble was pumped back up every time it threatened to burst. It was a grand failure, both of leadership and political economy.

Meanwhile, in the everyday life of the largest banks, human behavior was exerting its power. It has been observed that the patterns of group behavior look just like the flocking of wild animals. With the story of global opportunities, rapidly rising personal pay, and explicit government support all urging it on, the financial herd stampeded into the boom with unprecedented energy and aggression.

When a herd stampedes, individual animals may peel off, able to see a danger looming in the distance, but no one follows. These were the fools in the corner, the Cassandras of the crisis. Back with the herd, one more peels off, then a few more. They can see the danger ahead but the majority still hasn't noticed. Then suddenly, without warning, the mass of the herd turns. This is the majority, the critical mass. They did not peel off early, and their eyes were opened only as the crash became real. Finally, left behind, are the animals that carried on regardless, that separated from the herd. They are the sorry few who couldn't face up to the severity of the crisis, who hoped against hope and reason that it would just be a blip.

Looking at the turning point in this way helps understand how bubbles burst: unpredictably, and with uncertain timing, but in a recognizable pattern that has happened many times before. Elegant histories have been written of past bubbles, from the collapse of the moneylenders in fifteenth-century Florence to the Dutch tulip bubble in the 1630s and the British railway mania of the 1840s. Our goal is to recognize the patterns of human behavior that underpin financial bubbles, for history suggests they are an inevitable consequence of group psychology, which can no more be abolished than society itself. Bubbles are appearing, growing, and bursting all the time. Our job is not to abolish them but to mitigate the harm they can do, before, during and after.

A study of past bubbles also shows how different their impacts can be. Many bubbles, for example in an individual stock price or an individual commodity, can deflate relatively harmlessly. Some can have distorting effects. Yet others can bring down whole economies: nearly always when the bubble is financed through debt. As history shows, recessions caused by the bursting of debt bubbles are deeper, longer lasting, and have more dramatic consequences.

The growth of a bubble is usually driven not only by how people behave but by who is misbehaving. As a bubble grows, past experience suggests that the most bullish optimists tend to be promoted, gaining power at the expense of the cautious and the prudent. Psychological studies show that groups reinforce each other in playing down anxiety or risk. The body's physical response to imagining a great prize is physiologically the same as winning the prize. So we shun those who try to break the mould, and who challenge the group's imagination that they will win the prize. During a boom not only are the people most likely to acknowledge the risks shunned, but those least likely to worry are promoted. And so the bubble inflates.

Economists tend to analyze the flawed decision-making that led to the crash as a purely intellectual phenomenon. Yet the evidence increasingly suggests that in shaping our attitudes towards risk, body matters as much as mind. No issue illustrates this more clearly than sex. Sex determines human behavior more than any other single factor. Our sex affects how we grow, think, and behave. Does it matter, then, that the senior echelons of finance are almost exclusively male?

Some say that because finance requires aggressive, risk-loving, stereotypically male characteristics, it is consequently dominated by men. Let's set aside the immorality and incivility of much trading-floor behavior. Physiological research into trading room performance shows that irresponsible risks are reduced when more women are around, but that people tend to hire, reward and promote people similar to themselves. Evidence from Wall Street trading floors bears this out. But crucially, recent analysis shows that companies with more women on boards tend to perform better, compared to those with boards dominated by men. So rather than being male-dominated because finance is by nature aggressive and risk-loving, the evidence suggests that the culture of finance is aggressive and risk-loving *because* it is dominated by men.

Around the world, very clear interventions have successfully broken the male-dominated culture in finance. The evidence shows that once women reach around a third of a group, the culture tends to change and the male bias is replaced with a meritocracy. Because the problem is of culture obstructing merit, changes are needed to benefit fully from the capabilities of half of our population.

Many people react with horror at the thought of quotas on boards. Since it is in a company's interest to promote merit, surely, they ask, the best thing to do is to leave it in the hands of the company? But this argument falls foul of the central insight of this book: that in the design of policy, we need to recognize how people actually behave, not how we might wish them to.

This argument also applies to pay. If banks always acted in their shareholders' best interests it is not obvious their pay should be so extraordinarily high, or that it should have risen so quickly in recent years. Compared to most organizations banks pay a huge proportion of their profits to employees, rather than their owners, the shareholders. Worse still, they entered into contracts with senior managers which effectively reward failure. So-called 'incentivization' packages can be both financially dangerous by encouraging higher risk-taking and morally outrageous when they reward performance which, whether implicit or explicit, relies on taxpayer subsidy. Given the extremes that such rewards for failure reached, there can be both an economic and a moral imperative to act. In a world short of capital, banks need to keep cash as capital to support the economy and make their balance sheets safer.

The widespread assumption that a self-interested decision must always be the right one also wrongly implies that business activity should be amoral and divorced from ethics. Yet businesses do not operate in a moral vacuum. They are made up of human beings who all play their role in society. Like any other group of people, business leaders need to take responsibility for their actions, right or wrong. Whether legal or not, immoral actions within businesses should not be tolerated just because there's a logo on the door. So people who behave without integrity, like the traders who attempted to rig the money markets by fiddling the Libor index, should not only be targeted by the regulators. Like anyone acting immorally, they should also be socially shunned.

At the same time we must recognize the reality of the financial services industry. A very small number of very big banks pose risks to the whole economy should they fail. They should be distinguished from the thousands of smaller finance companies that pose no such risk, can claim no taxpayer support, and contribute enormously to the economy. While people in smaller companies also have a responsibility to behave ethically, their behavior was more tangential to the causes of the crash.

The historic failure to design policy reflective of actual human behavior is not a narrow problem. It spreads across vast swathes of the academic economics profession. Whole careers have been built in modern economics by building mathematical models based on assumptions known to be hopelessly flawed. Models can, of course, be helpful and bring insight to unexplained problems. But the march of the model through economic academia has come to displace the search for an understanding of how economies really work. The consequence has been both to infuse policymaking with impractical models, and to take resources away from the crucial task of understanding better how people really behave.

With modern technology, such empirical study can be very powerful. Modern corporations use detailed information to understand what their customers are likely to want before they even set foot in the store. They design every aspect of their business by observing the behavior of their customers. It's no accident, for example, that supermarkets always locate fresh fruit and vegetables rather than say cleaning products nearest the entrance. In the coming decades our ability to understand human behavior is set to make huge new advances. We should harness its power to design an economic framework that is more robust, stable, and prosperous.

Nevertheless, our understanding will never be complete. Even if we can predict, on average, how an individual will respond to a change in the economic environment, predicting the dynamics of a herd, whether human or animal, is impossible. A group of humans is molded by their collective experience, which cannot be directly observed or easily quantified. Groups constantly react, interact, evolve and adapt in response to change, including to changes in policy. This renders the future state of groups, markets, or the economy as a whole inherently uncertain. When it comes to designing policy we have to recognize this fact, not pretend otherwise.

This implies we should be cautious about a regulatory approach based on increasingly complex rules. People adapt to new rules in unexpected ways, which may exacerbate the very problem the rule was designed to solve. In nineteenth-century India the British colonial government became concerned about the number of cobras in the Delhi area. To combat the problem officials offered a reward in exchange for the head of a dead cobra. Once this system was introduced however, the rate of cobra attacks actually increased, as local entrepreneurs began to breed the snakes in order to maximize their returns. Equally, financial regulation is all about limiting risk, but financiers know that risk is directly linked to profit. This conflict creates a perpetual 'cobra effect' at the heart of the financial system. The discretion to react to circumstances and adapt the rules to fit a changing world is necessary and valuable.

Cobra effects aside, trying to regulate a complex system with complex rules leads to an infinite loop of complication to the point where no one understands either the system or the rules, including those who have devised them. Instead complex systems should be managed with clear, simple rules which can hold up in the face of our ignorance, so even though no one can predict the precise future of the system, everyone knows where they stand within it.

Above all regulators must realize that their job is not to prevent the banks from making mistakes. Failure is the secret of capitalism's success; without it there can be no useful innovation. Instead their role is to protect the public from the consequences of those mistakes. This means ending 'Too Big to Fail' once and for all.

But in a complex and uncertain world no system of formal regulation will ever be perfect. For this reason, culture and a revived sense of professional integrity are likely to be the best financial regulators of all. Designing policy to change culture for the better is difficult because outcomes are subjective and hard to measure. But again, research into human behavior can help guide us. We know that our behavior is heavily influenced by social norms. We know too that leadership can shape a culture based on what a leader pays attention to, and what he or she ignores. Policymakers must seek to engender a culture of responsibility, where the social norm is to behave responsibly, but real change is more likely to come when shareholders wake up to their responsibilities as owners rather than speculators.

In America changes have already been put in place by the Dodd–Frank Wall Street Reform and Consumer Protection Act. However, to stop the crisis happening again we also need to understand that bubbles will grow and will burst, and we must therefore change our whole economic philosophy, and with it the culture and morality of finance, so that it reflects not how we'd like people to behave but how we really do, warts and all.

Chapter 1

FOOLS IN THE CORNER

When a true genius appears in the world you may know him by this infallible sign: that the dunces are all in confederacy against him.
– Jonathan Swift, 1711

On a dark January night in 2004, the Deputy Governor of the Bank of England took the short trip from the Bank's headquarters on Threadneedle Street in central London, to the London School of Economics on the Strand. As he wrapped himself up in his coat and skipped up the steps to the newly refurbished lecture theatre, an audience of economics students waited patiently.

Sir Andrew Large stood to deliver a speech that, in hindsight, was one of the most powerful and eloquent warnings about the coming crash.

A full three years before the freezing of the money markets and the first run on a British bank since 1866 and four years before the collapse of Lehman Brothers and the biggest financial crisis in the history of capitalism, a man at the top of one of the most respected institutions in the world laid out what was happening, and the risks that it posed to us all.

If the financial crisis were a Shakespeare play it would be *King Lear*. Like the economists of our own time, Lear is a rationalist who insists, against all reason, that a person's inner life can be reduced to a neat little formula. In the opening scene he asks his three daughters: 'Which of you shall we say doth love us most?'[1]

---

1   William Shakespeare, *King Lear*, I.i.51

When Cordelia, his youngest, challenges this grotesque attempt to quantify the unquantifiable she is disinherited. Satisfied nonetheless with the rehearsed answers offered by the other two, Lear abandons his formal powers and cedes them to his children, believing they can be trusted to behave in the kingdom's best interests. He's wrong. During the course of the play we see the collapse of traditional authority, unrestrained greed in the ascendant, and the livid exposure of a series of flawed assumptions about human nature.

This chapter is about Lear's Fool.

In the play, the loyal court Fool repeatedly warns Lear of impending catastrophe. First he's laughed at, then ignored. Lear won't listen because to do so would mean accepting that he's made a mistake – and that there will be a terrible price to pay. It's far easier to dismiss the fool in the corner as a mad contrarian.

In November 2008 the Queen of England famously asked economists at the London School of Economics: 'Why did no one see it coming?' In doing so she crystallized the mood of a nation aghast at the near collapse of its financial system, the onset of the deepest recession in living memory, and the shattering of public trust in the financial establishment.

But Her Majesty the Queen was wrong. Some did see 'it' coming. Each piece of the jigsaw that together built the banking crisis was identified, and some people put the pieces together. Speeches were given, and presentations delivered.

In the years before the crisis a small number of economists, regulators and finance workers discovered they had been inadvertently cast in the role of the Fool. They saw what others chose not to see and they spoke of what they saw. But they found that no one with the power to act wanted to listen.

Fool Number One
Since 1982, central bankers and the world's most distinguished

economists have gathered each spring in the mountain valley of Jackson Hole, Wyoming. Here they exchange frank views on the latest economic theories, try then fail to agree on international policy frameworks and swap stories about the personal oddities of their respective finance ministers back home. The conference is set against a melodramatic backdrop of mountains, lakes and pine forests, giving members of the world's most urban profession a chance to play at being American frontier folk for a week. Seminars and formal discussions are interspersed with white-water rafting sessions and long hikes through rough terrain where the latest growth figures are breathlessly discussed while the party stops to admire the view. The location of the symposium was originally chosen by the organizers, the Kansas City Fed, for the quality of its trout fishing: part of an effort to entice along the then Fed chairman and noted angling enthusiast Paul Volcker.

In 2005, Raghuram Rajan, the IMF's talented young Chief Economist, had been invited to deliver a paper at Jackson Hole. His subject 'Has Financial Innovation Made the World Riskier?' His conclusion: yes. It was a daring and iconoclastic argument, for in the audience looking up at Rajan through his huge trademark spectacles was the most powerful man in global finance: Alan Greenspan, the chairman of the Federal Reserve, known to admirers as 'the Maestro'.

A popular legend about Greenspan claims that when he needed to think he would sit in his bath, poring over sheaves of economic data, looking for tell-tale patterns about the future in the raw numbers. A hard-line free marketeer, he had overseen an era of transformational deregulation in the financial sector. Having safely steered the American economy through the 1987 stock-market bust, the global panic of 1998 and the bursting of the dot-com bubble in 2000–2001, he felt under no obligation to justify his legacy.

Rajan stepped up to the lectern, took a deep breath, and politely told his audience that they had made the world a more dangerous place.

Originally Rajan had been asked to the conference to argue that Alan Greenspan's eighteen-year tenure at the Fed had made the financial system safer. But the more he considered the evidence, the less convinced he became of his own argument.

Instead he contended that a combination of technical change, institutional change and deregulation had supplanted the traditional banking virtues of stewardship and prudence. In their place had arisen a more high-stakes, hyperactive and unpredictable style of financial management, as banks fought each other and rival institutions like mutual funds to attract investors' cash.

Rajan explained that because pay was increasingly tied to short-term returns in this more competitive world, investment managers would want to take so-called 'tail risks': risks that would nearly always pay off with higher returns, but which would be catastrophic if they went wrong. That way the managers would take home a higher pay packet most of the time. If the risk ever materialized they might be fired, but this was a small cost compared to the super-sized bonuses while the going was good.

Similarly, because these managers' pay was set relative to their peers, financial managers were incentivized to follow the herd. Tail risks have the additional attraction of being easily concealed in the fine print from the undiscerning investor. To the casual observer, a manager who assumed them was simply a more skilled investor then his peer group. We will explore in later chapters how the natural human instinct is to follow the herd. These incentives reinforced an existing behavioral bias.

Rajan did not pursue his argument to its logical conclusion. What he overlooked was that when combined, these two behaviors multiplied. On its own, herding causes groups of people to move or act in fits and starts, meaning the behavior of the group is unpredictable and liable to sudden, violent change. Taking tail risks increases the fragility of the system when a gamble goes wrong. When a herd takes a tail risk that goes wrong, the results are spectacular.

Nevertheless it was a brilliant analysis of what Rajan would later term the 'fault lines' which ran through the global financial system, and it was a daring stance to address the taboo subject of pay in front of some of the best-paid people in finance.

The speech did not go down well. 'I felt like an early Christian who had wandered into a convention of half-starved lions,'[2] he later wrote.

One of the first members of the audience to respond was former US Treasury Secretary and then President of Harvard University Larry Summers. He called Rajan a 'Luddite' and said he found 'the basic, slightly lead-eyed premise' of the paper 'to be largely misguided', citing the Swedish and Japanese banking crises of 1990s as evidence that systemic risk was caused by irresponsible lending from plain old retail banks, so-called 'vanilla banking', rather than the financial alchemy practiced by high-rollers on Wall Street. Summers argued that had new forms of insurance like credit default swaps been available to investors back in the 1980s then the situation following the 1987 stock-market bust would have been a lot more stable.

But Summers had missed one of Rajan's central points. The supposed impregnability of the modern financial system depended on assumptions that had not been tested, indeed, that were seemingly unfalsifiable: the past twenty-five years of market behavior were no guide at all to the next ten, too much

---

2 Raghuram Rajan, *Fault Lines: How Hidden Fractures Still Threaten the World Economy* (Princeton: Princeton University Press, 2010)

financial innovation and systemic change had happened in the interim. Gesturing back to the three major market shocks that occurred on Greenspan's watch, Rajan asked, 'can we be confident that the shocks were large enough and in the right place to fully test the system? [...] Perhaps we can sleep better at night if we pray "Lord, let there be shocks, let them be varied and preferably moderate so we can test our systems."'[3]

Why were these warnings disregarded? What is it about human behavior that meant those with most to lose turned a blind eye to the growing storm? Why were those who warned of the risks treated as the fool in the corner? And what can we learn to help ensure they get a better hearing next time?

For Raghuram Rajan was not alone.

Fool Number Two

In his LSE speech a year earlier Sir Andrew Large had attacked the central assumption behind two decades of explosive growth in global finance. His argument rested on a simple distinction between two concepts: technical sophistication and progress. According to Sir Andrew, they might be related, but they were emphatically not the same thing.

Since the late 1980s bankers, economists, regulators and politicians had generally assumed that growing technical sophistication in the finance system would translate into greater stability across the economy as a whole. Computer technology, which allowed financial assets to be whizzed across the globe at the touch of a button, supposedly ensured that the riskiest assets would always find their way into the hands of those most able to bear the risk. Financial crises, it was assumed, occurred because risk was too concentrated, yet recent financial

---

3   Raghuram Rajan, 'Has Financial Development Made the World Riskier?', Kansas City Federal Reserve, 2005

innovation meant it would be safely diffused across the system, like chlorine molecules in a swimming pool. In the US, this belief in the system's majestic advance towards self-regulatory perfection became known as the Greenspan doctrine, after its most powerful proponent. In Greenspan's view, the market's growing ability to 'self-correct' meant that in time 'market-stabilizing private regulatory forces should gradually displace many cumbersome, increasingly ineffective government structures'.[4]

But according to Sir Andrew, all these heroic arguments about efficiency and risk dispersion hinged on a big 'If'. The system was only safer *if* everyone knew what they were doing, that is, if they properly understood the risks they were dealing with. Yet the very nature of the modern financial system conspired against such an understanding. In spite of 'steps forward through enhanced disclosure and improved accounting standards, there [had] been other steps back towards opacity: the result of the sheer complexity, speed of movement of risks, and in some cases obfuscation through Special Purpose Vehicles, or other off-balance-sheet devices.'[5]

He noticed that, for some firms, cultivating complexity had become an end in itself. After all, the more complicated a product or institution became, the harder it was for investors or regulators to track the underlying risks. Furthermore, the less risky an institution appeared to the outside world, the more easily it could borrow to take on even more risk.

Sir Andrew's insight was that financial institutions were not only gaming the regulatory framework but also eroding trust in one another. Financial liberalization and increased savings

---

4 Financial Crisis Inquiry Commission Report, 'Final Report of the National Commission on the Causes of the Financial and Economic Crisis in the United States', January 2011, p. 28

5 Sir Andrew Large, 'Financial Stability Oversight, Past and Present', 22 January 2004, speech to the London School of Economics

flowing from the rapidly developing economies of the East meant that the West was awash with cheap money, so much so that it had become more difficult for banks to make any through traditional means. In response, financial institutions had developed ever more ingenious ways of doing business: risk was increasingly concealed from investors in complex 'structured' credit products, off-balance-sheet vehicles and other arcane devices. 'The existence of new concentrations of risk might not matter if their new holders are fully aware of the risk,' said Sir Andrew, 'but new holders of such risk may not have the same understandings of what the risks consist of, as those who generate them. And accordingly they may behave in unexpected ways when shocks arise.'[6]

No one knew if all parties would, or could, honor their obligations in the event of a market shock. This could lead to financial hysteria and a 'one-way' market at the very moment when calm was most needed.

The speech was warmly received by its undergraduate audience; questions were dutifully asked and patiently answered. The text was published on the Bank of England's website.

No one noticed.

When Sir Andrew returned to the Bank the next morning, the explosive speech was not the subject of heated debate. There were no seminars called. No research was commissioned. In the newspapers over the following days, there was no reference made to Sir Andrew or the speech.

Sir Andrew was a banker by trade. In policy circles, 'I was considered a bit of a maverick,' he told us, 'which was not particularly comfortable.' This isolation went right down to the level of language. He explained that Bank of England economists

---

6 Ibid.

would talk of 'the concept of cycles … and the concept of cyclical smoothing and all these soothing words that are used, which are rather foreign to me when thinking about financial stability, because financial stability has got nothing to do with smoothing at all. It's all to do with spikes and discontinuities. And also it's to do with uncertainty as to whether and when such discontinuities might arise.'[7]

Sir Andrew continued to make similar speeches and argue the system was unsustainable for another two years. Then in January 2006 he quietly retired, before his term was up.

His speeches infuriated the British government because they warned of the dangers of excessive public borrowing. And yet he felt compelled to make them. 'The reason I did so', he told us, 'was because I said to myself, "look, the one thing I can do is at least to point out that if all this carries on it's all going to end in tears. I can't tell you how, no one can say how, but if you have a combination of ever-rising indebtedness and unknown events that will test your system one way or another, then sooner or later all these things will come together and it *will* end in tears."'[8]

This point about uncertainty is important. Rajan and Sir Andrew were right to argue that while financial innovation had dramatically increased what it was possible to *do* in financial markets, it had seriously undermined our ability to *know* what it was those markets were doing. Their focus on the essential *novelty* of the financial system confounds the argument that they were backward-looking Luddites. On the contrary, it was their critics who were too fixed on the past, convinced that they could use it to peer into the future like Greenspan sitting in the bath with his tables and charts.

One of the problems with the economics profession's

---

7 Sir Andrew Large, private interview
8 Private interview

approach to history is that it tends to be used as a narrow forecasting tool rather than a powerful echo of human experience:
'history doesn't repeat itself, but it does rhyme,' as Mark Twain
puts it. We will see more of this in Chapter 3 when we come to
think about bubbles, but first let's imagine if mainstream economists would have thought differently if they had considered
the historical precedent for ignoring warnings of impending
catastrophe.

In 1913, commentators who argued that war between Britain
and Germany was impossible deployed familiar arguments.
Technology had made the world a safer place: Britain's vast
fleet and state-of-the-art dreadnoughts meant no European
power would dare provoke a general conflagration. No general
or politician would be so irresponsible: the world's economies
were too well integrated, rational self-interest would prevent an
immensely destructive war between the world's great powers.
And where was the precedent? Britain hadn't been involved
in a European conflict since the Crimea sixty years before, so
why would it suddenly abandon its long-term strategy of non-
interference in European affairs?

The symmetry is eerie. The lesson is that people in all ages
dangerously overestimate their ability to remain in control of
events, when all too often it's the mad internal logic of the
system they've created which is really in control. Far from
making the system safer, technical development actually
augments this effect. The historian John Keegan writes that in
the years before the First World War the generals of the great
European powers had been told to draw up detailed war plans
in anticipation of an event no one wanted, or believed could
happen. Their guiding philosophy was to prepare assiduously
for the worst-case scenario. The war plans were enormously
complex documents designed to mobilize millions of men
rapidly; they operated on a 'use it or lose it' principle whereby

the first army to call up its troops and speed them towards the front would be able to smash the enemy while he was still asleep in the barracks. As a result, logistics fatally undermined diplomacy during the summer of 1914. In Berlin, Paris and St Petersburg the generals harassed politicians to give the order to mobilize as soon as possible – convinced that delay would have meant losing a crucial early advantage. And so events assumed their own lethal momentum, at the very point where calm reflection was most needed.

Sir Andrew Large and Raghuram Rajan saw that a similar dynamic was lurking in the global financial system. Perverse inner mechanics could easily hijack people's best intentions. The modern financial equivalent of the generals' war plans were the computer models which told traders what to buy and what to sell in times of market stress. Gerald Ashley, a former bullion trader at the Bank of International Settlements, explained to us what happened during the crisis: 'When markets fall the only thing that goes up is correlation. If everyone is using the same model and all the models are saying 'sell' then who else is buying?'[9] What the generals found in August 1914 is that because everyone was working on the same 'use it or lose it' principle, nobody captured the advantage it was supposed to bring. France and Britain mobilized quickly enough to intercept the German Army on its way to Paris. Similarly, because the banks were all working on the same assumption that they suddenly had to sell their mortgage-backed securities, nobody wanted to buy them. In the crisis their value collapsed and hundreds of billions of pounds were wiped off the books. Panic had been unwittingly hard-wired into an ostensibly risk-free system.

To return to Large, the fact that a Deputy Governor of the Bank of England with an acute sense of where the risks lay felt

9 Gerald Ashley, private interview

that all he could do was make speeches is a serious indictment
of the regulatory framework. Here was a man with an impeccable track record who, after a career in banking, had become
Chairman of the UK securities regulator. As Deputy Governor
of the Bank of England he occupied a position of weight, and
he spoke with great clarity about the problems that we faced.

He was ignored.

Fool Number Three
In 2006, a year after Rajan's speech at Jackson Hole, two years
after Large's speech to the LSE, another man took to the stage,
this time at an IMF seminar in Washington DC.

He had an unreadable stare and an utterly elusive accent.
His name was Nouriel Roubini and he was about to deliver the
speech that would make him famous.

In early 2007, Roubini announced, America would fall into
recession. And it would hurt.

He cited several causes: an oil price shock, declining
consumer confidence, a once-in-a-lifetime housing bust and
higher interest rates from the Fed. But that wasn't all; even
armed with Roubini's predictions the Fed would still be power-
less to prevent a recession. Lowering interest rates would have
no effect on growth because America had acquired a glut of
housing and consumer goods. The only place for banks and
firms to invest their money would be an economically unpro-
ductive share buy-back 'bonanza'.

Savoring the audience's dismay at this gloomy prognosis,
Roubini proceeded with his argument. The oil shock was safely
assured by constraints on supply and rising political instability abroad. Meanwhile the housing bust would be devastating
because American consumer spending had become so dependent on home equity withdrawal. He also drew the vital link
between the housing sector and financial markets, noting that

the banking system was highly exposed to the risks associated with mortgage debt and that this risk was dispersed elsewhere through the system through other financial institutions which had purchased mortgage related assets from the banks. Ominously he noted that 'You could not rule out some systemic effects if one of those institutions goes belly-up'.[10] Finally, he stated that a recession in America might have a knock-on effect given that so much of the rest of the world moved to the rhythm of the US economy.

Roubini concluded his speech. As he stepped down from the lectern the IMF moderator moved in to thank him, remarking 'perhaps we will need a stiff drink after that'.[11] The audience laughed and perhaps they were laughing at Roubini too. After all, he was a professional pessimist. He'd built an entire career at New York University prophesying doom. This was exactly the kind of Nostradamus act they'd expected to see that night.

In support of his argument Roubini provided several historical analogies featuring identical economic conditions – an oil shock, monetary tightening and the bursting of a bubble – which had tipped the US into recession; he focused particularly on the stock market crash of 1987. But as another economist present, Anirvan Banerji, pointed out, for every analogy Roubini dealt, it was possible to counter with a different one in which America had weathered the storm:

> In the fall of 1998 in the wake of the Russian default and the LTCM crisis, many predicted a recession. As Nouriel might recall, President Clinton himself called it the worst financial crisis in fifty years, and *Time* magazine had Alan Greenspan, Robert

---

10 Nouriel Roubini, 'The US and Global Outlook', transcript of an IMF seminar, 7 September 2006, Washington DC

11 Ibid.

Rubin, and Larry Summers on its cover as 'The Committee to Save the World'. But, once again, a recession was averted. Using our retrospectoscopes we can explain why there was or was not a recession in each case, why some shocks were that potent and not others, but that is not so easy before the fact.[12]

Michael Mandel writing in *Bloomberg Businessweek* was equally dismissive: 'I'm far less worried about the possibility of a steep recession than Roubini is. Economists don't know much, but they do know how to cushion downturns through sharp cuts in interest rates and injections of liquidity into the financial system.' The central bankers knew what they were doing. Even if all the events Roubini predicted came to pass, the Fed would pump enough money into the system to avert disaster.

In many ways Roubini was vindicated. Belatedly the world did sit up and pay attention. An article published in the *New York Times* in August 2008, while the subprime crisis was in full swing, showered praise on his IMF speech, even though the same newspaper had ignored it two years before. Roubini was suddenly cast in the role of America's grim oracle. The paper called him 'Dr Doom', the man who had seen a financial nightmare coalescing in the margins and tried to warn the world. Unlike Sir Andrew Large he was catapulted to fame. Roubini was invited onto primetime news programs to dispense his wisdom to reverential journalists, his online consultancy business made millions counseling shaken bankers while his book *Crisis Economics* became a bestseller. Most ironically of all he became a confidante of central bankers and finance ministers, those who had helped propel the system into the very recession which he had predicted. New York University's dismal

---

sage was always a phone call or an email away when a forecast was needed about which bank or market would go under next.

This last point is important. Roubini now occupies an immensely powerful position because he was noticed by the media. Given this fact, it is important to be clear about exactly what he did and didn't predict and why of the handful of economists who saw imminent catastrophe he was the one who became famous.

Roubini predicted a recession in the US which he thought might spread to the rest of the world. What he did not foresee was a global financial crisis so severe that only a multi-trillion dollar rescue package from governments across the world could prevent the destruction of free market capitalism. He did not perceive that the financial system had become hopelessly addicted to cheap credit, that it had become impossibly complex and dangerously opaque. He made no mention of the rise of the shadow banking system – that invisible network of unregulated or lightly regulated entities where banks hid their riskiest assets from regulators, investors and each other – nor did he cite the rabid short-term speculation fuelled by skewed pay incentives. Like a doctor diagnosing a migraine in his patient, he had noticed some impaired cognitive function and erratic behavior but missed the monstrous tumor behind it.

So why Roubini? We would argue that there was something oddly reassuring about the way Roubini predicted the recession. He couched his argument in the language of traditional economics, citing huge impersonal forces – oil, housing, monetary policy – as causes. These forces could be seen, measured and tracked by the experts. There is something remarkably comforting about a man who can claim there is a seventy percent chance that the global economy will enter recession next year, however unpalatable the prospect. For it confers a certainty on events which media commentators and policymakers alike find highly attractive. Even though, as Roubini himself admitted, he pulled the seventy percent figure out of his nose:

> I think if you had said 'fifty percent' you look like a wimp, it means you are not sure. So if you have the guts of believing there is going to be a recession, you should say something higher than that, and that is where the seventy percent comes from.

In other words, Roubini became a celebrity because his analysis of the crisis was most sympathetic to the economic framework which dominated thinking before the crash, even though he predicted a recession and not a global financial crisis.

Sir Andrew Large told us of the intellectual vanity which characterized the pre-crisis policymaking community: 'it was a rather funny sort of time, everyone felt they knew everything.'[13] Monetary policy, which central bankers believed they had finally perfected, became the prestige policy area, tending to crowd out the financial stability agenda. Price stability was assumed to be the only necessary precondition for financial stability. In the models central banks used to predict inflation, for example, it was taken as a given that the balance sheets of the banks would always drift back to a sustainable level. In this way, the aura of precision and objectivity associated with targeting a single headline inflation figure was projected onto the more complex and diffuse realm of financial stability.

In contrast to professional forecasters, Sir Andrew made one of the best pre-crisis analyses of the risks inherent in the system because he made fewer assumptions about what he knew. Finance was doing too many new things, and on an unprecedented scale, to make any sound predictions about how people would respond when things went wrong. Accepting this

---

13 Sir Andrew Large, private interview

argument however requires economists and policymakers to reconcile themselves with gaps in their knowledge, and recent work in psychology has confirmed the inability of experts to admit their own ignorance.

Groupthink

In 2009 two cognitive psychologists, Lisa Son and Nate Kornell, devised a study to show how expertise might lead to overconfidence.[14] Experts in two fields – mathematics and history – were provided with a list of names divided into three different categories. The task was to say whether a given name belonged to a particular category. For example, when given the following information: 'Mathematician – Rene Descartes', participants had to decide whether Descartes was a famous mathematician and could answer 'Yes', 'No', or Don't know'. The three categories were mathematicians, historians, and athletes. Within each category a third of the names actually belonged to the category, i.e. were real mathematicians, historians or athletes; a third belonged to a different category, for example, 'Mathematician – Muhammad Ali'. The final third were made-up names – 'Mathematician – Benoit Thoron'.

During the trial, Son and Kornell found that the experts were less likely to answer 'Don't know' in a category featuring their area of expertise. More interestingly they were more likely to say 'Yes' to made-up names attached to their specialist subjects. Mathematicians answered 'Yes' nineteen times to made-up mathematicians but only seven times to fictional historians; historians said 'Yes' eight times to made-up historians but only four times to invented mathematicians. In the words of Son and

14 Lisa Son and Nate Kornell, 'The Virtues of Ignorance' in *Behavioural Processes* no. 83, 2010, pp. 208–11

Kornell, 'experts were fooled into endorsing falsehoods because they failed to admit that they did not know'.

As a commentary on the caliber of economic analysis in the years leading up to 2007 this is pretty hard to beat. But there were other reasons relating to the way economists think and work which resulted in the dismissal of Sir Andrew's views.

In the second half of the twentieth century academic economists came to regard their subject as something akin to a hard science and adopted many of the conventions of the scientific community. Modern science works by establishing a consensus, hence its huge emphasis on peer-reviewed research. Modern economics has followed suit, even though as a discipline it is far more dependent on assumed first principles and educated guesswork than the controlled experimentation of the scientific method. The great Austrian economist Friedrich August von Hayek was famously ambivalent about his receipt of the Nobel Prize in Economics, because it 'confers on an individual an authority which in economics no man ought to possess'.[15] But despite this view, taking on the economic consensus has come to be seen as tantamount to challenging the scientific consensus: absurd.

Beneath the ideological surface of a group consensus there is a more fundamental emotional need for a shared vision. After all, the human capacity for group cooperation has played a huge role in our evolutionary success story. Professor Jared Diamond has argued that the major turning point in the fortunes of *Homo sapiens* was not the rise of higher cognitive functions in the brain, but the perfection of the human larynx, which allowed for the take-off of language which brought the exchange of ideas and

---

15 Friedrich August von Hayek, 'Nobel Banquet Speech', 10 December 1974

unprecedented social organization.[16] Our desire to conform, rooted in the deep structures of the human psyche, is powerful enough to subordinate more rational considerations. In the 1950s Solomon Asch conducted a famous experiment into the nature of conformity. He showed his test subjects three different lines of obviously different length. Then he surrounded them with a group of people who were in on the experiment, whose job it was to insist that the lines were all of the same length. Confronted with the pressure to abide by group expectations, over 70 percent of the subjects misreported the length of lines at least once.

This phenomenon is not confined to the faculty lab. In 1995, three teams of climbers combined and attempted to climb K2, the second highest mountain in the world after Everest, on the border of Pakistan and China. The group persevered despite worsening weather conditions. Tragically, six of the group died on the mountain. In one study, the impact of groupthink was identified in the desire to press ahead. As one of the survivors is reported to have said, 'the most dangerous thing about groups is that everyone hands over responsibility for themselves to someone else. You lose a sense of personal responsibility, and feel less able to express dissent.'[17] Indeed, it's been shown that mountaineering groups of four or more are more likely to suffer fatalities. This is because once the weather starts to turn no one in the group wants to be the lone spoilsport who suggests they turn back.

A set of shared assumptions can foster a real sense of camaraderie. This is our evolutionary reward for helping to define the group identity. Soldiers have described the 'pervasive well-being'

---

16 See Jared Diamond, *Guns, Germs and Steel: A short history of everybody for the last 13,000 years* (New York: W. W. Norton, 1997)

17 A. Searle 'Group Psychology: Valuable Lessons from our "New-Fangled" Subject', in *Psychology Review* 1996, pp. 2–34

and the 'strange sense of personal enlargement'[18] they experience when performing military drill. Sharing a professional consensus is, perhaps, the intellectual equivalent of this.

In the case of pre-crisis economics the professional consensus was to build economic policy on the assumption of perfect rationality. Banks were allowed to operate with no limit on the amount of debt they built up, and were asked to decide for themselves if their business models were sustainable. We know that this was a false assumption. And we have seen how some people questioned it.

Crucially, regulators felt these pressures too. As Lord Turner, Chairman of the UK Financial Services Authority, admitted, 'Regulators are also taken in by an intellectual framework that explains the bubble as rational, because humans have a bias to optimism to believe the world has improved for the better'.[19]

The United States Federal Reserve typified this mindset. J. Kyle Bass, a hedge fund manager and former Bear Stearns executive, worried that the housing market was headed for a fall. He took his concerns direct to the Fed:

> Their answer at the time was [...] home prices always track income growth and jobs growth. And they showed me income growth on one chart and jobs growth on another, and said, 'We don't see what you're talking about because incomes are still growing and jobs are still growing'. And I said, 'Well, you obviously don't realize where the dog is and where the tail is, and what's moving what'.[20]

---

18 William McNeill, *Keeping Together in Time* (Harvard: Harvard University Press, 1995), p. 2

19 Private interview

20 Financial Crisis Inquiry Commission Report, 'Final Report of the National Commission on the Causes of the Financial and Economic Crisis in the United States', January 2011, p. 19

Why did no one with the power to act do so?

Stories

Answering that question explains why one economic theory and not another is allowed to become the consensus. In science a given hypothesis gains influence because it provides the best possible explanation for the existing evidence; in economics the most popular theories are those which provide us with the most compelling stories.

Every culture tells itself stories. A narrative imposes form and causality on what would otherwise be the random chaos of experience. Stories provide us with the reassurance that we, and not the universe, are in control. The crime novelist P. D. James once said: 'What the detective story is about is not murder but the restoration of order.' It's just as aesthetically important that the serial killer's motives are psychologically explicable as that the killer eventually gets caught, so that by the end of the novel it's not only the crime that gets solved, but the criminal.

Economic narratives perform a similar function. Consider the astounding popularity of Marxism, which formed the official ideology of half the world's governments at the height of the Cold War. The Marxist view of the world gained traction not because it provided the best analysis of the facts, but because it purported to identify and resolve the fundamental cause of social injustice: private property. This narrative was so compelling because it moved the most intractable problems of human nature out of the subjective realm of ethics and politics and turned them into a simple question of technical administration. It followed that Utopia was around the corner: we no longer had to change ourselves, merely the laws surrounding property ownership and access to power.

Before the financial crisis economists and governments in the West were telling a different story, albeit one that was no less beguiling in its simplicity. According to this narrative deficit-spending would lead to sustainable long-term growth. Debt 'smoothed consumption', allowing banks and individuals to buy today what they would pay for tomorrow. Even though neither experienced a rise in real income this was possible because the value of the asset purchased, whether a house or another bank, would inevitably rise in value, allowing the debt to be paid off over time. Debt financing ensured that there need never again be a slump in demand which is why Chairman Greenspan was able to talk of a new era of economic management.

The twentieth century had been an age of economic extremes: the great slump between the wars, skyrocketing inflation in the 1970s, but now we had entered the 'Great Moderation'. Armed with nothing but a credit card, Man had tamed the economic cycle. This turned the nation's debt managers, the banks, into both the brains and beating heart of the economy. In consumer nations, the US and the UK, it meant we no longer had to feel insecure about being out-exported by Germany and Japan, or out-competed by the Far East; we had a new way of creating wealth, and it was just as good. The link between this story and Marxism was that both laid emphasis on private property, in one case a source of evil, in the other a source of aspiration and a means of unqualified good.

In two of the countries worst hit by the crisis – Iceland and Ireland – the nationalistic appeal of this narrative was even more overt. Iceland, whose banks held assets worth an eye-watering 1,000 percent of GDP on the eve of the crisis, appeared to have transformed itself from a small, economically negligible fishing nation, into a frozen Hong Kong of the North Atlantic, while the Republic of Ireland, which styled itself the 'Celtic Tiger' economy, was finally able to end seventy years of humiliating comparisons with its former colonial ruler, thanks to a booming financial sector.

Where there were questions of national pride, or political prestige, involved, challenging the financial mythology was difficult. Once personal profit was introduced into the mix it became all but impossible. This is what Patrick Evershed discovered in the years before the boom.

Evershed was a veteran London-based asset manager who had been following the business cycle for over fifty years. He told us how he had come to learn that 'people are backward looking when making investment decisions. You can only sell things that have been going up, but it's wrong to sell shares which are good value simply because the share price has crashed.'[21] In contrast to consumer goods, 'when people see the price of an asset rising, they don't reduce their demand for it, they want to join in'.[22] As a result he came under intense pressure from clients to buy financial assets during the boom. Evershed was convinced, however, that the debt financing which had driven up the price of assets could not go on forever. Debt had made the system so fragile that the tiniest market tremor could send the entire economy spiraling into recession.

But, just like Lear's Fool, when he stated the nature of the problem he found that 'people thought I was mad'.[23] The more convinced Evershed became that the economy was headed for disaster the more urgently he felt that the public needed to be warned. In 2005, in the run-up to a UK general election, he spent £100,000 on newspaper advertisements warning about the problem, 'but the consequence was people thought I was madder than they'd thought before'.

In the final months before the crisis erupted, the American hedge fund manager Jim Chanos took his concerns to the

---

21 Private interview
22 Ibid.
23 Ibid.

very highest level. A specialist in rooting out shady accounting practices, Chanos had made his name on the Street by betting against what he believed to be overvalued Enron stock a year before the Enron scandal broke. In April 2007 at the World Bank in Washington he had been asked to brief the G8 on the growing turbulence in global financial markets.

In the fortnight leading up to the conference, Chanos's fund had been combing through recently published 10k filings, the annual reports listed companies are required to file with the Securities & Exchange Commission (SEC). His staff noticed sinister concentrations of 'structured' finance products tied to the US residential real estate market weighing down the balance sheets of the biggest banks – a market which by this time had already begun to deteriorate. As Chanos tried to explain to G8 policymakers, this meant the next crisis would likely not be confined to a small clique of professional speculators with only themselves to blame: large banks bearing household names and containing the savings of real households were also under threat.

In an effort to drive his message through to an unresponsive audience Chanos took an unlikely step for a hedge fund manager, disclosing that his fund had made large bets against the world's leading financial institutions. If at this point policymakers had decided to act on his advice he believes that his fund would have lost a lot of money for his clients. But action was not forthcoming. Chanos was thanked for his presentation, papers were shuffled and the meeting moved on to the next item on the agenda: the insurance industry. 'I left the room sort of incredulous that the presentation ... really elicited no official questions or comments'.[24]

John Maynard Keynes famously remarked that 'markets can

---

24 Rob Johnson, interview with Jim Chanos, published on www.nextnewdeal. net, 1 September 2009

stay irrational for longer than you or I can stay solvent'. After the First World War, Keynes had taken up currency trading, speculating on margin that the German mark was overvalued. Even though Keynes was eventually proven right he had challenged the judgment of the market too soon and his fund was wiped out in the summer of 1920. If Keynes were alive today he might say that markets can stay irrational for longer than you or I can stay credible.

The case of Tony Dye is an instructive example to politicians and financiers alike that no one can afford to be right at the wrong time. Dye had worked as a pension fund portfolio manager at the Phillips and Drew fund. During the late 1990s he had refused to invest in American equities, convinced that they were massively overvalued. For several years his fund languished at the bottom of performance charts as more bullish rivals cashed in on the US stock market. Dye intended to bide his time and reap the rewards of the inevitable bust, but the managers of his parent firm UBS eventually lost patience and fired him in 2000. Dye's successors scrabbled to reverse his contrarian investment strategy. A month later the dot-com bubble burst and the US stock market plunged. Phillips and Drew hadn't had enough time to load up on as many US equities as their competitors and quite unwittingly found themselves catapulted to the top of the league, all thanks to Tony Dye.

Dye continued to call problems with the market in the years after the crash. Towards the end of 2002, in a letter to the *Financial Times* he predicted an imminent housing crash in the UK, on a similar scale to the house-price slump of the early 1990s. Up until his death in March 2008, Dye was warning that the boom was unsustainable. No firm would rehire him, so he started his own fund. Although posthumously proved correct, the economics were against him. Dye was right at the wrong time, and his fund was not a success.

Most bubbles take time to develop. Indeed the biggest and most dangerous bubbles gestate for many years. These long bubbles are exacerbated by changes in the profile of key decision-makers. To understand the crash, we should pay attention to what kind of people were on the up in the boom years and who languished on the lower rungs of the corporate ladder.

Richard Bowen became Citigroup's head of business underwriting in 2006. Part of Bowen's job was to supervise the quality of the mortgages Citigroup's investment wing was buying up, bundling together and selling on to Fannie and Freddie. When he arrived at his new post Bowen was shocked to discover that up to 60 percent of the loan applications he sampled were missing crucial documents or had been initially rejected then waved through anyway. Bowen repeatedly tried to alert top management to the dangers: if the loans went bad then investors had the right to force Citigroup to buy them back. He even sent Robert Rubin, the former US Treasury Secretary and chairman of Citigroup's board, a memo titled 'URGENT – READ IMMEDIATELY'[25] spelling out the risks. For his trouble Bowen went from supervising 220 people to just two, had his bonus reduced and his performance downgraded in a staff review.

It's significant that before joining the Treasury, Rubin had worked as an investment banker while Bowen's background was in consumer lending, historically one of the more conservative areas of banking. In the boom years the bulls of the financial world made great strides up the corporate ladder while the cautious tended to be left behind. With few exceptions, Britain and America's 'universal banks', the institutions that took savers' deposits but also speculated on the securities market, came to be managed by people who built their careers as buccaneering investment bankers. AIG's Financial Products division, which

---

25 Financial Crisis Inquiry Commission Report, 2011, p. 19

would go on to insure as much as half the American subprime mortgage market, was dominated by traders rather than insurance specialists, and at the three credit-rating agencies salespeople rather than analysts were promoted to the most senior positions. Mark Froeba, a former senior vice president of Moody's, summed up the consequences of this imbalance:

> When I joined Moody's in late 1997, an analyst's worst fear was that we would contribute to the assignment of a rating that was wrong. When I left Moody's, an analyst's worst fear was that he would do something, or she, that would allow him or her to be singled out for jeopardizing Moody's market share.'[26]

As the system began to overheat, those most predisposed to see the dangers were marginalized in favor of their more aggressive colleagues, thereby exacerbating the cycle. Regulators too were dazzled by the boom, backing off at exactly the point where intervention would have been most effective. The Fed's Roger Cole reports that Fed supervisors did occasionally query whether banks were growing too fast or taking too much risk, but such discussions always ran into pushback. For Cole, 'frankly a lot of that pushback was given credence on the part of the firms by the fact that – like a Citigroup was earning 4 to 5 billion a quarter. [...] When that kind of money is flowing out quarter after quarter after quarter, and their capital ratios are way above the minimums, it's very hard to challenge.'[27]

Wall Street's tradition of sidelining pessimists is by no means new. Roger Babson (1875–1967), an early theorist of the business cycle, was described by J. K. Galbraith as an 'educator, philosopher, theologian, statistician, forecaster and friend of

26 Ibid., p. 208
27 Ibid., p. 307

gravity'.[28] He was also a fool in the corner. Babson used intuition and common sense in his approach to the markets. His 'ten commandments' included instruction not to be fooled by a name, and to keep speculation and investment separate. He forecast the Great Crash but thanks to his less than orthodox approach he was dismissed by the Street. As Galbraith writes: 'In these matters, as so often in our culture, it is far, far better to be wrong in a respectable way than to be right for the wrong reasons. Wall St was not at a loss as what to do about Babson. It promptly and soundly denounced him.'[29]

As Galbraith described the period before the Great Crash of 1929: 'Never before or since have so many become so wondrously, so effortlessly or so quickly rich.'[30] This fantasy of wealth without work combined with the rags to riches narrative of the American Dream to ferment the toxic speculative frenzy which led to the Wall Street Crash. Then, as now, economic theory is what gave the story its shape, but it is the profit motive which lent it emotional momentum, and led to the promotion of the bulls and the rejection of those who sounded caution but were right at the wrong time.

This mindset is exemplified by the hapless speculators who piled their money into Madoff Investment Securities. An estimated $17.3 billion dollars was invested with Madoff.[31] The 8 to 12 percent annual returns, risk free, his company promised investors were far in excess of the average offered by competitors. Even in the barren year of 2008 one of his S&P 500 funds reported an annual return of 5.6 percent, when the average return on the index was minus 38 percent. Of course, as we

---

28 J. K. Galbraith, *The Great Crash 1929* (London: Hamish Hamilton, 1955), p. 84
29 Ibid.
30 Ibid.
31 *New York Times*, 20 December 2012

now know, these returns were entirely fictitious. As early as 1999 a financial analyst named Harry Markopolos had tried to alert the SEC after he took just four hours to prove that Madoff's purported monthly returns were statistically and mathematically impossible.

Yet Markopolos struggled to be heard: by the time Madoff was arrested in December 2008 he had already brought his concerns to the SEC five times. And although many insiders suspected Madoff of wrongdoing the market still ploughed money in. It was simply too mouthwatering a story to let facts get in the way. As the psychologist David Tuckett has said: 'even though intelligent investors knew that the returns were basically impossible, they thought he was a superman. In the pursuit of returns all rationality was lost.'[32]

In 2006 UBS's head of mortgage research wrote an article about that year's American mortgage crop entitled, 'Is this the worst vintage ever?' This was not a new theme. In 2003 she had written: 'Is the US Housing Market a Bubble?' But as a former colleague related: 'she went to the board and said "this is crazy. As soon as rates go up, these will default." Meanwhile the rollover was getting bigger and bigger. The board said "thanks very much", and bought more subprime-backed securities. In the end, she resigned out of disgust.'[33]

The Backfire Effect

We know from everyday life that it is very hard to tell people something they do not want to hear. If a friend is infatuated, the awkward conversation where you try to explain their beloved is absolutely wrong for them is often futile. If they are

---

32 David Tuckett, 'Addressing the Psychology of Financial Markets', IPPR, May 2009
33 Private interview

emotionally invested in the story of romance your intervention doesn't stand a chance.

Deep psychological processes subliminally reinforce our faith in the stories we tell ourselves. One of these processes has recently been described as the 'backfire effect' by the American political scientists Brendan Nyhan and Jason Reifler. When we confront a threat to our worldview, that complex mesh of belief, story, prejudice and habit which we use to define ourselves and make sense of our experience, the backfire effect snaps into action. It's an unconscious defense reflex, helping to shield our preconceptions against incoming hostile ideas, working as an information filter to confirm our prejudices and soothe our doubts. The tragicomic consequence of the effect is that the more we learn about the things that are important to us the less we know. In his wide-ranging study of self-delusion *You Are Not So Smart,* David McRaney describes several studies which observe the backfire effect in action.

In 1997 Geoffrey Munro and Peter Ditto devised a study in which people were divided into two groups depending on their attitude towards homosexuality.[34] The group who said they were pro-gay were given a spurious scientific study (devised by Munro and Ditto) which employed cutting-edge research to show that homosexuality was in fact a form of mental illness. The anti-gay group was given an equally fake study which suggested that homosexuality was an entirely natural form of human behavior with a solid biological basis. McRaney reports the backfire effect: 'On either side of the issue, after reading studies which did not support their beliefs, most people didn't report an epiphany, a realization they've been wrong all these years. Instead, they said

---

34 Geoffrey Munro and Peter Ditto, 'Biased assimilation, attitude polariza- tion, and affect in reactions to stereotype-relevant scientific information', *Personality and Social Psychology Bulletin,* 1997

the issue was something science couldn't understand.' When asked about other contentious topics later on, both groups said 'they no longer trusted research to determine the truth'. Rather than allow core ethical beliefs about what it meant to be human come into question, the backfire effect dismissed the very validity of the scientific method.

In 2006, Nyhan and Reifler performed a series of experiments to demonstrate how the 'ghost' of misinformation lives on, even after it's been formally debunked. They showed test subjects a series of studies about the existence of WMDs in Iraq. One article made the claim that the United States found weapons of mass destruction in Iraq, the next accurately reported that WMDs were never found. Unsurprisingly, those who supported the war and tended towards the conservative end of the political spectrum tended to agree with the first article and dismiss the second. Crucially, the conservatives reported that not only did the genuine news article fail to dilute their belief in the discovery of Iraqi WMDs but the second article positively enforced that belief. Nyhan and Reifler repeated the study with other controversial issues like stem cell research and abortion. Once again they found that if the second article contradicted a participant's ideological convictions their belief in the initial fictitious report was only strengthened. This held true all the way along the political spectrum.

When we look back at the raw numbers, it's difficult to see how policymakers were not more suspicious of the boom. Startling statistics leer out of tables and graphs. US household debt rose from 80 percent of disposable income in 1993 to 130 percent by 2006; three quarters of this was mortgage debt and yet incomes had barely risen. Surely this couldn't go on?

Then factor in the backfire effect. The more the evidence mounted the more strongly people clung to their cherished worldview, the belief that complexity meant progress, that in the modern age high indebtedness was not only normal but necessary, that if nothing else self-interest would ensure the stability of financial markets. As UK Prime Minister Gordon Brown declared in a speech to London's financial elite in 2007, 'a new world order' had been created, and we were witnessing the dawn of 'a new golden age for the City of London'. The backfire effect also explains people's preference for short-term historic analogies to make the case both for and against the crisis. One of its effects is to heighten our belief in evidence we have already acquired while at the same time making us skeptical of new evidence. When challenged we look to our past for reassurance.

In laboratory conditions it is impossible to demonstrate ethically what the psychological effects of abandoning a worldview might be, to force an override of the backfire effect in other words. But we can infer it would be devastating. The extreme emotional distress that results when the veil is torn and the true nature of things revealed forms the dramatic climax of *King Lear*. This is ultimately why so few people could bring themselves to believe what they were told by those who saw it coming.

Even as the evidence mounted, people found it hard to accept the coming storm. This was the tension most eloquently expressed by Chuck Prince, CEO of Citigroup, who saw the early tremors in the markets in July 2007 but said: 'When the music stops, in terms of liquidity, things will be complicated. But as long as the music is playing, you've got to get up and dance. We're still dancing.'

Just a few weeks later, the music stopped and the fools were vindicated.

There is something of Lear in Alan Greenspan's famous testimony to a congressional hearing on the banking crisis in October 2008. He can see the fault lines and fissures in his worldview but the backfire effect cannot repair them.

I made a mistake in presuming that the self-interests of organizations, specifically banks and others, were such as that they were best capable of protecting their own shareholders and their equity in the firms... I have found a flaw. I don't know how significant or permanent it is. But I have been *very distressed* by that fact... *I was shocked*, because I have been going for forty years or more with very considerable evidence that it was working exceptionally well.[35]

Greenspan could not, however, claim that he had not been warned. Like others, he had not listened. The bubble had been allowed to grow unchecked, and the bursting was upon us.

---

35 Alan Greenspan, testimony to the House Committee on Oversight and Reform, 23 October 2008

Chapter 2

TIPPING THE BANDWAGON

In abnormal times, in particular when the hypothesis of an indef-
inite continuance of the existing state of affairs is less plausible than
usual, even though there are no express grounds to anticipate a
definite change, the market will be subject to waves of optimistic
and pessimistic sentiment, which are unreasoning and yet in a sense
legitimate where no solid basis exists for a reasonable calculation.
– John Maynard Keynes, 1936

'**S**enior Goldman people have loaded up on firearms and are now equipped to defend themselves if there is a populist uprising against the bank,'[1] reported *Bloomberg*'s Alice Schroeder in December 2009. In London and New York bankers were stocking up on guns, gold and canned goods, anticipating anarchy on the streets. One City of London survivalist recalled the mood: 'I couldn't afford a bunker, but I looked at it... You can get bunkers made, or buy an ex-Ministry of Defence one. Best toilets, blast doors and air supply come from Switzerland. Best bunkers are made in the US.'

Visceral fear gripped the same world that had sidelined Sir Andrew Large, dismissed Roubini, and scoffed at Rajan. How did we get from the ritual lampooning of anyone who sounded a note of caution to guns and bunkers?

In this chapter we look at how people behaved as the world swooned from unsustainable boom to earth-shattering bust. The

---

timing and exact nature of this sudden, violent reaction could not be predicted, but its shape is common. We see it throughout history in bubble after bubble with the same tipping-point dynamic. We see it in nature when a herd suddenly turns or a flock takes off as if as one. Every time it involves a combination of rational and irrational behavior that is both inevitable yet impossible to predict with any precision.

The behavioral dynamics observable in the final year of the boom and during the shift from boom to bust are vital to an understanding of how financial markets work, for they reveal important truths about the way people tend to act when faced with uncertainty. If we are to design a policy framework that is more effective in mitigating the effects of the economic cycle we must understand these truths.

The most commonly cited point of no return is the fall of Lehman Brothers on 15 September 2008. For everyone, both those inside and outside the financial world, this was the game changer. When the bank was left to fail the inaction of the US government tipped the system over the edge. For those looking on from outside, what had been a series of market jitters and a credit crunch became an international obsession. For those on the inside, their confidence was shattered and their faith in the system undermined.

Yet this popular analysis of the tipping point overlooks the fact that the market collapse was first revealed well over a year before, in the early summer of 2007. First, in June, amid a raft of shocked headlines, the investment-banking powerhouse Bear Stearns was forced to bail out one of its hedge funds because of exposure to investments in subprime mortgages – securities which had been given a top AAA rating by the three major credit-rating agencies. A month later, with less fanfare but of equal importance, the lesser known German bank, IKB, collapsed when two of its funds faced a severe funding crisis after investor confidence drained away. As we will see, these two events between them foreshadowed the financial crisis, yet it didn't strike with its full force for another fourteen months.

Herding & What It's All About

Like the animals we are, groups of humans behave like herds. This should not be surprising; we are a naturally social and cooperative species, so the ability for individual humans to align their sentiments with those of the group conferred a major survival advantage early on in our evolutionary history. The limbic system, a structure in the mammalian brain closely implicated in herding behavior, is also responsible for the production of emotional responses to the outside world, including our strong desire to seek out cues and signals from others when we are unsure of ourselves. Crucially, the limbic system features a number of neural hotlines which circumvent the neo-cortex, the part of the human brain responsible for reasoning, learning and higher thought. This means the herding it inspires is often likely to be unconsidered and unreflective.[2]

Imagine, as a relentless sun beats down on the African plain, a herd of wildebeest graze peacefully together. All is calm. Suddenly, one animal senses a threat. Instinctively it moves closer to the herd for protection, fearful of being isolated. Then a couple more notice and jostle for protection looking for safety in numbers. A few more realize, and some more, until suddenly, fear rips through the whole herd. As if guided by one mind, with each individual looking to shield itself among the others, the herd stampedes. As the herd gathers momentum, it takes on a collective character.

For all our modern sophistication, humans continue to

---

2 See Robert R. Prechter, *The Wave Principle of Human Social Behavior* (Gainesville, Georgia: New Classics Library, 1999)

evince herd-like behavior. In fashion, for example, very few of us choose to stray too far from the herd. From time to time a few extroverts will leave the pack with outlandish new ideas. And while we may enjoy the sight, most of us will not take their lead. But occasionally, they catch on and people imitate them, until we reach a tipping point of respectability and the herd of mainstream shoppers follows.

Herding behavior also occurs in financial markets. Drawing on his own experience as a professional investor, John Maynard Keynes was one of the first economists to describe financial herding. Keynes argued that certain assets were subject to 'conventional valuation':[3] because relatively uninformed investors make up the bulk of the market their views are likely to determine the price of that asset. This gives the minority of informed investors an incentive to follow the herd, even though they may have a different view as to the true value of the asset. Tipping points occur when there are not enough strong roots of conviction to hold a conventional valuation steady. In their absence prices are liable to change suddenly and violently in response to fluctuations in market sentiment, or what Keynes termed the 'animal spirits'.

Keynes's insight was that financial herding will be more pronounced where knowledge is scarce because nervous investors will consult the 'opinion of the market' for reassurance. This is increasingly borne out by empirical research. Robert Olsen conducted a study of 4,000 corporate earnings estimates by financial analysts and found that the greater the difficulty in forecasting a company's earnings per share, the more the analysts were influenced by the opinion of the market as a whole, as expressed by the company's current share price.[4]

---

3 In the *General Theory of Employment, Interest and Money* (London: Macmillan & Co., 1936)

4 Robert Olsen, 'Implications of Herding Behavior' in *Financial Analysts Journal, July–August* (1996), pp. 37–41

Just as important, as forecasts became more dependent on market sentiment, more optimistic projections were produced. Herding, then, has a self-reinforcing dynamic, which has serious implications for finance.

After a series of incidents in June and July 2007, the coming crisis was inevitable in the eyes of those who were paying attention. They saw loss pile on loss, they saw confidence curdle to doubt and they watched in anticipation as feelings of unease grew more intense. The final failure of Lehman was the denouement: the moment that doubt turned to despair and the truth was unavoidable. The herd tipped; and we are now beginning to look back with fascination at how long the crisis took to work its way through the system.

Why did the system tip when it did? How can we explain the timing? The answer can be found in the combination of natural human behavior in an unsustainable system, which simultaneously perpetuated the boom, heightened the tipping point, and accelerated the bust.

What Happened

To get to the root of the tipping point, we need to rewind to early 2007, when the true flaw of subprime mortgages began to emerge. The concept of 'subprime' meant mortgage companies were explicitly lending to people who were deemed risky. The loans were marketed attractively to encourage people to take them out, but they masked hidden fees and a higher future rate of interest than traditional prime mortgages.

Subprime lenders, keen to maintain the high volume of sales, started to offer mortgages with 'teaser rates': a lower interest rate that would only last for a limited period. These were snapped up, even though once the discount period had ended, the interest rate would be jacked up to a much higher level. The S&L Golden West, which was acquired by Wachovia in 2006, specialized in Option ARMs. These were adjustable rate mortgages that gave people the option to choose between payment of principal and interest, interest only, or a low teaser rate which would cause the loan balance to actually rise, meaning much higher rates later on. People who would not previously have been able to get a mortgage signed up in droves. They were persuaded to pay the upfront fee and take the teaser rate in the expectation they could always re-mortgage on another teaser rate. This process is similar to the '0 percent on balance transfers for 6 months' that credit card companies offer, where people can rack up their credit card debt but pay no interest on it by immediately transferring it to a new card – until the offers run out.

Those uncomfortable with lax access to mortgages faced a moral tussle with the federal government. In a resonant speech delivered from the White House in 1995, Bill Clinton told the American people:

> You want to reinforce family values in America, encourage two-parent households, get people to stay home? Make it easy for people to own their own homes and enjoy the rewards of family life and see their work rewarded. This is a big deal. This is about more than money and sticks and boards and windows. This is about the way we live as a people and what kind of society we're going to have.[5]

Questioning the credit that made homeownership possible meant pitching yourself against this ideology, ideology that was backed up by public policy. In 1977 the Carter administration had introduced the Community Reinvestment Act (CRA),

---

5   William J. Clinton, 'Remarks on the National Homeownership Strategy', 5 June 1995

which encouraged banks to lend more to low-income neighbor-hoods. The enthusiasm with which banks pursued their CRA lending targets would be taken into consideration by regulators when deciding whether to approve a proposed merger or acquisition. The 1990s and early 2000s were a period of major consolidation in the finance industry, which meant the CRA came into its own as a tool of political leverage. A recent study of lending before the crash found that banks undergoing a CRA examination issued 5 percent more loans than a control group which was not being scrutinized by regulators over the same period.[6] Crucially, these extra CRA loans were 15 percent more likely to become delinquent a year after origination. Ominously, Bear Stearns was the first Wall Street investment bank to securitize Community Reinvestment Loans in 1997.

As we shall see, there are plenty of other reasons why banks lowered their underwriting standards in the years before the crash. Some of the worst abuses were committed by institutions which were not subject to the CRA. Yet the fact remains that government had given its blessing to a culture of risky lending, and that plenty of firms were delighted to cash in on the rhetoric. Take Countrywide. In 2003 Angelo Mozilo, chief executive of the US's largest mortgage lender, proudly proclaimed in a speech to mortgage professionals in Washington DC that, 'Expanding the American Dream of homeownership must continue to be our mission, not solely for the purpose of bene-fiting corporate America, but more importantly, to make our country a better place.' Responding to those who were calling for tighter regulation of the subprime sector, Mozilo warned that 'subprime lending and predatory lending are not the same

---

6   Sumit Agarwal, Efraim Benmelech, Nittai Bergman and Amit Seru, 'Did the Community Reinvestment Act (CRA) lead to a culture of risky lend-ing?', NBER Working Paper No. 18609, 1 October 2012

thing. Brushing them with one broad stroke only wipes out the opportunities for homeownership to too many deserving low-income and minority home buyers.'[7] Five years later only a hurried acquisition by Bank of America allowed Countrywide to avoid bankruptcy.

We should never seek to eliminate risk entirely. A modern economy could not function without banks prepared to put savings to use by financing useful activities like enterprise and homeownership. Many valuable projects, like helping a new business grow, will always involve a degree of risk that the loan will not be repaid. In the past, however, banks had been cautious about whom they lent to because they stood to bear the first loss if things went wrong.

Now, not only were banks being strongly encouraged to make loans that might not be paid back, but they used new technology to pass on the loans. So the people making the original decision to lend were not the ones that ended up being owed the money. The idea was to improve the efficiency of finance, and ensure that risk was more effectively distributed throughout the system, enhancing stability.

Alongside the new technology, a new language was born to describe this brave new world. The new language was convenient shorthand for those who worked in these markets. But it also conspired against external scrutiny of the new developments. Many people, including senior management, did not want to admit they didn't know what the alphabet soup of new acronyms stood for, as use of the new language implied confidence that you knew what you were talking about. It is now abundantly clear that the new technology merely meant different ways of doing the same old things: lending and investing

---

7 Angelo R. Mozilo, 'The American Dream of Homeownership: from Cliché to Mission', John T. Dunlop Lecture, 4 February 2003

money for a fee or interest. In effect, the new technology and language that went with it made the system more complex, avoided regulatory and tax rules, and made prudent management of banks yet more difficult. The emperor had no clothes.

It is not necessary to be bamboozled by the language.

The first piece of new technology used by banks was the mortgage-backed security, known as an MBS. Their purpose was simple. The bank would package up a group of loans, and sell them to an investor – or even another bank – as an MBS. The investor might want to purchase one of these securities to get a higher return than that offered by less risky securities, like government bonds. The bank might want to sell them in order to move them off their own balance sheet, thus freeing up capital, and enabling it to earn new fees by using the money to make more loans.

An MBS did not consist of just one person's mortgage. Banks took individual mortgages, and bundled them together. They then separated them into different tranches by level of risk, and a credit-rating agency was approached to give a top AAA rating to the least risky tranche, which would be paid back first in the event of a default. Middle tranches, called 'mezzanine' in the new language, were given lower ratings like BB, and the most risky called an equity tranche would be paid back last, so investors would lose out first if any of the borrowers defaulted. By chopping up bundles of mortgages in this way, investors could pick and choose the level of risk they wanted: they could take the risk on the lowest tranche, where homeowners might not pay their mortgages each month, but gain a higher yield than that offered by higher-rated assets. From 1997 to 2007 new issuance of these so-called MBS almost quadrupled from $600 billion to over $2 trillion.

An efficient market was thought to have been developed: those willing to bear the risk would snap up the riskier tranches, while those who wanted to play it safe would buy the higher-rated tranches. Everyone was a winner.

In old-fashioned language, an MBS was merely a loan book that could be bought and sold at a market price.

Clearly not all of the loan could be rated AAA. So banks started grouping the lower-rated tranches of MBS into new securities known as collateralized debt obligations, or CDOs. This allowed part of the riskier parts of MBS to be given the gold-plated AAA rating. The idea was simple: surely even all the riskiest homeowners wouldn't stop paying their mortgages all at once? Complicated mathematical models were created to map the likelihood of this happening, backing up the conclusion of the banks that someone somewhere would still be paying their mortgage, even if interest rates moved higher. Once again, the CDOs were divided into tranches, and once again, investors could select the level of risk they wanted to own. By creating layers of different debts structured by different levels of risk it was believed that risk was then in some way averaged out. Risk had been diversified by spreading it out through the system, so that it sat with those most willing to bear it.

In the old language, a CDO was a combination of the weakest parts of several loan books, in which it was harder to calculate the default risk.

Next, the banks set up special purpose vehicles (SPVs), to hold the CDOs. This took the whole process off their balance sheet, meaning they could sit back and reap the rewards without worrying about where the risks were, or allocating any capital in case things were to go wrong.

An SPV sounds clever, but in layman's terms it is simply a part of a set of loans the bank didn't want to admit to having in their accounts. The technique was not restricted to the private sector. In the euro area countries like Greece also used off-balance-sheet accounting tricks to hide liabilities from investors and European Union regulators.

Finally, the banks created a further clever twist. Enter the credit default swaps (CDS). These are a form of insurance to protect the lender in the case of a debt defaulting. When investors bought CDSs, they paid protection payments to insurers, like AIG. In exchange, should there be defaults, the insurers must deliver the original value of the bond in full. The owner of the CDS is effectively paying an insurance premium to cover for a fall in the bond's value in the event of a default. CDSs were therefore used by investors to hedge against a fall in the value of MBSs – even if all homeowners did stop paying their mortgages, you could still rest easy as you would receive a payout from owning a CDS. The issuers paid the credit-rating agencies to give the insured bonds the AAA rating. Once again, banks made money from the sales of CDS, and also used them to hedge risks on their own balance sheets. AIG became hugely profitable from selling this insurance cheaply, so capturing a massive market share in the sale of CDS.

The problem was that all the packaging up, the slicing and dicing, had obscured where the real risk was in the system. What if homeowners started to default more quickly than expected? What if vast swathes of homeowners all defaulted at once? Would the insurers be able to pay out? Wouldn't the supposed AAA tranches suddenly be exposed to a greater risk than the models had suggested? Even worse, would the legal structures be solid? Who would know what each tranche was really worth?

At the time, though, the financial sector was seduced by innovation, not realizing that the new technology of MBSs, CDOs, SPVs and CDSs had obscured where the risks really lay.

To put it in context, it was so complicated that when PricewaterhouseCoopers went in to administer Lehman's bankruptcy, it took teams of ten about ten days just to start to understand the products they were dealing with, let alone the deals that had actually been done.

Or think of it this way. The Bank of England's Executive Director for Financial Stability, Andrew Haldane, has calculated how much due diligence a diligent investor would need to read to make sense of the various products on offer. Staggeringly, your standard CDO investor would have to read over 30,000 pages on average to understand the product. This is nothing compared to the CDO-squared investor, who ought to be looking at about 1,125 million pages.[8] As a point of comparison, Tolstoy's *War and Peace* is a mere 1,358 pages. The complexity of the system simply cannot be overemphasized.

The new language that shrouded the system confused not only those looking on from outside, but those actually working for the organizations that crafted it. Stephen King, Chief Economist of HSBC, put it like this: The financial sector has created its own language. This bamboozles the public and to be honest even many in the industry... People tend to go along with it because they do not want to be the one who says they don't understand.'[9]

This fast-paced Wall Street lingo strengthened the hand of those who spoke it and excluded those who did not. Conservative MP Greg Hands, now a member of the British Government, worked as a derivatives trader for eight years. He told us how experienced traders could exploit the language for personal advantage.

As a typical example, he described a salesperson informing a trader that a client needed an updated price on a security they had been looking at the previous day. The trader would

---

8 Andrew Haldane, 'Rethinking the Financial Network', speech delivered at the Financial Student Association, Amsterdam, April 2009

9 Private interview

know there was a strong chance the client wanted to deal, or they wouldn't have returned for an updated price. To net a bigger profit the trader would therefore increase the price of the security, even though nothing about it had changed. At first the salesperson would be confused, but if they queried the decision they would get a dismissive reply like: 'Oh, it's because of the *theta*'. The salesperson would hesitate: 'Oh ... what is that again?' 'It's the time decay,' the trader would reply. At this point, still confused, the salesperson would be too embarrassed to ask any more questions and would retreat back to the client to try and explain the price change.

Amid the confusion of the new language, the central justification for the changes was that those willing to bear risk were being matched with those willing to offload it. Again, this was meant to help spread the risk in the system to those who could best bear it. This principle was based on the attitude and preference of the investors. If investors rationally knew how much risk they could absorb, only those able to bear the potential losses would take on the most risky debts. But this of course overlooks two fundamental flaws. First, that, thanks to the recent explosion in complexity, it was unlikely investors would have full information and understanding. Second, the fact that investors are not paragons of rationality, capable of exerting flawless judgment. They are swayed by human emotions and desires as much, if not more, than the rest of us. As the economist John Kay wrote in August 2007, a full year before the balance tipped, 'if trading was motivated not by differences in attitudes and preferences but by differences in information and understanding, risk would gravitate not to those best able to bear it but to those least able to comprehend it'.[10] His observation would be revealed as painfully prophetic.

In turn, the authorities took comfort in the belief that a self-interested decision was always a rational one. The Fed was aware that underwriting standards were lower in the subprime sector, but it assumed that the banks who bulk-bought these mortgages would only deal with responsible firms. After all, it wasn't in their interests to try and offload toxic waste onto valued customers. Nor was it in the credit-rating agencies' interests to assign high ratings to junk bonds. In the worst-case scenario all these CDOs were insured. Why would firms like AIG underwrite claims they couldn't afford to honor? When they looked at the total exposure to subprime mortgages, they saw the net exposure was relatively small. What they did not see, or want to see, was that because bets had been laid on the back of the subprime mortgage market, the gross exposure was huge. With the network of CDSs on the back of CDOs, you would only need a few CDOs to go bust to bring major institutions to the brink of bankruptcy. The consequence of the complicated new system was close to financial alchemy: it was to turn a risky mortgage into an AAA-rated bond, a gilt-edged security. It meant that the balance sheets of banks still stood up to scrutiny, which meant they could borrow still more money, to fund still more of these money-making tricks.

Of course, at the bottom of all of this were the proud new owners of houses across America. But as long as interest rates stayed low, house prices didn't fall and people kept paying their installments, everyone benefitted.

Between 2004 and 2006, US interest rates rose by over 4 percent, from 1 percent in June 2004 to a high of 5.25 percent in June 2006. On a variable rate mortgage this of course increased the cost of repayments. This also coincided with many mortgages coming to the end of the initial low-interest period, which prompted a huge jump in the monthly payments debtors owed. In July 2006, US house prices began to fall.

The United States is unlike many European countries in that mortgages are tied to the property not the borrower. For individuals this ensures that bankruptcy is a relatively painless process, but it has big implications for the financial system at large. If you can't meet your payments, or your house is worth less than your debts, you can simply walk away. If you relinquish it to the original owner, in this case the bank, you can avoid the foreclosure process.

Sure enough, thousands of US homeowners began to send back their title deeds. The early-morning post in mortgage banks across America became known as the 'jingle mail' – as keys were physically and metaphorically sent back to the bank. As rates rose and prices fell, more homes were abandoned. The impotent sets of keys came in a steady flow into the banks' mailboxes.

As entire streets of newly built housing were abandoned, prices fell still further. Banks across America became the unintentional owners of more and more houses, almost all worth less than they paid.

There was going to be a point of no return. As 2006 turned into 2007, it came.

The impact on the banks at first seemed to come out of nowhere. HSBC started the ball rolling when it wrote down $10.5 billion in goodwill and fired its US Head of Mortgages in February.

More dramatically, on 2 April New Century Financial, one of the biggest subprime mortgage lenders in the US, filed for bankruptcy after a month of difficulties.

In response to worry in the market, government-backed secondary mortgage market firms Fannie Mae and Freddie Mac offered new long-term fixed-rate mortgages designed to let typical subprime owners switch and divert the potential crisis.

Meanwhile, UBS closed its new hedge fund arm after it was hit by subprime losses.

These incidents weren't isolated, but few thought they were systemic. By June, the warning sign flashed brighter from one of Wall Street's most infamous institutions: Bear Stearns. The fifth largest securities firm on Wall Street announced it had spent $3.2 billion bailing out two of its funds that had been exposed to the subprime market. The so-called Timberwolf CDOs, packaged by Goldman Sachs, were only launched in March 2007. By the end of June, $100 worth of investment was worth $83, and by the end of July just $15. ABN AMRO, then about to be purchased by the UK's largest bank, Royal Bank of Scotland, was another significant buyer of the flawed Timberwolf CDOs.

Like HSBC, Bear Stearns also fired its head of asset management and launched an inquiry into the failure of the funds.

The collapse of the Bear Stearns funds sent shockwaves throughout the finance sector. It called into question the value of the CDOs that flooded the system, which had been bought and sold on the basis of their supposedly secure AAA rating. Bear Stearns funds had invested in securities it thought were safe. But thanks to the dramatic rise in subprime mortgage defaults, the value of these securities dissolved.

A source who at the time was close to Jimmy Cayne, bridge-enthusiast and Chairman and CEO of Bear Stearns, stripped it down to the essentials: 'This stuff wasn't triple A. There's going to be a big debate about this'.[11]

He was right with the first part but seriously understated the second.

The realization that the AAA assets could be almost worthless caused alarm in all corners of the financial sector. As Brad Hintz, analyst and ex-CFO of Lehman, questioned publicly at the time: 'How many other hedge funds are holding similar,

---

illiquid, esoteric securities? What are their true prices? What will happen if more blow up?'[12]

This was loudly reported around the world with alarm, but it wasn't clear what the immediate effect on the financial system would be. For those watching closely, it soon became clearer. The key is found not with an American mortgage giant or a high-risk investment bank, but with the relatively unknown German bank IKB.

On 20 July 2007, IKB announced happily that it had had a successful year. It was confident with its earnings forecast. It publicly dismissed rumors of a credit downgrade. Looking back, it is the epitome of pride coming before a fall. A mere ten days later, on 30 July, the bank was forced to admit that its earnings were 'significantly lower' than forecast. The German banking sector produced a rescue package worth €9 billion over the weekend in an attempt to protect itself and its national reputation.

IKB's losses had been sustained by two off-balance-sheet SPVs, called Rhineland and Rhinebridge, which had been set up to buy long-term mortgage-backed securities, funded by short-term wholesale borrowing. This SPV, like most, was linked by a credit line to the bank that owned it, so while it was off the balance sheet for accounting purposes, the bank was liable to make good its borrowing if it lost money. The credit lines were invoked. IKB didn't have enough funds to bail them out. The bank was set for collapse. Much to the relief of all concerned, in the immediate term the situation was hurriedly resolved. Germany's government and banking sector rallied round, bailout money was provided, and calamity postponed.

To an outside observer, this looked like the collapse of one provincial German bank. In comparison to Bear Stearns running into trouble, IKB's difficulties seem a smaller part of the tipping point. But the ramifications of the two were immense.

If you look at the combined effect of the Bear Stearns hedge fund and IKB collapse, the prognosis is fatal. It clearly showed, at least to those who were looking, that AAA ratings were meaningless, that off-balance-sheet debts were still the responsibility of the bank when things went wrong, and that investor confidence had started to curdle.

In September 2007, before being purchased by Royal Bank of Scotland in what was the largest financial acquisition in history, the Dutch bank ABN AMRO, for example, had over $100 billion of credit lines to off-balance-sheet vehicles, more than any other bank in Europe. Many of the losses on these vehicles will never be recovered.

So these early collapses were clear warnings of what was to come. From then onwards, banks increasingly realized that the risks they thought they had transferred to the off-balance-sheet 'shadow banking system' were in fact still on their books. Off-balance-sheet vehicles were brought back onto banks' balance sheets, and the value of AAA debt across the financial system was brought into question. Reassessing their balance sheets in this light, it became clear that the banks had a lot of the bad debt, and not nearly as much capital as they thought. As banks realized how exposed they were to bad debt, they became unwilling to lend to anyone else because no one knew who held what bad debt. Everyone was in the same position. The breakdown in lending of the credit crunch began.

Despite this dawning realization at the heart of the sector, the finance machine bulldozed on. Astonishingly, the RBS acquisition of ABN AMRO was completed, and signed off by British regulators. Many in the markets continued to assert that this was a short-term liquidity problem. In part, this was because many of the AAA debts were insured, so holders of the debt expected to be compensated if they defaulted. It took time to understand that a very small number of companies had cornered the market for writing such insurance, so when all the claims came at once they could not possibly cover them all.

So the crisis continued to work its way through the system: next to go down was American Home Mortgage, one of the largest independent mortgage lenders in the US. Meanwhile, during a testimony to the US Congress, Ben Bernanke, head of the Federal Reserve, admitted this crisis could cost America between $50 and $100 billion.

And then focus switched sharply back to Europe. On 9 August, the French banking giant BNP Paribas announced it was having to freeze three of its funds because it was simply unable to value them. The announcement sent the London stock market tumbling. The biggest faller was RBS, which despite all these warnings was still pursuing its high stakes takeover strategy.

The crisis was about to hit the UK. On Thursday 13 September, the BBC's business editor Robert Peston announced the biggest scoop of his career: Northern Rock, the UK's fifth-biggest mortgage lender had been forced to approach the Bank of England in its capacity of lender of last resort. Highly dependent on short-term funding from the money markets, Northern Rock had struggled to find others willing to lend to it, which triggered a short-term cash-flow crisis. With Peston's broadcast, the subprime crisis moved from an abstract problem affecting Wall Street and the City of London to something that threatened the lives of savers throughout Britain. Overnight, millions of savers removed their funds on the internet. By Friday morning, the run on the bank started in earnest. In the leafy suburbs of Surrey 250 people queued to retrieve their savings, with the police on hand to control the crowds. Even in the City, London's financial district, one branch had a queue, which only increased when City workers circulated online photos of it they had taken in their lunch break.

The share price tumbled by 32 percent in a day.[13]

The first run on a retail bank in the UK for 150 years meant that Northern Rock became a global emblem of the crisis. After a weekend of national panic, the British government finally attempted to reassure people that their deposits were safe. By Tuesday 18 September, with a promise that retail deposits would be protected, the crisis passed and calm was restored. The financial crisis retreated to the upper echelons of the investment banking world, where losses continued to accumulate. Huge losses were announced by almost all major banking groups as the values of assets were written down. The US Federal Reserve and the Bank of England cut interest rates in an attempt to stimulate the economy, while Citigroup, Bank of America, and JPMorgan Chase attempted to restore confidence to the market with a proposed superfund to act as a vehicle for troubled funds in order to wind down operations in an orderly fashion without a panic sale of assets. It never took off. Nothing stemmed the tide of loss. At the end of November, Freddie Mac announced the sale of $6 billion of its shares to cover its losses, only to be trumped by Fannie Mae about a week later selling $7 billion.

Then came another blow: Bear Stearns had announced its first ever quarterly loss on 9 January 2008. Throughout February, it continued trading, confident of its prospects. But it finally collapsed on Friday 14 March, when its hedge fund clients panicked en masse and withdrew their assets. Even on the evening before its collapse, most Bear Stearns employees had no idea of the severity of the crisis. As with most business failures, though, while the debts were the substantive cause of the collapse, the immediate trigger was simply that it ran

13 Bloomberg data

out of cash. Armed with the promise from the Federal Reserve
of whatever liquidity was required, JPMorgan stepped in and
bought the bank. Employees with their life savings in Bear
Stearns stock lost everything. It was in effect a government
bailout with JPMorgan as the middleman.

While a body blow to confidence rippled through the financial
world, the US Government had acted to keep the system afloat.

Losses carried on rising throughout April, and confidence
sank ever lower. The Fed and the Treasury dispatched full-time
examiners to monitor liquidity risk onsite at the big five investment banks. The industry referred to these as 'SWAT teams'.

August 2008 became the month of warnings. HSBC
announced that conditions in financial markets were at their
toughest 'for several decades' after suffering a 28 percent fall in
half-year profits. The Office of the Comptroller of the Currency
(OCC) downgraded Wachovia, noting its strong exposure to the
subprime mortgage market through its recently acquired lending subsidiary Golden West. And then, on 7 September, Fannie
Mae and Freddie Mac, which guaranteed or owned about half
of America's mortgage debt, valued at $5.4 trillion, were bailed
out. The impact of Bear Stearns was nothing compared to this.
These two firms were iconic institutions. They were part of
America's psyche. And they were bust.

When you look at 2007 and 2008 like this with hindsight,
it is surprising the balance didn't tip before it did. The pattern
set out so clearly by the early collapse of the Bear Stearns and
IKB funds was repeated across the financial world as more
and more pieces of the puzzle fell into place. The original
observers of Bear Stearns and IKB watched the truth gradually
dawn on the financial sector. But, while the pattern was the
same, no one knew if or when the whole system would fall.

By September 2008, though, people were primed for
panic. All that was needed was a trigger. The US government's

decision to take a stand and let Lehman Brothers fail provided that trigger.

Lehman Brothers was the fourth-largest Wall Street investment bank, and its reputation drew on over 150 years of history. The bank proudly traced its origins back to 1844 when a German immigrant, Henry Lehman, founded a dry-goods shop in Montgomery, Alabama. He was later joined by his two younger brothers who evolved the business into a cotton brokerage, and, after the Civil War, an investment bank. With total assets of more than $630 billion and over 3,000 operating subsidiaries by the time of its downfall, Lehman had a digit parked in every pie that global financial markets had to offer. It's been estimated that it was counterparty to a notional $5 trillion of CDS contracts, though at the time there was no way for anyone to compute which firms had made these deals with Lehman, or in what quantity. Like its competitors, the bank was overexposed to an overcooked American real-estate market, but it had borrowed more to fund its bets and was much slower to acknowledge its losses when the market soured.

By the fall of 2008 denial was no longer tenable, and in the week before its collapse Lehman posted a quarterly loss of $3.9 billion. Confidence tumbled and like IKB, Bear Stearns and Northern Rock before it, its funding dried up. The vultures began to circle, with Bank of America and the British bank Barclays looking to buy. The most feasible emergency takeover bid, from Barclays, stalled late in the weekend. The Fed, citing an obscure provision of the 1934 Federal Reserve Act, argued that it only had the legal authority to provide emergency lending to Lehman if the bank first posted high-quality collateral such as cash or government bonds. But Lehman did not have enough collateral to cover the size of the loan required, nor did it have any means of raising it. 'The only way we could have saved Lehman would have been by breaking the law,' said Fed

Chairman Ben Bernanke. 'I was not prepared to go beyond my legal authorities.'[14]

In the early hours of Monday 15 September 2008, Lehman Brothers filed for bankruptcy. There is a handful of recent events that everyone remembers in terms of where they were when they heard the news, like the death of Princess Diana, or the attack on the twin towers. This was the financial equivalent.

To the outside world, watching the sudden shift in the fortunes of finance was like seeing a flock of birds, until now settled calmly on the ground, suddenly, without warning, take off in flight. The amounts of money were so huge, the names so renowned, and the human pictures of despair so striking that it gripped the media and the public in equal measure. In the UK, we watched from a distance as the great American legend crumbled. The press immediately went into overdrive. The *Sunday Times* reported the newly prestigious Dr Doom, Nouriel Roubini, warning: 'It's clear we are one step away from a financial meltdown.'[15]

It was hard to believe what you were reading. 'Lehman Brothers Holdings Inc., the fourth-largest U.S. investment bank, succumbed to the subprime mortgage crisis it helped create in the biggest bankruptcy filing in history,' announced *Bloomberg*. 'The 158-year-old firm, which survived railroad bankruptcies of the 1800s, the Great Depression in the 1930s and the collapse of Long-Term Capital Management a decade ago, filed a Chapter 11 petition with U.S. Bankruptcy Court in Manhattan today.'[16] After that, we hurtled into freefall and there was no going back.

When Bear Stearns was salvaged by the government-backed

---

14 Ben S. Bernanke, testimony to the Financial Crisis Inquiry Commission, 2 September 2010
15 *Sunday Times*, 16 September 2008
16 *Bloomberg News*, 15 September 2008

JPMorgan buyout earlier that year, Bear's shareholders had seen the value of their investments dwindle to almost nothing. But the bondholders – the owners of the bank's debt – hadn't done too badly, as JPMorgan assumed Bear's obligations. This was because bondholders have stronger contractual rights to get their money back and is why investing in debt is perceived as much safer than investing in shares. When Lehman was allowed to fail, shareholders and bondholders alike were wiped out, and in an instant all bets were off. Investors with impeccable conservative credentials like Norway's government pension fund, which had invested heavily in Lehman debt, suddenly found themselves cast in the role of fly-by-night speculators facing nine-figure losses. A bankruptcy as fiendishly complex as Lehman's might take years to resolve; those who had invested in what appeared to be safe-as-houses, liquid assets now had no idea if they would ever get their money back.

Investors, particularly the powerful money-market funds – which finance the day-to-day borrowing of non-financial corporations, alongside banks – concluded it was no longer safe to lend. The cost of insuring bond defaults recorded its largest ever one-day rise; ailing capital markets began to enter a state of rigor mortis. As the Nobel Prize-winning economist Paul Krugman commented, 'Letting Lehman fail basically brought the entire world capital market down'.[17]

On the same day that Lehman filed for bankruptcy, Merrill Lynch surrendered itself to a $50-billion takeover by Bank of America. The following day the tottering insurance giant AIG, which had insured $440 billion of bonds for the world's biggest financial institutions, saw its credit rating downgraded. A clause in AIG's CDS contracts stipulated that a downgrade would require it to put up extra cash as collateral to guarantee that it could meet its obligations to CDS-holders. With its share price swooning, AIG was unable to raise the money and faced ruin. It was rescued in an $85-billion intervention by the Federal Government, in exchange for an 80 percent stake in the firm.

Wall Street's last two independent investment banks, Goldman Sachs and Morgan Stanley, now peered into the abyss. By Wednesday, Goldman's share price had fallen by 14 percent; Morgan Stanley's had dropped by 24 percent.[18] On Saturday 21 September, both banks applied to the Fed to become bank holding companies. The change in legal status meant they now had access to emergency borrowing from the Federal Reserve, but this would come at a price. The freewheeling era of light-touch Wall Street regulation was at an end.

Attention had now turned to the so-called 'universal banks', like Bank of America, Wachovia, and Citigroup. These vast institutions were where most Americans kept their savings, but they too were exposed to subprime debt through their invest-ment banking and mortgage lending subsidiaries. Under no circumstances could they be allowed to fail.

Over the next fortnight a close-knit group of Fed and Treasury officials hammered out a $700-billion plan to clean up the balance sheets of the American banking system by purchas-ing their bad debts or buying shares. After a heart-stopping rejection on 29 September, the rescue package known as TARP (Troubled Asset Relief Program) was finally approved by the House of Representatives on 3 October. Financial armageddon had been narrowly averted, a global economic recession was about to begin.

The Bystander Effect
In the fall of 2008 the global financial system resembled a scene

---

in an old Road Runner cartoon. Wile E. Coyote has raced out into the void above a canyon, but gravity only takes hold when he skids to a halt and looks down. The week beginning Monday 15 September was the moment when financial markets looked down, yet they had long since careered over the precipice. Given that the weaknesses in the financial system had been exposed more than a year earlier, why did the crisis take so long to play out? Why did the tipping point occur when it did?

One explanation for the first question is that the largest financial institutions were massaging their figures. As we shall see later on, the banks' bespoke mathematical models give them considerable discretion in valuing the assets on their books and in particular in estimating how many loans were likely to go bad. Economists have found that banks with the largest exposures to MBSs in 2008 were likely to report lower expenses set aside for bad loans. From 2007 onward we can see a growing discrepancy between the 'book value' (a bank's own valuation) of mortgage-related securities, and the market's valuation.[19] But this doesn't answer the second question. If investors were wising up, why didn't the panic occur sooner?

In our view, the myriad forces at work under the surface, the forces which determined when the aggregate confidence of the financial system tipped over the edge, have their roots in human behavior. And that is why it is so important we learn the lessons, for while banks may have disappeared or been transformed out of all recognition, bankers have not.

The same factors that kept the majority ridiculing the fools in the corner earlier in the boom were still in play in 2007. The backfire effect, for example, shows how difficult it is for people

---

19 See Harry Huizinga and Luc Laeven, 'Bank Valuation and Regulatory Forbearance During a Financial Crisis', European Banking Center Discussion Paper No. 2009-17, available at SSRN, 22 March 2010

to reconcile themselves with facts that threaten their worldview. But this was not the only cognitive bias at work on Wall Street. To get to grips with human behavior in 2007, we need to go back to group behavior.

As early as the fifth century BC, Plato observed the phenomenon of young orators being swept away by the forces of a crowd: 'the rocks and the whole place re-echo, and re-double the noise of their boos and applause. Can a young man be unmoved by all this? He gets carried away and soon finds himself behaving like the crowd and becoming one of them.'[20] In the nineteenth century, the Scottish journalist Charles Mackay wrote that, 'Men, it has been well said, think in herds; it will be seen that they go mad in herds, while they only recover their senses slowly, and one by one.' In 1841 he published his classic work, *Extraordinary Popular Delusions and the Madness of Crowds*, about the South Sea Bubble and other speculative frenzies. In the twentieth century, group psychology became the focus of academic study. Within a growing field of social psychology, criminal psychology homed in on the way our sense of personal responsibility is diminished in a group, because responsibility is shared by the group as a whole. This symptom of group behavior is called the 'bystander effect'.

The name was coined by psychologists in the years after the rape and murder of Kitty Genovese in New York on 13 March 1964. Winston Moseley, the man convicted of the crime, admitted in court that he stabbed Kitty seventeen times before sexually assaulting her and leaving her to die. He attacked her as she walked from a car park in Queens to her apartment, in a residential area. Her screams and cries for help were heard around the neighborhood but, despite this, no one so much as

20 Plato, *Republic*

called the police. No one intervened. The entire neighborhood was a bystander to the crime.

The inertia of Kitty's neighbors sparked horror and disgust around America. Everyone asked the same question: why did no one help? Psychologists in particular seized on it. Against a background of news reports and commentators pointing vehemently to the moral decay and dehumanization of the modern age, psychologists sought to delve deeper and identify what it is in us that would let us stand idly by a crime and say nothing. The result was labeled the 'bystander effect'.

We all know that when we see something happening that we know is wrong, we are thrown into conflict. The reasons to intervene are morally strong – our human tendency to empathize sparks our natural desire to stop the harm we see being done. We know it is wrong, and we ought to do something to stop it. But fear often holds us back. We face a rational fear of the risks of intervention: that we might be physically hurt, verbally abused or blamed. Then there are the irrational fears, like our acute desire to avoid social embarrassment: what if we are judged for interfering with something that may be none of our business?

In the wake of Kitty's murder social psychologists developed the now famous theory that, as discomforting as it is to admit, if there are more people witnessing an event, fewer people will intervene. It is not a question of 'moral decay', nor that the people watching are psychopaths who lack normal levels of situational engagement. If you witness something alone, you know that the only source of help is from you. The responsibility and the blame for inaction lie with you. This knowledge may still be outweighed by the arguments not to intervene, but it is a powerful incentive to act. If, on the other hand, you know that you are one of many witnesses, the responsibility and the blame of inaction are diffused. Not only that, but inaction becomes increasingly easy to reason away: someone else has probably done something already, so to intervene now will only confuse the situation.

The classic study into the bystander effect was conducted by John Darley and Bibb Latané in 1968.[21] Darley and Latané's crucial insight was to observe the inverse relationship between intervention and the number of bystanders. Importantly, they found that those who did not intervene were largely undecided. They were not indifferent, but were in a constant state of conflict even as they did not act until it was too late.

Forty years on, swapping social psychology for behavioral finance, there is evidence of exactly the same principle at work in the finance sector. We know that there were many witnesses to the pandemic of irresponsible lending. The impending crisis was widely reported in the financial press, many people wrote papers informing their peers. A growing number of people knew something was wrong. But the collective body of the finance world did not act.

We spoke to one banker who had occupied a senior position in Lehman's European operation. Several months before the crash that would engulf the firm he realized that he was no longer being sent the profit and loss sheets for the fixed-income part of the business. Fixed-income is a category of finance which includes mortgage-backed securities. 'This is a bit Enron-esque,' he thought to himself.[22] But as his responsibilities lay elsewhere in the business he didn't take steps to puzzle out the implications.

The anonymous Wall Street banker who runs the Epicurean Dealmaker blog explains how the diverse, diffuse and dizzyingly

---

21 John Darley and Bibb Latané, *Bystander Intervention in Emergencies: Diffusion of Responsibility* (New York: Columbia University Press, 1968)
22 Private interview

complex structure of modern investment banking conspires against a sense of collective responsibility:

> Senior bankers, from corporate finance, to M&A, to sales and trading, each run little businesses focused on tiny segments of the global financial markets, whether it be healthcare M&A, mortgage-backed securities trading, or investment grade debt underwriting. Most of these businesses have very little to do with each other, and each requires a different focus and business model for success. Strange as it may seem to the uninitiated, a giant, trillion-dollar asset business like Goldman Sachs, when properly understood, looks a lot like a very large, very awkward aggregation of hundreds if not thousands of tiny little cottage industries.[23]

In one of the less subtle ironies of the crisis, Dick Fuld's quarterly webcasts to his Lehman workforce always included a reminder that 'You are all risk managers'. This hollow slogan is emblematic of the problem thrown up by the bystander effect: if everyone is held equally responsible then in practice responsibility lies with no one at all.

The expectation that blame would be safely dispersed has been vindicated by events. No senior Wall Street figure has ever been prosecuted for the decisions that led to the crash. Responsibility and blame is diffused across the sector as a whole: between risk managers, regulators, credit-rating agencies, company boards, central bankers and CEOs, so that no single individual can really be called to account. Those who designed the system and promoted the flawed ideology may be equivalent to the

---

23 The Epicurean Dealmaker, 'Three's a Crowd', www.epicureandealmaker. blogspot.com, 19 March 2012

perpetrators of the crime, but the whole finance sector, with safety in numbers, were the silent neighbors.

But just as in the Darley and Latané experiments, the bystanders were not calmly watching events of 2007 and 2008. The majority were worried, unsure of what to do, fearful of embarrassment and, more importantly, afraid of losing their jobs. On Wall Street, the power of peer pressure should not be underestimated. In a world where power and prestige depend on access to networks, failure to conform is a dangerous and costly exercise. The social norms of finance perpetuated this exclusive atmosphere. No fund manager wants to miss out on the best deal, the best investment. If everyone is in on something, you don't want to be the one who misses out. The downside of this is a groupthink mentality. As Stephen King, HSBC's Chief Economist, put it to us: 'People behave in herds. If you try and regulate when you see a bubble forming, the vast majority of the sector will say "it's not a bubble, don't interfere".'[24]

When we discussed this question with the head of the UK Financial Services Authority Adair Turner, he pointed out that 'at the end of a boom there are fewer people who have seen a crash and therefore more who think "it" can't go wrong'.[25] The history of finance doesn't occupy much time on modern economics courses, but even if it did, historical understanding is not nearly as powerful as personal experience. And the majority of the workforce had no memory of a crash with which to frame their experience. They may have been nervous and fearful, but they didn't know of what exactly they were fearful. As long as you don't have an object for your fear, it is hard to act on that fear. Instead it stays a nagging, nebulous worry without real power. When finally crystallized in the fall of Lehman, unspoken fear found its outlet,

24 Private interview
25 Private interview

and exploded across the sector. Put more prosaically, when a large downside risk has been ignored for some time, all valuations will be shocked downwards at the moment the risk is exposed.

Just as the bystanders of Kitty's murder didn't take responsibility and intervene, so too was it hard for those wrapped up in the system to know exactly what could be done. When Lehman fell, the time for inert internal conflict was over.

Herding behavior and the bystander effect are closely linked because individual attempts to evade responsibility can induce herding effects. Economists have found that company boards are most likely to fire executives in response to poor performance of a firm relative to its industry, whereas industry-wide failings are less likely to result in sackings at individual firms.[26] This gives managers an incentive to follow the herd since they will be safe if they implement strategies that are failing elsewhere.

It's an unfortunate fact of the business cycle that, during a boom, company boards are liable to mistake a responsible business strategy – such as a refusal to lower lending standards – for underperformance. Bill Dallas, the co-founder of subprime mortgage lender First Franklin, explains the commercial pressure to conform:

> If I had said to the borrower, 'fully document your income or you won't get this loan', [the crisis] would have ended. But I'm one lender right, right? So you know what happens to my volume if I do that and no one else does? It goes to zero.[27]

In a market offering few rewards for anyone reluctant to join

---

26 Randall Morck, Andrei Shliefer, Robert Vishny, 'Alternative Mechanisms for Corporate Control', *American Economic Review*, September 1989

27 Quoted in David Faber *And then the Roof Caved In: How Wall Street's Greed and Stupidity Brought Capitalism to its Knees* (New York: John Wiley & Sons, 2009), p. 52

the stampede, the herd mentality urged on ever more reckless behavior. According to former Treasury Secretary Hank Paulson, at a dinner in June 2007 Citigroup's CEO Chuck Prince even pleaded with him: 'Isn't there something you can do to order us not to take all of these risks?'[28]

But we should be wary of overstating the more self-conscious, calculating aspects of herding. We are prone to underestimate the extent to which irrational considerations guide our decision-making. In one study, the behavioral economist Dan Ariely asked MIT students to write down the last two digits of their Social Security numbers. On the same piece of paper he then asked them to record how much they would be willing to spend on a bottle of wine, a book, and a box of chocolates. After collecting their papers Ariely asked them whether the number had any influence on their bid. The students dismissed the idea. But the data told a different story. Those with Social Security numbers in the lowest group, from 00 to 19, were willing to pay $67 on average for the items combined. Those in the highest group, with numbers from 80 to 99, bid $198 on average, or three times as much.[29] Neuroscience also suggests that the more rational areas of the brain will collaborate with the limbic system to provide a convincing alibi for the actions we our unconsciously compelled to perform.

At the time few in finance were consciously aware of taking their cues from the herd, even fewer saw themselves as unwilling participants in the madness. A former Morgan Stanley man recalls that with hindsight: 'The herd instinct was just amazing. Everyone was looking for yield. You could do almost anything you could dream of and persuade people to buy it.'[30] Nor was it

---

28 Henry M. Paulson Jr., *On the Brink* (New York: Business Plus, 2010)

29 Dan Ariely, *Predictably Irrational: The Hidden Forces that Shape our Decisions* (New York: Harper Perennial, 2010)

30 Quoted in Gillian Tett, *Fool's Gold* (London: Little, Brown, 2009) p. 35

impossible for individuals to break away from the herd before it rampaged over the cliff. In October 2006 Jamie Dimon of JPMorgan ordered his staff to sell off large CDO positions, at the height of the market. In the long run this proved to be a far more competitive policy than the 'all in' attitude adopted by his rivals.

Finance as a Complex Adaptive System

When Bear Stearns and IKB faced bailouts in the summer of 2007, individuals on the edge of the herd were startled. Gradually throughout 2007 and 2008 more people noticed, but the bystander effect, the backfire effect, and the dynamics of group psychology kept widespread panic at bay. As Ron Brater, another Morgan Stanley man, described it: 'in banks you have this kind of mentality, this groupthink, and people just keep going with what they know, and they don't want to listen to bad news'.[31]

Finally, with the fall of Lehman, the crisis took that one fatal step too far, and triggered panic.

But why was Lehman so different? The backfire effect, the bystander effect, peer pressure, and herd behavior all explain why the delay lasted as long as it did, but they don't explain why the fall of Lehman had such a spectacular effect. It's particularly striking that the direct losses resulting from the Lehman bankruptcy were so limited. Net payouts to holders of Lehman CDS contracts were only around $5 billion.[32] So why were the effects so far-reaching?

To answer that question it is useful to think of the financial sector as a complex adaptive system. A growing field of research

---

31 Ibid.

32 Andrew Haldane, 'Rethinking the Financial Network', speech delivered at the Financial Student Association, Amsterdam, April 2009

into complex adaptive systems brings together psychology, anthropology, math, economics, and neuroscience to study group behavior. Groups of people are complex because of the almost infinite variations of behavior: adaptive, because we respond to experience, so history matters; and a system because the actions of the group has feedback, so the group acts in a recognizable or systemic way. Within the system, rules in turn develop with characteristics distinct from those of the individuals involved.

The world of politics is another complex adaptive system. The sum of individual behavior, while complex and unpredictable, is shaped by experience and history, and fits into recognizable and repeated patterns. Leadership matters, of course, but there is a group dynamic that persists outside any individual's control. The peer pressure, herd behavior, and bystander effect that we noticed earlier can all be recognized within this system.

The patterns of complex adaptive systems lean heavily on the mathematical field of chaos theory. Made famous by the image of a butterfly flapping its wings in Tokyo to cause a hurricane in Florida, chaos theory is the study of dynamic systems that are both unpredictable yet follow repeated patterns. These so-called chaotic patterns are highly sensitive to initial conditions, or history. Their unpredictable nature comes not from random shocks but from an unfolding of the internal dynamics of the system. After the fact, chaotic patterns can look inevitable, even though they are almost impossible to predict in advance.

It is illuminating to think of finance in this way – as a system – because it draws together the human behavior ideas we have already covered with key structural features. Using this model in a brilliant analysis of the crisis, Andrew Haldane identifies four key mechanisms at work within the system: connectivity, feedback, uncertainty and innovation.

It is clear that in the last two decades the scale and

interconnectivity of the finance sector increased dramatically. This has had countless consequences, but one of them is that something which starts as a local problem is now far more likely to become a global one. The conscious interdependence of institutions within this framework meant that as risk became recognized in 2007 and 2008, individual banks rationally attempted to stock up their liquidity. But, because of that same interdependence, this in fact increased the difficulties facing each institution. The uncertainty that dogged the sector began to reach unparalleled heights as everyone realized that, thanks to the dramatic innovations of the last ten years, the level of counter-party risk simply could not be calculated. The new technology of securitized assets and credit-default swaps had transformed risk from an abstract concept into a commodity, allowing it to be bundled up, sliced, diced, priced, traded, and traded again. Up to a point, this game of pass the parcel had allowed risk to be safely dispersed across the system. Indeed, in the years before the crash, the financial system proved remarkably resilient in the face of oil-price shocks, the dot-com bust and 9/11. But as time went on and more of these instruments were passed around, the exact source and location of the underlying claims became harder to trace. All of this resulted in a system that, although hugely more complex, was in fact far less robust.

The result was a dense, interconnected world of finance balanced on a knife-edge. Up to a point, all these different properties helped to absorb and disperse shocks. But after a certain point they simply increase the shock and magnify its effects. Hence the sudden tipping point.

The authorities, too, are not separate from but part of the system; their expected reaction informs behavior, while the authorities' behavior is itself informed by the rest of the system. As George Soros has pointed out: 'In the past, whenever the financial system came close to a breakdown, the authorities rode to the rescue and prevented it from going over the brink. That is what I expected in 2008 but that is not what happened.'[33]

If we think back to the Kitty Genovese case, Greenspan's approach to mopping up after crises is a bit like the police arriving, telling everyone to stay calm. For a long time finance had been lulled into a false sense of security by the interventions of central banks. As a group, they had been encouraged to believe that they would be rescued. Charlie Bean, then Deputy Governor of the Bank of England has spoken out honestly about expectation within the Bank: 'We knew [elements] were unsustainable and worried that the unwinding might be disorderly, though I don't think anyone could have guessed the course that events would actually take.'[34]

The Lehman failure banished the assumption that the authorities would intervene to prop up a failed bank. Given widespread public concern that bailouts reward irresponsible risk-taking, this may have been exactly what the Treasury and the Fed had intended. What they failed to foresee was that the resulting shock to so many well-informed individuals would tip the balance of the financial system from introspection to panic.

However you look at it, the collapse of Lehman came as a direct shock. But the reason it came as a shock was not because of some external event that intruded upon the system. Rather, it was a shock because the system's internal dynamics had blinded everyone to its essential fragility. And it was structured in such a way that once it tipped, the cascade was violently disproportionate to the direct financial impact of the trigger event. Fear was contagious, and the herd mentality worked rapidly to undo what little confidence was left in the market by September 2008.

---

33 *Financial Times*, 28 January 2009

34 Charles Bean, 'Some Lessons for Monetary Policy from the Recent Financial Turmoil', remarks at Conference on Globalisation, Inflation and Monetary Policy, 22 November 2008

None of this is to say that financial crises, or the behavior that drives them, are inherently unpredictable. Dan Ariely writes that 'our irrational behaviors are neither random nor senseless – they are systematic.'[35] On a long enough time frame, a freak occurrence becomes a pattern. It is to these freak patterns, otherwise known as financial bubbles, that we now turn.

35 Dan Ariely, *Predictably Irrational: The Hidden Forces that Shape our Decisions* (New York: Harper Perennial, 2010)

Chapter 3

FOREVER BLOWING BUBBLES

I acknowledge I have made great mistakes. I made them because I am only human, and all men are liable to err. But I declare that none of these acts proceeded from malice or dishonesty, and that nothing of that character will be discovered in the whole course of my conduct.
– John Law, letter to the Duke of Orléans, 1720

I apologized in full, and am happy to do so again, at the public meeting of our shareholders back in November. I too would echo [Lord] Stevenson's and Tom's comments that there is a profound and unqualified apology for all of the distress that has been caused.
– Fred Goodwin, to the Treasury Select Committee, 2009

Fred Goodwin, former Knight of the Realm and former CEO of Royal Bank of Scotland (RBS) – at one time the biggest bank in the world – might well qualify for the title of world's worst banker. After all, his two rival contenders made the worst of their mistakes before the crisis. Upon examining Lehman's books SEC officials testified that Dick Fuld would have had to start selling subprime securities as early as 2006 if he'd wanted to avoid bankruptcy. Similarly, AIG's Joe Cassano stopped writing CDS contracts in late 2005, when it was discovered that up to 95 percent of the CDOs his division was underwriting consisted of subprime loans.

Goodwin, on the other hand, waited until November 2007 to stamp his name on the annals of financial misadventure. By then Bear Stearns had been forced to bail out two of its hedge funds, the money markets had frozen over and, by the end of September, Northern Rock had suffered the first run on a British bank in 150 years.

Yet in November Goodwin completed RBS's takeover of the Dutch bank ABN AMRO. It was, in the words of Merrill Lynch which advised on the deal, 'the world's largest bank takeover and one of the most complex M&A transactions ever'.[1] A subsequent investigation by UK regulators discovered that RBS's due diligence on the deal amounted to 'two lever arch folders and a CD'.[2] As it turned out, ABN had been a latecomer to the subprime madness and had invested in some of the most poorly underwritten CDOs. To make matters worse, RBS had paid for the acquisition in cash raised by issuing debt, eroding its capital position and increasing its reliance on short-term wholesale funding. After the fall of Lehman, that type of funding dried up and by 7 October 2008 the bank was on life-support, wholly dependent on emergency borrowing from the Bank of England. Its 2008 loss was later revealed to be £24.1 billion ($34.2 billion): the biggest corporate loss in UK history. On 13 October, it was part nationalized by the British taxpayer. At the time of writing the UK Government still owns an 82 percent stake in the bank. Goodwin was stripped of his knighthood in February 2012.

Goodwin stands out because he was no freebooting investment banker like Dick Fuld or Jimmy Cayne. RBS's traders could count on their fingers the number of times he had appeared on the bank's trading floor in London. His background was in the more conservative retail side of the banking

---

1 Quoted in *Slate*, 1 December 2008
2 'The Failure of the Royal Bank of Scotland', Financial Services Authority, 2011, p. 7

industry. And yet he had fallen victim to the oldest delusion in finance: 'this time it's different'.

It wasn't. And neither was he.

John Law was the Fred Goodwin of his day. Like Goodwin, Law was an ambitious self-made Scotsman who became one of the most powerful financiers in the world. Like Goodwin, he would become a poster boy for the greatest financial disaster of his generation. And like Goodwin he would end his career in disgrace, stripped of his noble title.

Goodwin began his career in financial services as an accountant. Law's origins were less respectable though no less relevant. Having tired of his father's well-to-do banking firm in Fife he headed south where, in the murky taverns and cobbled back alleys of 1690s London, he became a professional gambler. Law enjoyed playing for high stakes but his gambler's impulsiveness got the better of him and in 1694 a nasty incident involving a woman, a duel and a conviction for manslaughter, required him to leave the country. The following years were spent shuttling between continental Europe's major financial centers, Brussels, Amsterdam and Paris, where the card-sharp gambler turned financial speculator.

It was at this point that Law took an interest in economic theory. Then, as now, the great issue of the day was government debt. Governments wanted to spend – on war and colonies in the New World – but holes in the public finances limited their room for maneuver. Law's big idea was consolidation. Not just of the debt, but the entire economy. His scheme had two parts. The first was to enable government to take control of the money supply, replacing gold and silver, whose price was ruled by the markets, with something more stable. Law suggested that a central bank should be created, something along the lines of the new Bank of England which had been founded the year he left England. In return for deposits of gold and silver, it would issue paper money. As more people deposited at the state-owned central bank, government debt would diminish. The next trick was to give people an incentive to exchange their cold, hard metal for paper by passing a law requiring people to pay their taxes in central bank notes – much more easily achieved in an absolute monarchy, where the King didn't first have to consult Parliament.

This novel idea would now be regarded as conventional. The second element of the plan involved creating a state-controlled investment opportunity so incredibly profitable that the public would be mad not to risk their cash on it.

Law first approached the Scottish government with his scheme, but was thwarted by the Act of Union with England in 1707. France, on the other hand, was open to new ideas. As the economists Ken Rogoff and Carmen Reinhart found in their wide-ranging study of the history of government debt, when it came to fiscal policy eighteenth-century France was the basket case of Europe, having defaulted on its debts four times between 1648 and 1715.[3] By the time Law turned up in Paris with his outlandish proposals, the French crown was tottering on the edge of bankruptcy. In the French Regent, Philippe Duke of Orléans, Law found an eager audience.

This is an important parallel. Politicians with a desire to spend more than they can afford are often attracted towards powerful financiers. After all, the business of bankers is debt, so surely they know better than anyone how to deal with it? In the United States, Clinton installed Robert Rubin, the former co-chairman of Goldman Sachs, as Secretary to the Treasury. When running two expensive wars and a vast budget deficit, George W. Bush turned to the CEO of Goldman Sachs, Hank

---

3 Kenneth S. Rogoff and Carmen M. Reinhart *This Time it's Different: Eight Centuries of Financial Folly* (Princeton: Princeton University Press, 2008), p. 87

Paulson. In Britain Fred Goodwin became a key ally of Gordon Brown's on matters relating to the City. In 1999 Goodwin, then group deputy chief executive at RBS, chaired a Treasury taskforce on credit unions. According to *The Times* of London:

> His involvement ensured that he had cordial relations with everyone at the top of the Treasury, and he enjoyed praise from ministers and the benefits of being seen to promote Mr Brown's agenda.[4]

In 2004 Brown ensured Goodwin was knighted for 'services to banking'. Back in eighteenth-century Paris, John Law's powers of persuasion worked their magic on the Duke of Orléans and in 1716 he was given a position equivalent to chief finance minister. A French central bank was established exactly according to Law's scheme and a year later a new government-backed trading company, the Compagnie d'Occident, was floated on the stock market. The Compagnie was granted a monopoly over trade with France's new American colony, Louisiana. Shares were issued at five-hundred *livres* apiece and John Law was to own a majority stake. Frenchmen and foreigners were then strongly encouraged to purchase shares with banknotes issued by the new central bank.

So far, so good. The next stage involved driving those share prices up. Not only would this ramp up demand for the paper money with which to buy them but, as the majority shareholder, it would by coincidence massively increase Law's personal worth. The Compagnie therefore embarked on a huge spree of acquisitions, merging with the East India and China Companies to form the Mississippi Company in 1719, purchasing future profits from the Royal Mint and acquiring a monopoly right to collect taxes for the French Crown. Imagine Apple, Microsoft and the IRS merging into a single company and you have some idea of what drove French investors wild. The public clamored for a piece of the action and the share price soared, peaking at 20,000 *livres* by late 1719 – forty times the original value. Law's near-contemporary the Scottish philosopher David Hume wrote that at the height of Mississippi-mania a man with a hunchback on the Rue Quincampoix – the Parisian street where shares were traded – made a small fortune by renting out his back as a portable makeshift desk for frenzied speculators to deal over. Law became one of the richest men in Europe.

There was just one problem. Where was all the money coming from? The Mississippi Company hadn't yet turned a profit from the trade with Louisiana. Law had paid for all the acquisitions simply by issuing new shares. These in turn were funded with a reckless increase in the money supply. The French central bank, which Law controlled, was ordered to print more banknotes, allowing investors to borrow to buy more shares in the belief that they would keep rising in value. Law had effectively turned the entire French economy into a gigantic Ponzi scheme. Something had to give, and by December 1719 it did. Law had gambled wrongly on the true market value of his super-corporation and the share price started to tank. At the same time the new glut of paper money bloating the system caused inflation to rocket. By May 1720 most people had converted their paper banknotes back into the more trusted gold and silver. The currency crashed. Thousands who had tied up their wealth in Mississippi shares were ruined and the French monarchy's fiscal crisis rolled on for the rest of the century, directly contributing to the Revolution in 1789. Law was disgraced, the Duke of Orléans stripped him of his titles and property and he was forced once again to leave the country. He died in obscurity in Venice in 1729.

What went wrong? Why did the Mississippi Company's share price suddenly collapse? It turns out the root cause of John Law's problems is something we're rather familiar with. Answering that question brings us back to Goodwin.

Beneath the creaking edifice of the collateralized debt obligations, credit default swaps and special purpose vehicles which modern finance constructed around itself there has to be something capable of injecting long-term profits into the system – an economic fundamental. What RBS and the Mississippi Company shareholders had in common was their belief in a good news story – a dream termed a 'fantastic object' by the psychoanalyst David Tuckett. Under the influence of this object, 'beliefs about what is risky, what is desirable, what is possible and what is likely all shift in an expansive or excited direction'.[5] Sustaining the rise and rise of the Mississippi Company share price was a belief in the stupendous wealth supposedly locked up in Louisiana: gold, beaver hides, fisheries and agriculture. The modern-day equivalent was a belief that new technology had enabled them to create high yield, ultra-low risk bonds by lending to the subprime mortgage market. As Niall Ferguson said of the latter episode, 'as a business model, it worked beautifully – as long as interest rates stayed low, as long as people kept their jobs, and as long as real estate prices continued to rise'.[6]

The trouble is that both the riches of Louisiana and near risk-free returns on subprime mortgages turned out to be little more than clever marketing strategies. The settling of Louisiana in the port town of New Orleans – so named to flatter Law's patron the Duke – was an unmitigated disaster. Instead of lush meadows teeming with beavers and gold, the colonists found

---

5   David Tuckett, 'Addressing the Psychology of Financial Markets', Institute for Public Policy Research, May 2009

6   Niall Ferguson, *The Ascent of Money* (London: Penguin Press, 2008)

stagnant, crocodile-infested swamps and lethal clouds of malar-
ial mosquitoes. Eighty percent of the settlers died in the first
year. Three centuries later, excessive lending to Americans with
poor or non-existent credit histories turned out to be a similarly
faulty business model. The rate of default after twelve months
on American subprime loans rose from 14.6 percent for loans
made in 2005, to 20.5 percent for loans made the following
year, and 21.9 percent for loans made in 2007.[7]

This same pattern has occurred time and time again throughout history: belief in a dream; a new innovation that transforms
business and even entire economies; followed by a rapidly
inflating bubble and then a tipping point at which the bubble
bursts; then huge losses.

Bubbles have been as short-lived as a few months. Or as with
the bubble leading to the economic crash, a bubble can last for
years, their unsustainable nature hidden by outside effects such
as imported deflation and the inherent need in investors and
the markets to believe in that game-changing innovation.

What makes this happen over and over again? What does a
bubble look like? Can we spot them, and if we can why do we
fall for them again and again?

Anatomy of a Bubble

Bubbles begin with what the economist Hyman Minsky referred
to as a displacement, a change in economic circumstances which
creates new and potentially profitable opportunities. The more
exciting the innovation, the more alluring the dream.[8] So the
most famous bubbles have followed radical changes like the rise
of the railways, or the arrival of the internet. In the case of John

---

7 Chicago Reserve Bank discussion paper
8 Hyman Minsky, 'Financial Instability Revisited: The Economics of
   Disaster', prepared for the Board of Governors of the Federal Reserve
   System, 1964

Law and the Mississippi Bubble it was the settling of Louisiana that was hoped would change the economic fundamentals of the French economy.

The second stage of Minsky's bubbles framework is expansion. Expansion occurs as prices begin to rise in the game-changing business or sector. Initially the rises may be small and in line with the inevitably uncertain improvements in the fundamentals of the market. So the share price of a company will rise in line with realistic expectations of the new opportunity they have. As the price begins to rise more people begin to notice, leading to the next stage, euphoria.

Under euphoria, trading really begins to take off. Prices begin to climb, often fuelled by financial innovation and cheap credit. The South Sea Bubble of 1720 was Britain's answer to the Mississippi fiasco. The British government granted the South Sea Company exclusive trading rights to the whole continent of South America in return for its purchase of the entire national debt. The problem was that these trading rights were not the British government's to bestow. South America was a possession of Spain and Philip V had only agreed that Britain could send one ship a year to his colonies, limited both by tonnage and value of the cargo. Just as in the Mississippi Bubble, credit extended by the company itself allowed investors effectively to borrow the money to buy shares in the company. As the price skyrocketed they were able to sell their shares for a profit before their next installment was due, then recycle their profits to do it again and again. During the Wall Street Crash of 1929 financial 'innovation' such as broker loans and margin-trading accounts allowed investors to buy shares without having their full value to invest.

The euphoria stage often features a feedback loop, which sets in as expectations of the size of profits rise, leading to a corresponding rise in demand for the asset. This in turn leads to a rise in the demand for credit which, when met, simply fuels the rising price, beginning the cycle again and actually strengthening confidence. In March 2010 FSA Chairman Adair Turner described how this feedback loop works in commercial property:

> Increased credit extended to commercial real estate developers can drive up the price of buildings... Increased asset prices in turn drive expectations of further price increases which drive demand for credit; but they also improve bank profits, bank capital bases and lending officer confidence, generating favorable assessments of credit risk and an increased supply of credit to meet the extra demand.[9]

Minsky observed that as euphoria kicks in over-trading begins to occur, with prices heading far higher than the underlying business of a company can justify. The price climbs further as outsiders begin to enter the market attracted by the chance to make quick and easy gains. In the South Sea Bubble, early investors were the socially well-connected and those with insider knowledge: the aristocracy, MPs and the wealthy. But as prices started to rise, and as cheap and easy credit was extended to all, the type of investor changed. Suddenly maids and servants could enter the market with very little money and make amazing returns that transformed their lives. With shades of the later dot-com bubble, when the mere announcement of an online strategy led to a rapid rise in any company's share price, the *Original Weekly Journal* described the impact of the South Sea Bubble: 'Our South Sea equipages increase every day. The

---

9   Adair Turner, 'What do banks do, what should they do and what public policies are needed to ensure best results for the real economy?', lecture to Cass Business School, 17 March 2010

City ladies buy South Sea jewels, hire South Sea maids, and take new country South Sea houses; the gentlemen set up South Sea coaches and buy South Sea estates.' Indeed it was said that there were 200 new coaches and chariots in London and as many more being built.[10] In turn, this only drew more people into the market, attracted, as many throughout history, by the idea that they could get rich quick. A rumor emerged that the Spanish were offering to trade Gibraltar for some territory in Peru, allowing the Company to build and charter as many ships as they wished to trade in South America. It had no basis in fact but the share price soared.

At the height of the bubble, entrepreneurs looking to cash in on the mania set up dozens of fictitious trading companies to flog worthless stock to the gullible public. These included a company 'For improving the Art of making Soap', a company 'For furnishing Funerals to any Part of Great Britain' and a company 'For building and rebuilding Houses throughout all England. Capital, three millions.' In one notorious instance stock was issued on behalf of: 'a Company for carrying out an Undertaking of great Advantage, but Nobody to know what it is'.[11]

Apparently it sold very well. We may laugh at the credulity of the eighteenth-century investor, but were the purchasers of CDOs-squared any the wiser? If we think we have learned our lessons we are mistaken. Early 2011 saw a new bubble, this time in silver prices. During 2010 silver prices had been increasing slowly. From January prices suddenly shot up, almost doubling in just fourteen weeks. With silver prices at an all-time high, antique dealers on Portobello Road in London were approached

---

10 Malcolm Balen, *A Very English Deceit* (London: Fourth Estate, 2002)
11 Charles Mackay, *Extraordinary Popular Delusions and The Madness of Crowds* (1841)

by scrap-metal merchants, and accepted offers to melt down their antiques into silver ingots. Unbelievably they were worth more in the market as simple ingots than as beautiful antique candelabra and silver-service sets.

Then the bubble burst. During May silver prices dropped by 30 percent. The antique dealers were left with lumps of metal but had destroyed beautiful and historically important objects in the process.

In most bubbles, by the stage of rapidly rising prices, the fools in the corner have already started to point out the fallacies driving the market: the so-called missing fundamentals. In the dot-com boom it was the fallacy of promises rather than profits in company valuations. In the financial crisis it was the fallacy of ever-rising house prices. Ultimately a bubble can't be sustained forever. But as we have seen, prices continue to rise, in spite of observable evidence, on the back of the herd mentality of the market and those who need it to succeed, and those who speak out are ever more marginalized.

The next stage of Minsky's bubbles framework is the tipping point for insiders: distress.

In the distress phase outsiders continue to flood into the market, driven by watching their friends and associates make what appears to be free and easy money. But some insiders are brought down to earth, and remember the fact that an economy and a market need to have fundamentals.

Time and again, those with a vested interest in the success of the boom continue to bang the drum after the tipping point has been reached. British Prime Minister Gordon Brown told the House of Commons almost thirty times that he'd succeeded in abolishing boom and bust. At a congressional hearing in November 2002 Alan Greenspan insisted that mortgage markets were 'a powerful stabilizing force' in the American economy. Like John Law, who continued to talk up his paper

economy until the very end, and like Blunt, the lead director of
the South Sea Company who kept offering ever fantastical terms
for share offerings, the authorities continued to claim they'd
changed the economy forever. Similarly, Goodwin completed
RBS's ill-fated takeover of ABN AMRO in October 2007, after
the money markets had closed and the run on Northern Rock.
In 2008 he told shareholders, 'we are happy, we bought what
we thought we bought', while it was being discovered elsewhere
that ABN AMRO was exposed to $100 billion worth of dubi-
ous asset-backed securities including subprime mortgages.

   This was when John Law and Fred Goodwin should have
known better. As insiders they should have been well placed
to see the house of cards that their money-making empires
were based on, but instead they failed to get out early enough.
Goodwin knew about, and should have understood, the implications of the collapse of the German bank IKB after some
AAA-rated assets turned out to be worthless. Yet Goodwin
actually invested RBS further into the bubble, completing the
acquisition of ABN AMRO. Just as the Mississippi Company
investor sipping his spiced coffee in a Paris salon had no sense of
the real picture in Louisiana, the board of RBS drinking lattes
and cappuccinos had no detailed understanding of the business
decision it had just approved.

   Minsky referred to the final bursting of a bubble as the revulsion phase. As insiders flee the market, taking their profits with
them, the price begins to fall, leading to outsiders selling up to
minimize their losses. When a large number of people suddenly
appreciate a risk they had previously ignored or not known
about, the value of the asset in question can fall dramatically. As
they start to sell there are no new outsiders coming in to buy. So
prices fall swiftly, causing even more investors to run from the
market, which further depresses prices and leads to a downward
spiral. If at the same time cheap credit is withdrawn, the effect

can be multiplied as the supply of cash that has enabled outsiders to invest in the market disappears.

This bursting can happen incredibly quickly. As the South Sea Bubble collapsed, investors in businesses across the board saw their profits disappear fast. South Sea stock fell 51 percent in six days in September. The collapse of the bubble rippled through London. At the coach manufacturers whose books had swelled, orders were suddenly cancelled. One coach builder saw twenty-eight of its forty orders cancelled, while a newspaper correspondent foreshadowed the infamous portrait of the 1929 crash when he stated that 'weekly throughout the streets of London you may see second-hand coaches'.[12]

Like other bubbles, the Japanese asset bubble in the 1980s followed the Minsky framework. After the Second World War the Japanese people were encouraged by their government to save their income. This in turn created a large pool of cash for banks to lend, meaning that loans became easier to obtain. Stories abounded of the brilliance of the Japanese working culture, and how the Japanese economy was set to beat the world. The Yen increased in value against foreign currencies, so Japanese financial assets became extremely lucrative. This was the displacement: an enticing story of success coupled with easy credit and a change in financial circumstances. As speculators moved into the stock and housing markets, prices continued to rise, leading banks to grant increasingly risky loans. At prime locations in Tokyo's financial district a square meter of real estate could trade for as much as $215,000.[13] The Japanese market had reached the euphoria stage and over-trading kicked in.

At its peak on 29 December 1989, the Nikkei stock index hit

---

12 Malcolm Balen, *A Very English Deceit* (London: Fourth Estate, 2002)
13 Philip Shapira, *Planning for Cities and Regions in Japan* (Liverpool: Liverpool University Press, 1995), p. 96

38,957, closing that day slightly down at 38,916. At this time, it's been estimated that the total real estate of Tokyo, valued at $7.7 trillion, was worth more than twice as much as all the land in the USA.[14]

In the New Year the Japanese central bank triggered the distress phase. The bank came to the conclusion that the bubble was unsustainable and something had to be done. The solution was to tighten monetary policy by increasing interest rates, so withdrawing the cheap credit that had fuelled the boom. What was meant to induce a gentle deflation of the bubble turned into a giant bust as revulsion took hold. The debts that had fuelled speculation and growth defaulted as property and equity prices fell rapidly, leading to a cascade through the banking sector. Many banks and corporations could no longer afford their debts, but were considered too big to fail and given injections of liquidity to bail them out. In reality they simply became too indebted to carry on trading and were reliant on bailouts to survive. The so-called zombie banks were born.

On 15 June 2009, the Nikkei index closed at 10,040, 75 percent below its 1989 peak. Japanese property prices only started to rise again in 2004 and today are valued at levels last seen in 1983.[15]

So if bubbles are as inevitable as they are unpredictable, what can be done? The debate among economists on how to deal with bubbles has been conducted in the context of a crucial speech given in June 1999 by the then Federal Reserve Chairman, Alan Greenspan. Addressing Congress's Joint Economic Committee, Greenspan laid out his philosophy and thinking on bubbles, which was to define the economic policy landscape for the next decade.

Greenspan argued that bubbles can't easily be spotted as they

---

14 Ibid.
15 www.doctorhousingbubble.com, 6 January 2013

are forming, and that, even if they can be, they can't be stopped from inflating without causing a substantial contraction of the wider economy. 'Bubbles generally are perceptible only after the fact. To spot a bubble in advance requires a judgment that hundreds of thousands of informed investors have it all wrong,' he told Congress. He argued that you cannot confidently lean against a growing bubble, because investors get asset prices right.

In 2002, at Jackson Hole, he further extended his defense of being unable to slow a bubble when he pointed to a 3-percentage-point rise over the course of 1989 and another 3-percentage-point rise over the year of 1994. Neither saw stock-market growth slow. Therefore only a significant and rapid rise in interest rates, which would have a knock-on effect to the rest of the economy, and possibly cause a significant recession, could control a bubble.

Instead, the solution was 'to mitigate the fallout when it occurs and, hopefully, ease the transition to the next expansion', an approach known as mopping-up. The catastrophic effect of Japan's bubble bursting wasn't the demise of the bubble in itself, he explained, but the policy response to it afterwards. Effectively, he was arguing, just as he had after the dot-com boom, that if only monetary policy had been loosened then Japan would not have lost a decade.

Greenspan's explanation of his policy of mopping-up demonstrated an unyielding belief that the price investors are willing to pay is the only valid valuation of an asset. His argument that only a sharp change in interest rates could lean against a growing bubble revealed an ideology that no other tools should actively be used to manage the economy. Both were flawed.

The ideology that the only effective tool was the short-term interest rate grew out of the failure of 1970s regulatory regimes. It relied on the belief that no other tools would have an effect and that, so long as narrow inflation was controlled, everything else would take care of itself. This in turn relied on an assumption that people are rational.

Likewise, the belief that the only valid valuation of an asset was the market price for that asset was put forward because other valuations are necessarily less precise and based on subjective judgment. The decades-old principle that a valuation had to be a 'true and fair' reflection of the value of the asset was downgraded. But the market price of assets does not behave as for other, normal, goods. The theory that only the market price matters depends on the validity of the efficient markets hypothesis, which itself requires people to always be fully informed and to have realistic expectations about the future.

This central assumption of perfect rationality is riddled through the Greenspan doctrine. But the assumption is wrong, and the unrestrained bubble was of historic proportions. How policy should respond to bubbles depends crucially on the impact of its bursting on the wider economy. This in turn depends to a large degree on whether the bubble is funded by debt.

When a bubble only affects asset prices, like the silver bubble of 2011, or even the dot-com bubble, then the consequences may be fairly small. But when people borrow against the inflated bubble prices, as they did before the financial crisis, then the consequences of the bust can be calamitous.

Such borrowing against overvalued asset prices happens in the euphoria stage of a bubble – when trading takes off and when cheap credit starts to allow more investors into the market. As Adair Turner described it: 'The 2000 boom and the credit boom were the same structure. The difference is an equity boom might lead to some misallocation of resources but can be absorbed by the economy, whereas a debt boom causes economic crisis.'[16]

---

16 Private interview

So was the dot-com boom really structurally the same as that which led to the crisis in 2008? In effect, yes. In both, the essentials set out by Minsky are clear. First was an innovation, which led to a boom in prices. Euphoria kicked in, then over-trading followed by distress and finally revulsion as people fled the market. In 2000 the collapse of companies like boo.com – a media darling with ambitious plans to launch across Europe and transform the way we purchased clothes – showed the world that profit and loss really did matter. In 2007, the failure of AAA-rated securities was the first reminder to people of exactly the same thing: fundamentals matter.

What then was the difference? Why did the dot-com bubble disappear gently, while the financial crisis spawned in the US led to a worldwide economic recession?

It's All About Froth

As we have seen, in a bubble the value of an asset like a house or a share increases, often rapidly. As euphoria kicks in, the valuation becomes disconnected from the asset's underlying value. This gap between the real, underlying value and the value at the top of a bubble can be called the froth: the profit, on paper, gained by buying at a sensible valuation, and the market price at the right point of the bubble. In theory the bubble can collapse, and if you get out at the right time – which isn't as easy as you might think – then all you'll lose is the froth. Imagine a frothy cappuccino. If you blow the froth off the top then you're still left with the coffee underneath. In reality of course it's not that easy. Blowing the froth off is likely to mean that we slop some of the coffee out as well, leaving some of us with less than we started with.

Now imagine we'd borrowed that cup of coffee. What happens then?

In a debt bubble people borrow against the froth, taking out credit secured on over-valued assets in order to fund further speculation, which in turn drives the price up further, allowing for yet more borrowing. In a property bubble fuelled by debt, such as the Japanese bubble in the 1980s, you might take a mortgage out on the nominal value of one property to purchase another. Then after the price on that had gone up, you would take out a mortgage on the second property to buy a third, or even borrow against the value of the second property to pay the mortgage on the first.

The Italian-American con man Charles Ponzi gave his name to this strategy in the 1920s. In December 1919, Ponzi managed to convince New York investors that they could double their money in three months by commissioning him to purchase foreign postage coupons, which could then be redeemed for stamps of a higher value in the United States. In fact the overheads involved in buying up large quantities of low-value coupons negated any profits that might be gained from arbitraging the exchange rate. This didn't matter however, because a steady stream of new clients allowed him to pay out the promised returns to earlier investors while creaming off millions to line his own pockets. When the *Boston Post* ran a story about Ponzi's criminal past in August 1920 the scheme collapsed, bringing down six banks with it. Just as a classic Ponzi scheme works for only as long as new money keeps coming in to pay fraudulent returns, a debt bubble can appear stable as long as asset prices keep rising. If prices stop rising you're in real trouble.

The problem in a debt bubble is that the boom is on both sides of the balance sheet. Assets and liabilities are both increased. When the bubble bursts, asset values fall, but the debts remain the same.

In the South Sea Bubble this happened when the South Sea company started allowing investors to buy shares with just a 10 percent deposit. In the Wall Street Crash investors were able to use broker loans with little collateral. In the bubble running up to the credit crunch, banks lent against over-inflated property owned by people who had no way to pay the money back, even before the prices of their house crashed. These were all debt bubbles, and the economic consequences of their collapse were devastating.

Now compare some other bubbles. The dot-com bubble saw huge amounts of paper profits wiped out, but few had borrowed against the shares. The railway bubble in the 1840s saw share prices in railway ventures almost double in three years and, although there was a slowdown afterwards, the wider economy did not collapse.

Between 2005 and 2007 there was an economic bubble surrounding uranium mines where investors and then speculators first piled into uranium itself, then into mining companies with links to uranium, and then into mining in general. The price of uranium went from less than $20 per pound in 2005 to nearly $140 in 2007 and fell back to $40 by 2010. Uncannily, Galbraith predicted this little-known bubble with a throwaway line in his assessment of the Great Crash: 'Instead of radio and investment trusts, uranium mines ... will be the new favorites.'[17] It was a classic bubble, but most people outside of the markets didn't even know about it. Even if the credit crunch hadn't brought it to a premature end, it would have had little chance of spilling over into the rest of the economy.

Likewise, the late 1980s saw a bubble inflate and burst in classic cars. In 1985 E-Type Jaguars were worth around £16,000. Each year, prices then rose by half, and by 1989 the cars exchanged hands for over £100,000. In 1990 the bubble burst, and a decade later, the cars were worth only a third

---

17 J. K. Galbraith, *The Great Crash 1929* (London: Hamish Hamilton, 1955), p. 29

of their peak value. Fortunes were spent on restoration that could not be recouped, which, while technically economically inefficient, was good for Britain's heritage. Only classic car enthusiasts really noticed.

When Turner compared the 2000 asset boom and the credit crisis he used a technical expression, referring to 'a misallocation of resources'. This means money being spent where it won't create the most benefit for the economy. At the turn of the twentieth century, for example, telecoms companies were falling over themselves to lay fiber-optic cables to power the Internet traffic. They all presumed that Internet traffic would continue to increase at the pace it had at the beginning of the boom, and discovered that after the crash this wasn't the case. Demand simply couldn't survive at that level or at a price to support the cost to lay the cable. As a result companies like WorldCom went bust leaving millions of miles of unused fiber-optic networks strung not just across America but between continents and around the world. Those resources may have been misallocated at the time, but it's those same 'dark fiber' networks that power Google and many other corporate networks today.

The nineteenth century's answer to dot-com mania was a telegraph bubble in the United States. Between 1846 and 1852 the number of telegraph miles in America rose from 2,000 to 23,000. Excess capacity made the industry unprofitable and many telegraph companies folded, yet the country was left with a long-distance communication system that was cheap enough for businesses of all sizes to use. Britain's Victorian railroad boom also saw a misallocation of resources, with too much money funneled into railroad lines that served too few customers to be economical and multiple lines built between towns. After the bubble burst, however, the infrastructure remained. Speculation ensured that the world's first railroad network was delivered faster than would have been possible without a bubble. Of the 11,000 miles of railway track used in the UK today, 6,000 miles was first laid between 1844 and 1846. By contrast, the six main lines of France's centrally dictated railway network were begun in 1842 and not finished until 1860.[18]

So even when we get bubbles, they can still be positive, providing us with accelerated investment in a sector. The market may not be perfect at allocating resources, but a positive legacy can remain.

But when the bubble is financed by debt, the result is too often different. People are left unable to pay their debts, and the losses become concentrated in the financial system. If a debt bubble is big enough, then the losses make the banks under-capitalized or insolvent, leading to a credit crunch as the banks either collapse or try to repair their balance sheets. The collapse of such a debt bubble can therefore have a negative impact on the whole economy, much wider than the sector in which the bubble occurred.

So bubbles in themselves aren't always bad. But when they leave behind debts, they can be disastrous.

In the case of the bubble that led to the 2008 financial crash, the asset price rises were very clearly financed by debts. With a cover story of the wall of savings and imported deflation from Asia, and with regulatory controls over debt levels removed, debts were expanded to finance asset purchases almost without limit.

This insight into the difference between equity bubbles and debt bubbles gives us a clue as to how to deal with them. Bubbles are part of human nature. Driven by both rational and irrational impulses, they can no more be abolished than society itself. Indeed, in recent years, crises seem to be occurring

18 Christian Wolmar, *Fire and Steam: A New History of the Railways in Britain* (London: Atlantic Books, 2008)

more and more frequently.[19] It is more important than ever that by understanding that it is the debt that brings down an economy, we better prepare to stop bubbles inflating, control the expansion of debts that fund them, and better cope with their bursting.

19 Andrew Haldane, 'Capital Discipline', speech to the American Economic Institute, 9 January 2011

Chapter 4

IRRATIONAL ECONOMISTS

Experience of life tells us that people are imperfect. Sometimes we're rational, sometimes we're well informed. Sometimes we are both. Often we are neither. Neuroscience suggests that anywhere between 10 percent and 15 percent of our behavior is conscious; and not even all this is rational.

Yet for years students and teachers of economics made the assumption that people were well informed and rational. Huge effort was put into work that extrapolated these assumptions to make sense of the world. The gap between economists' models and the real world was not ignored. It was contemplated to try to make sense of what was going on, and to improve the models. Over time these models were not just used to try to predict the future and understand the economy, but became deeply embedded in the plumbing of how the economy actually worked. Yet the assumptions on which modern economics was based were eminently false.

Let's consider a game, where you can choose between a certain gain and the chance to gamble for more. If you were offered $550 now, or a gamble with a fifty-fifty chance of winning $1,000, but an equal chance of walking away with nothing, which would you choose?

Despite the fact that on average you would win more by gambling, most of us would probably choose the dead cert. We would prefer not to gamble, even though on average we would win more money, because there is still a chance that we might not win anything at all. We like the certainty. We can already think of the new iPad we could buy. Indeed neuroscience shows that our synapses would already be responding as if we have bought the iPad. Why risk throwing that away just because we *might* make $1,000?

Polling undertaken for this book shows that under those circumstances, of those who made a choice, just 8 percent of a representative sample of the population would take the risk. Breaking it down further, some groups are more likely to gamble: 19 percent of 18–24-year-olds would, compared to just 4 percent of over-60s. Twelve percent of men would gamble, but only 5 percent of women.

This risk aversion is widely understood, is intuitive, and can be added into an economist's model. But what if we turned this game into one where you lose, rather than win, the money. So either you lose $450 for sure, or you gamble, with half a chance you lose $1,000, but half a chance you lose nothing. In this second case the outcomes are exactly the same as in the first example, except that you are $1,000 worse off under all circumstances. Nothing else has changed.

Yet intuitively, this gamble starts to look a bit more attractive. Why would you let someone just take the $450 off you, when you could gamble for the chance to lose nothing? Whereas before we could feel the certain gain of $550 in our pocket and start to dream what we would spend it on, now we feel the harsh chill and indignation of losing money.

If you chose this time to gamble to avoid a loss, you wouldn't be alone. People are far more likely to take the risk when faced with a loss, but not put a certain gain at risk. It's intuitive: why not gamble if you're losing anyway? But why risk it if you can profit now with certainty?

The polling backs up the intuition. Of those who made a choice, instead of 8 percent who will gamble to win, fully 25 percent will make exactly the same gamble to avoid a loss.

Among young men, aged between eighteen and twenty-four, 57 percent will gamble to avoid loss – more than half.

This polling confirms a crucial insight of behavioral economics: loss aversion. We find it much harder to stomach a loss than to miss out on the chance of a gain. So even though the relative returns and risks are exactly the same, people are far more likely to gamble to avoid a loss than to make a gain.

Some of the most well known events in finance followed exactly this behavior. Nick Leeson, faced with huge losses from a gamble gone wrong, staked yet more in the hope of reversing his losses. Instead he lost even more money and eventually broke Barings Bank. As the man himself said, 'I was determined to win back the losses. And as the spring wore on, I traded harder and harder, risking more and more. I was well down, but increasingly sure that my doubling up and doubling up would pay off.'[1]

The trouble is, this natural human behavior is actually the reverse of that you should employ if you want to be a successful trader. The most successful traders gamble where they see the chance of a profit, and take their losses when they have to. To behave as most young men would in the previous examples is to be like a rogue trader.

The fact that we behave differently when confronted with gains and losses was first recognized in the academic world by the psychologists Daniel Kahneman and Amos Tversky, in their 1979 paper 'Prospect Theory: An Analysis of Decision Under Risk'. It became the most cited paper ever to appear in the journal *Econometrica*.

Yet more than a decade later, Barings, one of Britain's oldest and most respected banks, was brought down by exactly the human behavior they predicted.

---

1   Nick Leeson, *Rogue Trader* (London: Little, Brown, 1996), p. 63

In an interview with the *New York Times*, after being awarded his Nobel Prize, Kahneman explained that to understand the problem that prospect theory tackled you had to go back to the eighteenth-century Swiss mathematician Daniel Bernoulli, who in 1738 framed a problem:

> The question that Bernoulli put to himself was 'How do people make risky decisions?' And he analyzed really quite a nice problem: a merchant thinking of sending a ship from Amsterdam to St Petersburg at a time of year when there would be a 5 percent probability of the ship being lost. Bernoulli evaluated the possible outcomes in terms of their utility. What he said is that the merchant thinks in terms of his states of wealth: how much he will have if the ship gets there, if the ship doesn't get there, if he buys insurance, if he doesn't buy insurance. And now it turns out that Bernoulli made a mistake; in some sense it was a bewildering error to have made. For Bernoulli, the state of wealth is the total amount you've got, and you will have the same preference whether you start out owning a million dollars, or a half million or two million. But the mistake is that no merchant would think that way, in terms of states of wealth. Like anybody else, he would think in terms of gains and losses.[2]

This was Kahneman and Tversky's most important realization and led to the framing of loss aversion and its introduction to the economic lexicon.

Yet, since the publication of the theory, the economics profession has spent enormous resources constructing theories to explain away this behavior as entirely rational. Of course there may be some circumstances under which there are rational

---

2 'A Conversation with Daniel Kahneman on Profit, Loss and the Mysteries of the Mind', *New York Times*, 5 November 2002

elements to the explanation. For example, you can argue that once Leeson had lost a fortune, he was already going to lose his job unless his gamble paid off. But to understand this result fully, we need to understand that human behavior combines elements that are both rational and irrational, as Leeson's own testimony bears out.

The consequence of this finding is that instead of assuming *rationality*, we should observe *behavior*, and learn from empirical observation how people actually behave. For all the theories, it isn't possible rationally to explain why loss-avoidance tendency is so widespread.

The economist, Richard Thaler, known for advancing the cause of behavioral economics, probably described the assumption of rationality best when he said 'conventional economics assumes that people are highly rational – super-rational – and unemotional. They can calculate like a computer and have no self-control problems.'[3]

Yet human beings are not the rational agents that economic theory expects us to be. Accepting this has deep ramifications for the structure of economic policy, and indeed the economics profession itself. Over a generation we became increasingly obsessed with making the wrong assumptions about human behavior just so that we could model these wrong assumptions into increasingly complex mathematical models, thus curtailing the exercise of judgment. Wiser economists realized their assumptions were false, but argued that there was no better way to organize facts, and that the gap between the model and the reality would tell us something. Yet for decades this excused a failure to put enough resources into empirical observation of how people actually behave, and instead a whole pyramid

---

3 Quoted in David Orrell, *Economyths: 10 Ways Economics Gets it Wrong* (New York: John Wiley & Sons, 2010), p. 111

of economic theory and practice was built on false assumptions. Much of the work was worthless.

It would almost be funny were the consequences not so serious.

These flaws in the standard assumptions of economics are increasingly recognized. A growing academic literature supports the importance of understanding human behavior. Such insights are beginning to support policy changes.

In an incentive-driven pilot scheme that has paid people to recycle, Windsor and Maidenhead Council in the UK has seen an average increase of 35 percent in the weight of recyclable materials collected. Following their lead, the UK Government has now established a Behavioral Insights team to apply these findings across the Civil Service. For example, the British tax office asked behavioral economists to draft tax letters. When they used the understanding of the importance of social norms, and so emphasized in the letter that 90 percent of people in the city of Exeter had already paid their tax, the letters boosted repayments by an additional 10 percent compared to other letters, at no extra cost. The innovation will save millions in administration costs, and reduce tax avoidance by £280 million. In the same vein, an energy conservation program provided people with comparisons with their neighbors on their energy use. The program saw a 2 percent drop in energy consumption.

These innovations are important, and the early signs are that they work. Basing policy on observations of how people really behave is crucial. But they do not go far enough. So far, such insights have only been applied to fairly static areas of policy, like tax collection. In wider economic management, we must recognize that policy and expectations of policy have an impact on how the system operates. It is necessary, but not sufficient, to base policy on observations of how people behave now. We must also know as much as we can about how groups of people will react to policy, and take that into account. That is very difficult. It means being realistic about what we don't know about how groups will react. It is almost impossible to foresee the way that the dynamics of a system will unfold. So we must not be afraid of designing policy that can cope with all this uncertainty.

Losing Faith

The explosion of mathematics in economics did not happen by accident. The rapid advance of mathematical techniques and computing power were a seductive draw in a profession that had long struggled to justify itself as a science. This new analytical power coincided with a wider breakdown of traditional social structures based on trust. As the Western world was gradually liberated from hierarchical structures based on social position, and automatic respect for traditional institutions of governance was questioned, there was a need for a replacement.

Every institution was required to justify its existence. It was not good enough for an institution to argue that it had built up expertise in exercising judgments over time. The legitimacy of any subjective judgment that was not based on an apparently objective fact was increasingly questioned. Whether justified or not, where traditional institutions were broken down, something had to be put in their place. That something was the mathematical model. For while people could fulminate against vested interests, or protest inherited privilege, who was going to argue with the trained expert, or the impartiality of the silicon chip?

Subjectivity became tainted by distrust, and objectivity was deified as the solution. If we could all see the inputs and outputs of a process, then there was no need to place our trust in one another: we could place it all into the model. As computer power developed, so mathematical models came to be relied upon more and more as the providers of objective judgments. The problem was that models were only as good as the inevitably flawed assumptions underpinning them. But once we had repudiated our ability to make subjective judgments, it was difficult to legitimately question what had gone wrong.

The sheer extent to which objectivity had gained such a hold on economic policymakers was demonstrated by the reaction to the collapse of Long-Term Capital Management (LTCM) in 1998. This fund was a fund set up by esteemed Nobel Prize-winning economists, who had themselves created a model for working out the value of complex derivatives known as the Black–Scholes model. Their model, based on the traditional assumptions of economics, had become the industry standard over the years since it was published in 1976. Almost every derivatives trader used the Black–Scholes model to value their book.

Myron Scholes set up a hedge fund to make money from his renowned and complex risk management models. Scholes joined fellow Nobel laureate Robert Merton and John Meriwether, who had run Salomon Brothers' infamous bond trading operation until he resigned during a scandal in 1991. The new fund initially prospered. The models told them how to invest the money. Over five years LTCM grew to almost $5 billion in size and produced astonishing, world-beating returns for their clients of over 30 percent per year.[4]

Yet LTCM made a fundamental mistake. While they relied on their models to tell them where to invest, they forgot that their assumptions weren't an accurate reflection of the real world.

Specifically, they assumed that the price of US and Russian government bonds would be correlated and move together. They

---

4 Niall Ferguson, *The Ascent of Money* (London: Penguin Press, 2008)

made huge returns from observing movements in the prices of the two bond markets, selling US bonds and buying Russian bonds at the right time, and hedging their risks in derivatives. But when the Russian government threatened to default on her debts, the correlations assumed in the model broke down. The prices of the bonds they owned moved in a way their model had told them would happen only once in several billion times of the life of the universe.[5]

By August 1998, LTCM had lost 44 percent of the value of the fund. By September they were bust, and the Federal Reserve had to organize a bailout. Alan Greenspan called the heads of all the major Wall Street firms together and told them to cancel all of the trades they had made with LTCM. The alternative was that others exposed to LTCM would in turn go bust, and even those that would directly benefit from LTCM going bust would suffer from the ensuing crisis in confidence. So the trades were unwound, and the investors lost everything.

The lesson from this failure was that the models on which so much faith had been placed were built on flawed assumptions. It failed to take into account what happens when a crisis occurs. The models assumed markets worked smoothly but, in a crisis when a government can't pay its debts, markets are not smooth. The models failed to reflect how correlations change; how asset prices can move suddenly; how liquidity can disappear; and what happens when the herd shifts.

A trader worth his stripes, using judgment and intuitive understanding of human behavior, knows that these things can happen. But a hedge fund comprised of Nobel Prize winners was completely unable to predict it. The gut instinct of traders, with all its dirty and discredited association with subjectivity, should have seemed preferable to the fallible world of the

---

5 www.derivativesstrategy.com

objective output of computer modeling. As Merton pointed out in hindsight: 'only a crazy person would have a mathematical model just running, [and] go off fishing'.[6] Yet even after the failure of LTCM, the march of the models continued.

A decade later, almost the same mistakes were repeated in the credit crunch. The world of MBSs, CDOs, and CDSs grew rapidly, and relied heavily on powerful computers to model the risk that homeowners would fail to repay their mortgages, or that companies would fail to make good on their bonds.

Astonishingly, the models used to value the new instruments made exactly the same type of mistake as the models that brought down LTCM a decade before. How did this happen?

LTCM's collapse had brought into sharp focus the problem of assuming that the price on different bonds would move together. It mattered how much a likely default by the Russian government would affect perceptions of a default in, say, Mexico. Applying the new techniques of quantitative finance and using the rapidly developing computing power had made banks on Wall Street and in the City of London huge amounts of money. The collapse of LTCM had shown the risks. But the attitude remained: that mathematics could understand and therefore control risks, if only the right formula could be found.

In 2003, a Chinese-American called David Li appeared to have cracked the problem. Li had spent years in Canadian universities as an academic actuary, studying the so-called 'broken heart phenomenon'. Li had studied medical research which showed that after the death of a spouse, the brain of the surviving husband or wife would release chemicals into the blood that weakened the heart. Li looked at hundreds of medical records, and found that the effect was not uncommon,

6   Donald MacKenzie, 'Long Term Capital Management and the Sociology of
    Arbitrage', *Economy and Society*, vol. 32, no. 2, August 2003, pp. 349–80

but in fact widespread. In the year after the death of a husband, the chances of a wife dying doubled. And men, he discovered, suffer even more from broken hearts. In the year after a wife's death, husbands are six times more likely to die. In technical language, there is a strong correlation between the deaths of married couples.

Li's understanding of these models of real behavior made him rich. From the relative backwater of Toronto's Waterloo University, Li was hired to work for the Canadian Imperial Bank of Commerce. There he applied his formula to the market for life insurance. Because spouses are more likely to die a short time apart, the price of a joint life assurance policy which pays out more on the death of the first spouse was overpriced, compared to a policy for an individual. Understanding this mispricing allowed Li, and his bank, to arbitrage the market and make money. Li's bank cornered the market, and made a fortune, before his competitors recognized the correlation and changed their prices too.

Having successfully applied his understanding of correlation to life assurance, Li turned his mind to the broader question of correlations of bonds. He faced up to the flaw that had brought down LTCM. How likely, he asked, is it that one company or country defaults on their debts, if a different country does so? Li thought that by understanding and pricing the risk that had brought down LTCM, then that risk could be managed.

The goal was worth it. Could Li replicate the vast money-making of LTCM, while also protecting his bank from the risk that sank the hedge fund?

Li followed his approach to life assurance. He worked out the expected probability of defaults on bonds from market prices, and compared the likely default across different bonds. By applying the principle that had worked for life expectancy, he could then work out the impact that default on one bond, by a company or a country, would have on the likely default of another. His model was thought to price CDOs accurately for even the most complicated investment products. Even if an unexpected event happened, like the Russian default, any bank using Li's model should be protected from the knock-on consequences.

Specifically, Li applied the thinking to the new securitized instruments that had grown up over the past decade.

The model was an instant hit. The Canadian Imperial Bank of Commerce became one of the biggest players in the markets for the new securities. David Li was showered with praise on Wall Street, and asked to give presentations to the increasingly large number of mathematicians operating in banks across the financial world. He was poached as Global Head of Derivatives Research at Citigroup, which was to become the biggest bank in the world.

As the market grew, it wasn't just the banks of Wall Street who increasingly relied on the model. A year later, the rating agency Moody's changed the way they evaluated the risk on the new securities. Traditionally, ratings agencies had insisted that pack-aged-up securities included a wide spread of bonds, to reduce the risk that they would all go bad together. Instead, in 2004, Moody's changed to Li's formula to work out the risk of loans going bad. The result was that new securities could be issued with packages of very similar bonds – for example subprime mortgages – and still attract the very top rating from Moody's. Just a week later, Moody's competitor Standard & Poor's followed suit.

But there was a mistake in Li's model. The sad irony is that in attempting to solve the problem that brought down LTCM, Li had made exactly the same error: he had assumed that markets would broadly continue to operate as before.

How could such a wildly popular and scrutinized model be mistaken?

When working on the cost of life insurance, Li had relied

on real-world information about when husbands and wives died to work out the correlations between different events: in economists' language, the data was exogenous; it was not affected by the model. When he applied the same thinking to defaults on bonds, again he needed data, this time on the likelihood of defaults. But such defaults don't happen often enough to be directly measurable, in the way deaths are. There is no equivalent of the public records office. So Li made an assumption that the risk was accurately reflected in market prices for insuring the risk of such a default. He then based his model on that assumption.

But, crucially, this assumption made Li's model circular. The valuations that were the output of his model would be right so long as the market price of a default was an accurate reflection of the actual risk of default. But the more people across the financial markets used the model, the more the model itself defined the price of risk, which was itself the input to the model.

So long as the markets continued to behave as they had done in the recent past, the problem would build up, but the model would continue to work. Yet as we know, financial markets are characterized as much by spikes and tipping points as they are by smoothness and continuity. In addition, the data used in the model was gathered only from recent history. This bias towards the present was what had blinded the LTCM model. LTCM's data had stretched back only five years, a period which failed to cover any really significant events. In some cases the data fed into Li's model was even shorter. Li himself knew his model wasn't perfect. 'The most dangerous part,' he said, 'is when people believe everything coming out of it.'[7]

Yet not only did banks start to believe everything that was

7 'Recipe for Disaster: the Formula that killed Wall Street', *Wired*, 23 February 2009

coming out of it, but ratings agencies and then regulators, too, began to use the model to value these assets. The flawed model became part of the plumbing of the financial system.

By the time the flaw in the model became obvious, the whole financial system had come to rely on its valuations. This time, rather than just requiring the bailout of a hedge fund, the over-reliance on mathematical models had led to a bailout of the whole system.

Of course the flaws in this one model do not show that models can't be useful. Models and mathematics can be an important guide to the expected value of an asset, and the risk of a market position. Likewise, it's not unusual for a model to have flaws. Indeed, every model has its flaws, because all models need to make assumptions about the world to make it easy to understand.

The problem was not using a model. It was treating the results of a model based on imperfect assumptions as objective fact. Models can guide subjective human judgment but they cannot replace it.

David Li's model was not the only cause of the crash. But the story is symptomatic of an attempt to find objective answers to questions that must in part be based on subjective judgment. Given the complexity of human behavior, questions about the future of the economy are necessarily subjective. The appearance of objectivity can be soothing. Yet any appearance of objectivity is itself built on subjective assumptions, and so hides the true nature of a judgment. Surely it is better to accept a judgment as subjective than to try in vain to pretend otherwise?

So how did we come to a position where we made the same mistakes within the same decade? We lost faith in the power of subjective judgment. Like Icarus, we forgot ourselves, flew too close to the sun and saw our models burn up when exposed to harsh reality. Objectivity was so compelling that we ignored our instincts and believed that the computers must be right.

Models Built on Sand

While Professor Scholes and David Li's models went spectacularly wrong, it would be unfair to imply that they were unusual. Their assumptions and modeling were standard practice that had built up over decades. Indeed, much of the economics profession was engulfed, and remains engulfed, in a false paradigm.

Economics has always been a blend of art and science. Trying to understand how our economy works, how jobs are created and how scarce resources are allocated needs an understanding of mathematics, and an understanding of human behavior.

For almost 150 years after its birth in the late 1700s under David Hume and Adam Smith, the subject of economics was rooted in human behavior and morality. Indeed both Hume and Smith sat as Professors of Moral Philosophy at Edinburgh and Glasgow universities respectively. During the nineteenth and the first half of the twentieth century, economics continued to combine empirical observation of human behavior with analytical thinking about its consequences. Keynes was famous for highlighting the importance of 'animal spirits', and eloquent in his descriptions of the behavior of man.

But over the past fifty years, in the economics profession this concern with human behavior has sadly diminished. While earlier economists had used equations for shorthand, from around the 1950s economists began successfully to use mathematical techniques to come to very elegant and insightful conclusions. By making assumptions of rationality, telling and perceptive new economic theories were established. In 1954, Kenneth Arrow and Gérard Debreu proved mathematically how fully rational, fully informed people would best maximize their well-being if left to trade in perfectly complete, liquid markets. The free market would always lead to the best outcome for everyone.

It is a crucial finding that not only explains why Adam Smith was right 200 years earlier about the invisible hand but also helps tell us what kind of market failures get in the way of the successful operation of free markets. In addition, the elegance of the mathematical proof of Smith's invisible hand is striking and bold. Most economists will remember when they first understood the result.

It is easy to see why economists started to look at other ways to use similar techniques to repeat the success of Arrow and Debreu. To do this, assumptions were needed to make the problems tractable. Without gross simplifications of individual human behavior it is exceptionally hard to model how a group behaves.

Based on these assumptions, a raft of new conclusions inevitably followed. The economists who used the new mathematical techniques were honored with Nobel Prizes. More techniques were developed. Computing power widened their scope. This was progress!

At the same time, a new theory of rational choice developed. This theory stated that people's preferences and desires could best be measured not by anything internal but by observing choices actually made, and then assuming that the preferences people held were consistent. This theory was based on the philosophical construct, following Bentham, that human decision-making was based on conscious decisions that weighed costs and benefits of actions to maximize utility.

Such assumptions built on the philosophical tradition of the time. In the eighteenth century, philosophy saw decision-making as a binary choice. Rational choice theory – and the assumptions that underpinned it – was based firmly in this enlightenment conception of rational man. The philosophical insights of the later Wittgenstein, which emphasized instead the essential uncertainty and unknowability of mind, came too late to be embedded in the axioms of economics.

In the 1960s, economists including Milton Friedman and Robert Lucas developed the crucial insight that the development of the economy depends to a large degree on what people expect. They made the assumption that rational people would have rational expectations. Once this assumption was made, a number of very strong results followed, such as that the market price for an asset is the best possible predictor of its price in future, because all information is distilled into that price: the efficient-market hypothesis, put forward by Eugene Fama in 1970. To model expectations that are anything but rational is harder, so the assumption of rational expectations became standard.

Gradually, economics departments began to change too. Those with a strong grasp of the mathematics were promoted, while those who relied more on description were sidelined. Only those able to build the most complicated mathematical models were respected. The explosion of financial services from the 1980s onwards also developed the trend, with the opportunity to make huge amounts of money out of the modeling. Increasingly, economists were lured out of underpaid professorships in academia to work in finance. Of course, finance wanted the mathematical economists most, so courses were changed to focus on models and to teach the latest mathematical techniques, and mathematical research prioritized. This mathematical approach reached its zenith in the early twenty-first century, when universities taught postgraduate degrees in economics more to physics graduates than economists. In many of the world's most prestigious economics faculties, like Harvard, Yale and Stanford, postgraduate courses based on a richer, more historic account of economic history were abandoned. Given the economic fortunes of that country, it is ironic that the first step any economics student had to take to get to grips with all this math was to learn the Greek alphabet.

The result of the mathematical paradigm in economics, and the promotion of mathematical ability over and above a wider understanding of human behavior, was that people stopped questioning the assumptions. For to question the assumptions behind the mathematics was to undermine the use of the mathematics. And no one wanted to do that, because math was where the money was. Those who did question the math were stigmatized as not being up to it.

The changes in academic economics fed through into the world of policy. The efficient market hypothesis means that no asset can be fundamentally wrongly valued, because the market has already processed all the known information, and the asset will trade at 'fair value'. The theory implies that no one can beat the market – unless they know insider information that the market does not.

But we know that markets do not operate efficiently: for example house prices move gradually, with a lag, so even if fundamentals change sharply, tomorrow's house prices can be reliably predicted to be fairly close to today's. Likewise, rational-choice theory is undermined by the fact that we know people's preferences are not consistent. People can make different choices without changing their preferences, perhaps because of their mood or the choices of those around them.

This is confirmed by neuroscientific research. Most of the brain is concerned with subconscious processing, so most decisions are not choices but are automatic. In addition, neurologists point out that most behavior is guided by the 'often unrecognized influence of finely tuned affective (emotion) systems that are localized in particular brain regions and whose basic design humans share with many other animals'.[8] Furthermore, they find that without these subconscious processes, the conscious brain cannot function enough to 'get the job done alone'.

But those who opposed the rationalist school of economics faced a problem. In 1976, Robert Lucas first expressed his critique that has become famous for its eloquence in putting the case for rational expectations. The Lucas critique argues that any observation of behavior cannot be the basis for policy, because the policy itself will change behavior. In his words: 'any change in policy will systematically alter the structure of econometric models'.[9]

So long as people look to the future, the critique has no answer. Policy affects behavior, so changing policy changes behavior. So any model must take into account people's expectations. So far so good. Indeed as the economics profession increasingly looks to empirical observation of how people behave, it must not drop this vital insight.

Unfortunately, the Lucas critique had two unintended consequences. First, including expectations makes economic models much more complicated. So the simplifying assumption of rational expectations became much more attractive to make models tractable. Second, empirical economics was undermined, because any empiricist who could not adequately measure expectations could not predict people's response to a policy change. As the philosopher John Gray has written: 'The

---

8 Colin Camerer, George Lowenstein, Drazen Pralec, 'Neuroeconomics: How Neuroscience can Inform Economics', in the *Journal of Economic Literature*, vol. 43, March 2005

9 Robert Lucas, 'Econometric Policy Evaluation: A Critique', in K. Brunner and A. Meltzer, *The Phillips Curve and Labor Markets*, Carnegie-Rochester Conference Series on Public Policy, 1, (New York: American Elsevier, 1976), p. 41

decoupling of history from economics has led to a pervasive unrealism of the discipline.'[10]

Instead of shining light on the frailties of our understanding, as they should have done, these challenges drove the economics profession into an increasingly navel-gazing, mathematical spiral. So, for example, the size of banks' balance sheets were excluded from most economic models, and instead were confidently expected rationally to alter to fit what was happening in the real world. Such confidence was unwise.

There is an answer to the challenge laid down by the Lucas critique. It is to be realistic about the limitations of our knowledge, and humble about how little we can predict of the future. After the economics profession's experience of the past five years, a little humility is no doubt appropriate.

Exactly the sort of human behavior we observed in the crash meant that anyone who challenged the new orthodoxy was undermined. Economic papers were replete with pages of complex, obscurantist algebra, but the same lampooning of outsiders that we saw in the credit boom was exercised on those who questioned the use of complex mathematical equations. Rational expectations became the norm, and anyone who questioned the assumption of rationality was accused of being irrational themselves.

This assumption of rationality was applied directly to finance. A common assumption was that, based on the efficient markets hypothesis, the movement of market prices followed a normal distribution. Such an assumption allows you to draw some very strong conclusions. The special property of a normal distribution ensures that once you know the outcome of an event, and you know how far typical events diverge from that

10 John Gray, 'The Original Modernizers', in *Gray's Anatomy* (London: Allen Lane, 2009), p. 272

average, you can work out how confident you are of most events being within a certain distance from that average. The distance is called a 'standard deviation'. The consequence is that if you know a pattern has a normal distribution, you can work out the sorts of results you should expect 95 percent, or 99 percent, or 99.9 percent of the time.

The combination of the efficient-markets hypothesis and the normal distribution became intoxicating when applied to financial markets. The calculations they allow you to make help you to feel in control of any risks you might face, because you can put a specific figure on how likely or unlikely a certain outcome might be. Risk officers at investment banks became particularly consumed by a concept known as 'Value at Risk' (or VaR), literally, the value of the bank at risk under a 'worst-case scenario'. Mathematical calculations could provide the specific answer to the question: what is the maximum we could expect to lose over the next week? The computer would spit out the solution, something like 'you can be 95 percent sure that you won't lose more than $32.4 million'. Being able to put numerical values on risk was remarkably comforting for everyone, from the risk officer of a specific department, to the head of the trading floor, and all the way up to the CEO of the bank.

But these outcomes were based on crucial assumptions that are nearly always wrong. A set of outcomes can only be described as a normal distribution if what you are measuring is the product of random and independent causes. And as we have repeatedly seen, people are not perfectly rational. Even largely rational people behave irrationally in large groups. Events are not independent but dependent on history. But flaws in the model – model uncertainty – as distinct from risk in the underlying reality, is rarely taken into account, so these Value at Risks are presented not as the estimates they really are, but as fact.

There is further, more colloquial yet categorical proof that markets are not efficient: some people do buck the market. Warren Buffett and George Soros are the most powerful advocates. Buffett went so far as to say 'I'd be a bum on the street with a tin cup if the markets were always efficient'.[11] Soros pointed out that 'this interpretation of the way financial markets operate is severely distorted. That is why I have not bothered to familiarize myself with efficient market theory.'[12]

Despite this evidence, the financial world still clung to it as a simplifying way of making their models work. Look at the continued dominance of the model for pricing derivatives derived by Black and Scholes despite the fall of LTCM. The Black–Scholes model doesn't represent reality, and traders would lose money as long as they relied on it.

Empirical observation of how markets move shows how price changes do not follow a normal distribution but have more chance of being influenced by extreme, outlying events. This may be because of the herding behavior we have seen so much of. This increased likelihood is called a 'fat tail' as the outside ends of a distribution curve are fatter than normal.

But rather than jettison the model completely, or find a better set of assumptions on which to base their model, people operating in financial markets simply fudged it. Traders would add on an extra cost if someone wanted to bet on an extreme event, just to cover themselves in case it did actually happen. An experienced military sniper aiming at a long-distance target knows not to rely solely on what he can see through his hi-tech telescopic sight. He will often aim several feet above the target, to adjust the shot for wind speed and the pull of gravity on the bullet once it leaves the barrel. In the same way, traders

11 Quoted in David Knox Barker, 'Debunking the Myth of the Efficient Markets Hypothesis', www.seekingalpha.com, 10 September 2011
12 George Soros, 'Theory of Reflexivity', speech to MIT, 26 April 1994

often knew to mistrust the complexity and sophistication of a particular model and used their subjective judgment to aim off what it was telling them. Yet ratings agencies and regulators took the model as gospel. Despite the shortcomings of the Black–Scholes model, it is still in use today.

So even though we have shown ourselves able to question the validity of financial models, why did we have a collective bout of amnesia over the last decade? There are two broad reasons why mathematical models gained such a hold: because the rise of computer power made it possible, and second because human nature made it desirable.

The Rise of the Machines

For centuries, mankind has tried to manage risk. Fear over the future is part of our survival instinct, whether you hoard food, save money, or arm yourself for defense. We all want a world where there is less uncertainty. We all know that bad things can happen, but if we can understand how likely they are to happen, we start to feel more in control of our own destiny. We feel even more in control if we know that we can buy insurance to compensate for the risk. From this basic human desire arose the insurance market: by creating a market for risk, people could protect themselves against the slings and arrows the world throws at us.

Demand for this kind of protection fueled the growth in financial markets. If risk could be measured and priced, then you could mitigate the impact when something bad happened. Of course this didn't prevent bad things from happening: we still had stock-market crashes, or company losses. We all instinctively know that insurers, casinos, and bookmakers still lose out once in a while. Risk management can't stop destabilizing events, but it can reduce their impact. The world therefore became used to the idea that certain risks could be hedged away.

To understand why computers were so beguiling, let's consider something known as 'Monte Carlo simulation'. It's a method used for trying to predict how the world might look in the future, by running lots of different random scenarios. It was invented in the 1940s, by nuclear physicists, but it went on to be applied to many other fields, including financial markets. As the name suggests, its inventors were inspired by the casino of Monte Carlo, where gamblers were prey to many different scenarios depending on the probabilities they faced. There are some gambles where we all know the probabilities: the chance of a coin landing either heads or tails, for example. But what if we had to toss 100 coins in a row? And then play a round of poker, followed by blackjack? The possible future paths grow exponentially and we need help to work our way through the math. Monte Carlo simulation provided a way to deal with the vast numbers of different scenarios: the computer has the power to see all the different paths simultaneously and then spit out a prediction within seconds.

This kind of power was like a drug to the derivatives industry. Derivatives are all about what might happen in the future, and the future can be complicated. Rather than buying insurance now, you might want to buy it in the future if something else happens: so you want to buy an option on an option, for example. This kind of second derivative was beyond the capabilities of the Black–Scholes model. But computers could figure out what these new kinds of options might cost. Computers could look at what might happen if an earthquake were to hit at the same time as a collapse in the currency, or what might happen in a sequence of events, such as interest rates rising followed by employment falling followed by inflation rising. Computers could price up any kind of derivative a person might happen to want.

Consequently, with the march of the machines, the derivatives market exploded. In the six years to 2006, the global derivatives market quadrupled in size, to a total of around $400 trillion outstanding.[13] There was now an alphabet soup of products that relied on complex financial models for their pricing. The derivatives available became increasingly complex. And the more complex the product, the more complex were the models needed to price them.

The exponential rise in the size of the derivatives market was not a cause of the financial crisis, it was merely a symptom. It was a signal of problems in the allocation of risk – that we had become so overly reliant on the models we stopped looking at what assumptions had gone into them. Banks fell in love with what computers could achieve and, like infatuated teenagers, constantly pushed the limits of financial practice. Computers were seen as like us, only better. The modelers were dazzled by their own reflection, enchanted by their innovation – and ultimately doomed to self-destruction.

Models and math also penetrated the mortgage market. Previously a borrower's creditworthiness had been assessed manually, based on subjective factors like how a loan applicant came over in interview. In the 1980s the Fair Isaac Corporation developed new 'credit-scoring' software based on statistics like the historic rate of default in a given area. This sped up the process of granting mortgages but it also disguised the inherent risk of subprime loans, for which there were very few historical statistics.

Computers provided us with a false sense of control. If you can predict a risk, you can hedge it. If you can find a buyer of that risk, you can price it. The internet and advances in telecommunications meant that it became much easier to match up buyers and sellers, facilitating the growth in the derivatives market. So, the argument went, we had moved to a period of greater stability: if everyone knew what the price was at any

---

13 Bank for International Settlements Data, 2006

given point in time, and risks were matched up to those who could bear them, then what could possibly go wrong?

Feeding the System

For the private sector, a reliance on financial models was incredibly convenient. It meant they were left alone to do their own thing. If anyone challenged or questioned a bank, it could point to all its complicated risk models and show that it had everything under control. For those running the banks it was a blessed relief from having to worry about the minutiae of regulation: they had their cleverest people working on the job, leaving them free to plan their next acquisition.

More than that, there was a hubristic sense that the private sector had won the argument. Greenspan epitomized this attitude when he told Congress in 1999 that 'the self-interest of market participants generates private market regulation. Thus, the real question is not whether a market should be regulated. Rather, the real question is whether government intervention strengthens or weakens private regulation.' Financiers had long argued that being left alone to create wealth for themselves would lead to greater wealth for all. The celebration of light-touch regulation, without any prudential oversight, necessarily acknowledged that markets knew best.

In winning the argument, the private sector could feel superior. It fed their ego to know that their way of managing risk had won. Why should they even bother to think about the frailties of their models when every part of the system was so accepting of them? Even during the credit crunch, the illiquid assets that were causing so much trouble were valued on a 'mark-to-model' basis, where the accountants would routinely use the banks' own models to value assets.

Perhaps it is understandable that private banks would use models to best try to get a handle on the value of very complex assets. It is easy to see how the apparent certainty of a model valuation makes life easier. And as the models were making a lot of money in the short term, and your pay was linked to short-term results, why ask too many difficult questions?

More surprising is that regulators also asked banks to make their own valuations of the assets they held. They did so on the basis that the banks knew best. Since it was held that it was in the banks' interests to know the valuation of their own assets, they could be relied on to do just that.

During the boom, almost no one challenged the belief that the markets had it right. The relative success of allegedly efficient markets during this period appeared to confirm that markets really had entered a new period of stability. Regulators and Central Bankers subscribed to the growing belief that advances in mathematical pricing of risk and increased globalization had mitigated the chance of any shocks to the system. As Alan Greenspan said in 2005: 'The application of more sophisticated approaches to measuring and managing risk are key factors underpinning the greater resilience of our largest financial institutions.'[14]

With markets becoming apparently more and more efficient, Central Bankers, regulators and risk managers dangerously built their ideology blindly around this intellectual consensus. As Adair Turner commented in 2009, 'we have had a very fundamental shock to the "efficient market hypothesis" which has been in the DNA of the FSA and securities and banking regulators throughout the world'.[15]

How was it that regulators were caught up in the hubris too?

---

14 Alan Greenspan, 'Risk Transfer and Financial Stability', speech to the Federal Reserve Bank of Chicago's Forty-first Annual Conference on Bank Structure, Chicago, Illinois, 5 May 2005

15 Quoted in 'How to Tame Global Finance', *Prospect Magazine*, 27 August 2009

Once again, in the search for our answer we should discard the assumption that the regulators were perfectly rational, omniscient beings, and instead look to how human beings really behave.

Psychology gives us another clue. Cognitive capture describes how groups of people can become drawn powerfully to a given worldview, even when each harbors individual doubts. Economic regulators and indeed large swathes of the academic economics profession followed this capture.

Regulators tend to be less well paid, less qualified, and less aggressive than the bankers they regulate. They find it harder to query assumptions or stand up to banks acting irresponsibly. Good regulators are poached, and use their understanding of the regulations to game the rules. Increasingly, this has led to regulators hiding behind complex rule books, and insisting on adherence to detailed, prescribed rules rather than exercising their judgment.

But this standard explanation of low-paid and junior regulators does not tell the whole story. Most regulatory bodies also employ people from finance, often in senior positions. The problem is that the more financiers who become regulators, the more the regulator becomes captured in the prevailing paradigm of finance. The common psychological concept of groupthink then means that it's hard to challenge a dominant mode of thinking.

In the case of the Securities and Exchange Commission, such groupthink supported key assumptions which, consequently, went unquestioned.

The SEC assumed it was right to use banks' own models to work out how risky their investments were. Not only was the obvious conflict of interests ignored, but the other, external measures of risk were not taken into account. Work by the Bank of England's Andrew Haldane has showed that in the run up to the crisis, the risk measures used by regulators did not distinguish at all between banks that later crashed in the crisis, and those banks which survived without direct government support. By contrast, by using simple external measures of risk, like the ratio of the bank's share price to its total lending, the banks that went on to fail showed clear signs of distress in advance, while banks that survived the crisis performed much better.

But a deeper assumption by the regulators, again supported by the dominant groupthink, was that if the market was saying something, it must be right. As Adair Turner has explained, 'an organization like the FSA has worked on the assumption that it has to define that there is some specific market failure, or else our intervention is not legitimate'.[16] This allowed them to shed responsibility for being proactive.

The reliance on false assumptions, which allowed people to use models to give apparently objective answers to essentially subjective questions, also had a deeper, and still more damaging impact. By removing the link to humanity, the economics profession also removed the fundamental link between ethics and economics.

For the regulator, if the market was the ultimate arbiter then there was no need for the SEC, the Fed or anyone else to stand as a judge. The authorities pushed away any potential discomfort that might come from a subjective judgment, and left it to something objective – the market.

The SEC's own institutional history and statutory objectives led to a focus on micro regulation. It had been founded in 1934 as a law-enforcement agency with a mandate to protect investors against the fraud, dodgy accounting and insider dealing rife in 1920s Wall Street. It had only become a banking supervisor in 2004, in response to European legislation requiring all investment-banking activities to be regulated under a single authority. Its statutory objectives are to 'protect investors, maintain fair, orderly, and efficient markets, and facilitate capital formation'.

Unlike the Federal Reserve, which did not supervise the investment banks, the SEC had no mandate to promote financial stability. This meant that even though SEC staff raised concerns about the conflict on interest involved in letting the banks use their own risk models ('if anything goes wrong, it's going to be an awfully big mess,'[17] commented one SEC commissioner), nothing was done.

Michael Halloran was a senior advisor to SEC Chairman Chris Cox. Early in 2007 he had gone to Erik Sirri, the SEC official in charge of the banking supervision program, and asked him, of Bear Stearns, 'Why can't we make them reduce risk?' According to Halloran, Sirri replied that the SEC's job was not to tell the banks how to run their companies but to protect their customers' assets.[18]

We now know that this was a false dichotomy. There is no contradiction between protecting investors and protecting the financial system as a whole. But the SEC regulated as if they had to choose one or the other.

By focusing on the micro-level tasks, the SEC was allowed to shy away from putting forward subjective judgments about the big picture. Their objectivity fitted in with the wider world's view of the primacy of objectivity: if something could be measured, modeled and objectively understood, then it took precedence over intangible and subjective judgment. Again, they trusted what could be objectively proven, rather than trusting the

---

17 Financial Crisis Inquiry Commission Report, 2011, p. 153
18 Ibid., p. 283

institutions to make their own judgments. This viewpoint suited the prevailing political climate.

Powerful computer models were an example of the democratization of previously hierarchical elites: they could help smash down the 'white-shoe' network on Wall Street as new talents would be required. Although there were questions about subprime loans, no one wanted to challenge the laudable goal of extending the American Dream of homeownership to previously marginalized groups. Thus it was in the politicians' interest to embrace a world where humanity appeared to have conquered risk through the rise of mathematical models. Record profits on Wall Street seemed to provide the evidence that the philosophy was working, and the tax receipts to boot. Why would anyone question what that growth was built on? Why would anyone question whether efficient markets were working, when stock markets were booming and a wall of money was washing over the globe?

Consequences

The unmasking of this hubris finally came when the previously liquid mortgage-backed securities market suddenly dried up. Who actually knew what these mortgages were worth? There simply wasn't enough information, after they'd been sliced and diced and distributed through the system, to know.

Such a collapse in the market had not been factored into the mathematical models. They need prices to work; without prices, they had no data to work with. Like a car without petrol, they wouldn't start. The credit crunch began when BNP Paribas told investors they couldn't take money out of two of its funds owing to a 'complete evaporation of liquidity' in the market.[19]

There was initially a collective bout of incredulity. How could

---

the models have failed? Things that the models had predicted would almost never happen were now happening with frightening regularity. Even as the crisis broke, risk managers used the language of the models to express their incredulity: 'We were seeing things that were 25-standard deviation moves, several days in a row' said Goldman Sachs CFO David Viniar in August 2007.[20] Most of us would use the phrase 'once in a lifetime', but for those deeply embedded in financial markets, a lifetime would be a poor expression of experience when a model could simulate a multitude of lifetimes at once.

Thus the prevailing consensus of rational expectations, efficient financial markets, and normal distributions began to fall apart. So far there has been little for policymakers to fall back on in its stead. Supporters cling to the argument that, even if flawed, this paradigm is the best way to look at the world because of the lack of an alternative. Even Alan Greenspan, facing the breakdown of his lifelong ideology that markets are self-regulating, could only admit, 'Yes, I found a flaw'.

All the uncertainty banks thought they had tamed has been exposed. Risk management was a mirage. This was upsetting for those invested in the system.

Indeed the high level of consensus between central bankers, regulators and financiers was itself the cause of potential instability within the system. There must be more challenging of received wisdom, rather than an indolent acceptance of the prevailing ideology.

It is not that we should make policy less rational – far from it. But we must recognize the reality of human behavior, in markets and in regulators, and design policy with our eyes open to how people behave, recognizing that behavior is itself dependent on the system. We must use the power of models, but not be dominated by them.

Wiser financiers have long known that the application of mathematical models to financial markets was not a perfect science. The renowned investment manager, Peter Bernstein, points out that there is 'a persistent tension between those who assert that the best decisions are based on quantification ... and those who base their decisions on more subjective degrees of belief about the uncertain future'.[21]

This dilemma can be solved, but only by understanding the dynamics of how people really behave. By facing up to the reality of irresolvable uncertainty, by concentrating effort on how people really behave, and how individual behavior shapes societal behavior, we can improve the safety of our financial systems and the way we run our economy. We will turn in later chapters to the need for stronger institutions in which to embed discretionary decisions. And we must understand the impact of the personal incentives on individuals if we are to start to unravel the unsustainable system that over-reliance on technology has generated. But next, we turn to the single most important determinant of human behavior, which didn't feature in economists' models at all.

---

21 Peter L. Bernstein, *Against the Gods: The Remarkable Story of Risk* (New York: John Wiley & Sons, 1998)

Chapter 5

WOMEN ON TOP

If Lehman Brothers had been 'Lehman Sisters', today's economic crisis clearly would look quite different.
– Christine Lagarde

In June 2007, as the global financial system embarked on its long, careering journey towards the edge, a subsidiary of the German reinsurance giant Munich Re decided to reward its best sales staff with an 'incentive trip'.[1] The company's one hundred top performers were flown to Budapest where they were treated to a night at the city's famous Gellért thermal baths. Gellért is a lavish art nouveau spa complex built in the twilight years of the Austro-Hungarian Empire. That night, for the benefit of the insurance men, the baths had been especially converted into an open-air brothel.

Ornate four-poster beds were arrayed around the poolside. Twenty prostitutes were hired to work on the company's account. The women were color-coded with ribbon armbands. Red meant available for flirting, yellow for sex, those with white ribbons were reserved for senior company executives and top salesmen only. With the sort of efficiency for which the German reinsurance industry is renowned, the women were given a stamp on the arm for every service they performed – to ensure there was no haggling over payment at the end of the night.

This distasteful episode highlights the importance of confronting one of the single biggest determinants of human behavior:

---

1 *Daily Telegraph*, 19 May 2011

sex. The Munich Re 'incentive trip' could only have occurred in a corporate culture dominated by men, where sexism was normal. The cognitive scientist Stephen Pinker writes that 'The sexes are as old as complex life... Differences between men and women affect every aspect of our lives... To ignore gender would be to ignore a major part of the human condition.'[2] Whether we like it or not, in both our professional and our personal lives, sex makes a difference to how we experience the world.

Compared to almost any other skilled profession, the leadership of the financial services industry is overwhelmingly male and the culture of finance steeped in testosterone. Does this matter? How male is too male? And what could we do about it?

There is a view that discussion about women in finance is an irrelevance. That one issue is social policy, the other financial policy. But recent evidence shows that society has a direct incentive, for the sake of both financial stability and healthier profits, to see more women in the boardrooms of financial institutions. The unspoken assumption that finance, like war, demands such masculine behavior, and that gender has no place in discussion about economic policy, does not stand up to an honest assessment of the facts. Men's dominance does not exist because of the inherently masculine nature of finance. Rather the masculine nature of finance exists because of its dominance by men.

So as we move on from the crash and build a stronger, more stable financial system, we must not shy away from acknowledging that more women can play a key role in the solution. Once this has been accepted then the question becomes not whether to change the status quo, but how.

---

2 Steven Pinker, *The Blank Slate: The Modern Denial of Human Nature* (London: Viking, 2002), p. 340

Rare Commodities

Let's start with something that's impossible to dispute. In the upper echelons of finance women are rare.

In 2012, 2.9 percent of the CEOs working in the American financial services industry were women, rising to 15.9 percent of executive officers; 19.3 percent of the seats on boards of US financial firms were filled by women. Yet women make up a majority, 55.8 percent, of the industry's workforce.[3] The UK does no better. On one bank's London trading floor sampled in 2008, just four of the 260 traders were female.[4] Until 1973, women members weren't even allowed onto the floor of the London Stock Exchange. Even then, for the first six months they could only look around and make contacts, they weren't permitted to deal. In 2011 women occupied only nine seats on the group boards of the world's seven largest investment banks, out of a possible eighty-six positions.[5]

Today there are more than 6 million employees in American banking, and although more than half are female, most women 'tend to settle at the bottom'. Forty-five percent of women in banking and finance receive entry-level wages and only 7 percent earn $100,000 or more per year, compared to 31 percent of men earning more than $100,000.[6] Outside banking, the pattern is repeated. In the United States in 2011, for every dollar a man earned, women made only 77 cents: a 23 percent wage gap.[7]

The problem is that women are not progressing to the top. A British report into the lack of women on boards called it

---

3 Catalyst figures
4 J. M. Coates and J.Herbert, 'Endogenous steroids and financial risk taking on a London trading floor', *PNAS*, April 2008
5 *Dow Financial News* survey (March 2011)
6 www.americanbanker.com (1 October 2011)
7 American Association of University Women, 'The Simple Truth About the Gender Pay Gap' 2012 Edition, p. 5

the 'leaking pipe' syndrome. The lack of progress cannot be accounted for by the argument that, because women only entered finance relatively recently, they simply have not yet reached the top, so we just need to wait for the so-called 'cohort effect' to reach its conclusion. PwC commissioned research which showed that in most developed countries women and men enter the professional services sectors in equal numbers. Yet women are lost from the pipeline through voluntary termination at a rate two or three times faster than men once they have attained senior management level.[8]

This leakage explains why so few women get to the very top of corporate America. In 2012 women filled 14 percent of the board seats of S&P 1500 companies and 17 percent of the boards of S&P 500 companies. The numbers for the most senior leadership positions are even more sobering. Only 3.8 percent of all US CEOs are women, compared to only 1.1 percent of chairs of company boards.[9]

So why do more women not get to the top? After all, finance is an extremely competitive business. If talent is being held back, surely rational companies would promote on merit? As the chairman of a FTSE 100 company recently remarked, 'why would you deny yourself access to half the world's intellect? It's a no-brainer.'[10]

Francine Blau, a professor of labor economics at Cornell University, points out that 'we control for a variety of factors like experience, education, occupation, and industry ... those factors can explain some of the gap, but there is about 10 percent that can't be explained and could be due to discrimination. My

---

8 PricewaterhouseCoopers 'The leaking pipeline: Where are our female leaders?' (March 2008), p. 3

9 Ernst and Young, 'Getting on Board' (2012)

10 Cranfield, Female FTSE Index and Report 2010, p. 18

personal feeling is that discrimination has declined significantly but still exists.'[11]

Dr Ros Altmann, herself a successful investment banker, argues that rather than outright discrimination, women make slower progress to the top because the culture of finance subconsciously rewards masculine behavior:

> The criteria by which you are judged for getting higher up an organization tend to be the ones that are valued by the people at the top... You see at the very top it is this aggressive, sometimes short-termist, certainly highly risk-prone rather than risk-control attitude which is valued.[12]

How is this manifested in the workplace? As one example, women are generally less confident, or are less happy to assert confidence. In a survey of MBA students, 70 percent of female respondents rated their performance as equivalent to that of their co-workers whereas 70 percent of men rate themselves higher. Sharron Gunn, from the UK Institute of Chartered Accountants, told a committee of MPs investigating the issue: 'One of the things we come across is lack of confidence in females... Lack of confidence in moving up the corporate ladder. We see this happening before people enter the workplace.'[13] The irony is that unqualified confidence is far from a virtue in the finance industry. Brad Barber and Terrance Odean analyzed over 66,000 trades from discount broker accounts. The traders who were most confident, performed the most trades, but they

---

11 Treasury Select Committee, oral evidence, Q65, 14 October 2009

12 McKinsey & Co., 'Women Matter: Gender Diversity, a Corporate Performance Driver', 2008, p. 8

13 Treasury Select Committee, oral evidence, Q65, 14 October 2009

underperformed the overall market.[14] They also found that male investors underperformed female investors, in part because the men were more likely to overestimate their own abilities. In a 2010 study, 104 students were asked to judge strangers' personalities from their photos. They were then asked to estimate how well they had done. The difference between these estimates and their actual performance was used as a gauge of overconfidence. The students were then paired together randomly on a similar task, after which they were asked to rate their partners' ability. Overconfident individuals were perceived as more competent than they really were.[15] This effect may help explain why men rise faster to the top (one of the functions of testosterone is to help stimulate confidence).

This process is self-reinforcing. Because the status quo is dominated by men, confidence and assertion are deemed normal and necessary to climb the ranks. The predominance of aggressive men at high levels determines these social norms. Put it this way: can you imagine Dick Fuld ever stopping to think 'am I good at my job?' Yet people like Fuld set the tone for what was considered successful.

But the problem goes far deeper than the culture of finance. It has its roots in society's expectations that grow from childhood onwards. Research by Marta Favara in the UK has found that girls who attend single-sex schools are more likely to study traditionally 'masculine' subjects like math and science than

---

14 Brad M. Barber and Terrance Odean, 'Boys will be boys: Gender, Overconfidence and Common Stock Investment', *Quarterly Journal of Economics*, Harvard, February 2001

15 Cameron Anderson and Sebastian Brion, 'Overconfidence and the Attainment of Status in Groups', Working Paper Series, *Institute for Research on Labor and Employment*, UC Berkeley, 14 April 2010

girls who attend mixed-sex schools, even controlling for ability.[16] This is strong evidence for a gender 'priming' effect. The girls who attend mixed-sex schools become more aware of gender difference and so feel under greater pressure to conform to type.

We have spoken to women who agree that when they were growing up, they were no less ambitious than their male peers and no less successful academically. But when they thought ahead to their career, they expected that if they wanted to have children they would have to take a career hit while they were relatively young. In contrast, their male friends did not factor in family at all to their career expectations. For them, their trajectory was linear without interference from their personal lives. Among employers, the belief that child-rearing is still an exclusively female sphere survives. In June 2008 one of Britain's most high profile businessmen, Theo Paphitis, remarked in an interview that his pregnant colleagues' brains 'turn to mush' rendering them useless as employees for six months. He described paternity leave as 'a bit soppy'.[17] There is a deeply imbedded assumption that the choice between family and work is a choice that must be made by women and not by both parents. In the US this choice is reinforced by the absence of statutory paid maternity leave. As long as this attitude persists, there will always be a barrier for women in a career like finance, which traditionally demands extremely long hours and absolute flexibility.

Further evidence of the cultural bias against women comes from comparing pay. Despite a strong legal framework, there is still a discrepancy between the levels of pay between men and women. The gender pay gap is often explained in terms of women being more likely to leave work and have children,

16 Marta Favara, 'The Cost of Acting "Girly": Gender Stereotypes and Educational Choices', *Institute for the Study of Labor Discussion Paper No. 7037*, November 2012

17 *Daily Telegraph*, 3 June 2008

but this cannot readily account for the gap which already exists immediately after college graduation. In a 2007 study, the American Association of University Women found that just one year after graduation, women on average earn 80 percent of what their male counterparts make.[18] Government has long acknowledged the problem. The Equal Pay Act of 1963, a federal law prohibiting wage discrimination on the basis of sex, was a first step. Years later, in 2009, Barack Obama signed the Lilly Ledbetter Fair Pay Act into law that improved equal-pay legislation, changing the statute of limitations on discriminatory pay checks.

In theory, legislation ensures that men and women now compete on a level playing field. But as well as the pay gap in average earnings, when it comes to discretionary, performance-related pay – better known as bankers' bonuses – the spirit of the Equal Pay Act is all too easily subverted.

According to census data compiled by *Bloomberg*, Wall Street is the scene of one of the highest gender pay gaps in US, with women only earning between 55 and 62 cents for every dollar earned by their male counterparts.[19] This is in part reflective of the different roles that women occupy in financial services. But even when you take like for like, there is a discrepancy. Remarking on a 2003 General Accounting Office report into the pay gap, Democratic congresswoman Carolyn Maloney observed:

> After accounting for so many external factors, it seems that still, at the root of it all, men get an inherent annual bonus just for being men. If this continues, the only guarantees in life will be death, taxes and the glass ceiling. We can't let that happen.[20]

---

18 American Association of University Women, 'The Simple Truth About the Gender Pay Gap' 2012 Edition, p. 8

19 *Bloomberg News*, 16 March 2012

20 Congressman John D. Dingell, press release, 20 November 2003

One reason for the discrepancy can be put down to a particular feature of human behavior: reflexivity. People reward like with like. In new polling commissioned for this book, only 17 percent of men thought that if more women had been in finance the crisis would have been prevented or its impact lessened. But more than double this amount, 40 percent of women asked, thought that the presence of more women would have made a positive difference. Academic evidence suggests that this affects the evaluation of women's performances by their superiors, because most of them, as we have seen, are men. Louise Marie Roth, an American sociologist, has researched this aspect of the discretionary reward system, and concluded that 'perceptions of performance within teams of workers adversely affected women because of universal tendencies to prefer similar others'.[21] Lucy Marcus, chief executive of Marcus Venture Consulting, agrees. 'We feel a sense of kinship with people who are like ourselves. It's less risky to hire the familiar.'[22]

One trader told us that she came in to the office after the weekend of London Fashion Week and was making polite small talk; she was in the middle of describing something she'd bought when her boss turned round and shouted, 'Would you just shut the fuck up about fashion?' She was proud of her instinctive response, 'I will when you shut the fuck up about football,' until she realized it was bonus day and he was in charge of her reward package.[23] Because the system is so opaque and secretive, she couldn't tell what effect this did or didn't have. Only her instinct told her it hadn't helped.

Women weren't the only victims of this bias. In some cases risk managers had their pay determined by the very traders

21 Louise Marie Roth, *Selling Women Short: Gender Inequality on Wall Street*, (Princeton, 2006)

22 *Financial Times*, 25 May 2011

23 Private interview

they were supposed to be supervising. But the gender prejudice involved in the bonus payment formula has been particularly pernicious. Jessica Thompson described being at a bonus allocation meeting: 'They crossed the women off the list because the thought they might get pregnant, saying: "The money will be wasted, we won't get the work out of her."'[24]

So what are the practical consequences of a financial system dominated by men? In investment banking, the highly masculine culture has given rise to a working environment shaped by schoolboy pranks, pseudo-military posturing and an unhealthy dependence on the sex trade.

A former Merrill Lynch banker told us how trading divisions have established systems of hazing rituals for the new 'recruits'. 'You line them up in the morning, bark out the breakfast orders, but don't let them write anything down. If they make a mistake and get the wrong bagel then you throw it back in their face.' At other times the sales team would invite a hapless novice out to dinner. Once the group had racked up a thousand pounds on the bill the new recruit was made to pay. Provided they survived the shock, they would be reimbursed the next morning. In both cases the idea is to gauge how well they cope under pressure.

The purpose of other games is less obvious. We were told about suit-jacket sleeves being snipped off, unattended desks stuffed with rubbish, and a mobile phone injected with ketchup while the owner went off to fetch some lunch. This last-day-of-school atmosphere might sound fun, but imagine discovering your phone's been turned into a sauce receptacle minutes before an important client is due to ring, or being pelted with paper on a bank trading floor – where a moment's lapse in concentration can result in losses worth hundreds of thousands of pounds. This kind of unprofessionalism wouldn't be tolerated in other

---

24 'Sexism in the City', *Daily Telegraph*, 15 November 2009

high-pressure working environments, like hospitals or law firms, and yet it's openly accepted among the managers of the nation's wealth.

Venetia Thompson, who was fired for gross misconduct when she published an exposé of a year of excess in a top brokerage firm, put it like this:

> I had stumbled into and was now bolting around the school playground at an East End comprehensive, wearing stilettos, and there was no head teacher on patrol – just dozens of men in their thirties and forties, throwing things at me, all the while trading millions of bonds.[25]

Her schoolboy analogy is apt, but in parts of the financial world that culture has grown unchecked. Women must either dive in head first or not at all. As our Merrill Lynch banker put it: 'Short skirts, high heels, tits out – many women on trading floors do this to bring business in. Women can either copy men, or be aggressively feminine, there's no middle ground. They define themselves purely in relation to the men.'[26]

These are not isolated anecdotes. The reports of incessantly masculine banter, the overwhelming male presence and the attitudes of these men to the few women are exhausting. Trading is known as an extreme. One woman who has worked as a trader in the City for over a decade said her colleagues would go to strip clubs about once a week, to the point where they bestowed their own nickname on London strip club Stringfellow's – 'Chez Pierre'. These visits aren't just for recreational purposes. Kat Banyard of the Fawcett Society appeared before British MPs

---

25 Venetia Thompson, *Gross Misconduct* (London: Simon & Schuster, 2010) p. 33
26 Private interview

to testify, on the basis of extensive interviews with female City workers, that

> it was becoming frequent for meetings to be held in lap dance clubs... I also had women speak to me and say that prostitution was being used in client deals or in ways to generate business – and that all of this culture created a very hostile environment, as you would expect, for female employees of those firms.[27]

Meanwhile Jessica Thompson, who left a hedge-fund job in 2009, has publicly vented her frustration: 'Lap-dancing clubs, been there. Smutty, offensive jokes, heard them all... All night benders in anonymous clubs full of lecherous bankers, done that. Pornographic footage on the mobile, seen it all. Oh, and leering, personal remarks. I doubt there is one I haven't heard.'[28]

Gender stereotypes are diligently adhered to. In a survey of 25–35-year-old women performed by a female trader, female respondents reported being treated like admin staff. The incidents were minor in themselves but cumulatively show how deep-rooted the sexism still is. If someone called for a male colleague to organize a meeting and a woman answered the phone, they would ask the woman to book something into the male colleague's diary, instantly assuming she was a secretary. Male staff would routinely ask female staff to sort through their receipts for them in order to be processed for expenses. And one described how she was expected to collate and organize responses to events or dinners even though she occupies the same position as her male colleagues. Men, they all added, were very rarely asked to do the same.

Women are not alone in speaking out about the masculine

27 Treasury Select Committee, written evidence, September 2009
28 *Independent*, 21 March 2009

culture of finance. Stuart Fraser, the chairman of the Policy and Resources Committee for the City of London, a man who has worked in the City since 1963, summarized the situation succinctly as, 'a lot of alpha males with testosterone streaming out of their ears'. An experienced banker, codenamed Phillip in the *Daily Telegraph*, explained it this way:

> We're always in the business of wooing [clients] away from other finance houses or schmoozing them into staying with us. They are paying for us to do business for them. If that means taking the guy to a strip joint, so be it... And a lot of it is posturing: rival alpha males ... squaring up to each other.[29]

In the years before the crisis, this 'squaring up' was one of the most destructive consequences of unrestrained male aggression. The people at the top of banks making the key decisions were engaged in very masculine competition. It can be called the 'sexio-economic effect', or to put it more plainly, a 'my bank's bigger than yours' phenomenon. For people lower down in organizations, the social norm was set at the top where there were a handful of men whose names have entered financial folklore: Dick Fuld, the former CEO of Lehman Brothers, who was known as the Gorilla because of his combative attitude and aggression; Joe Cassano, head of the Financial Products division of AIG in London, nicknamed 'Patient Zero' because of his pivotal role in bringing down AIG; and Fred Goodwin, possibly the most notorious banker in the UK, who made twenty-seven acquisitions in seven years and completed RBS's acquisition of ABN AMRO after the credit crunch had started so as not to lose face by backing out.

Why is the masculine domination of finance a problem?

---

29 *Daily Telegraph*, 15 November 2009

Other professions with deeply ingrained gender disparities often point to special skills or attributes – typically more developed in one sex than another – which their careers happen to reward; like primary school teaching, or sheet-metal-working. So might it be that the traits required for a successful career in finance are more widely prevalent in the male population as a whole? More to the point, does it matter for good business?

Testosterone and Risk

We know that higher levels of testosterone fuel aggression and competitive behavior. We also know that they sedate risk aversion. Studies find there is a correlation between testosterone-dependent risk aversion and career choice: only a third of female US MBA students choose careers in the risky parts of finance like trading, compared to over half of men.[30] In home life, too, research confirms the common-sense notion that women, on average, are more risk averse than men when they make financial decisions.[31] As we have already seen, on average only 5 percent of women would rather give up $550 and gamble with a 50/50 chance of losing everything or winning $1,000. The figure for men is over twice that, with 12 percent opting to gamble. The only group in which over half of respondents said they would gamble was men aged 18–24.

So, the argument runs, men make better bankers for the same reason that they make deadlier soldiers: both professions reward higher levels of risk appetite. For finance this is true in a very material sense. The greater the risk, the higher the payout. The

---

30 Paolo Sapienza, Luigi Zingales, Dario Maestripieri, 'Gender differences in financial risk aversion and career choices are affected by testosterone', *PNAS*, 24 August, 2009, p. 1

31 James Byrnes, David C. Miller and William D. Schafer, 'Gender differences in risk taking: A meta-analysis', *Psychological Bulletin* 125, pp. 367–83, 1999

Wall Street investment banks hit hardest by the crisis comfortably out-performed their rivals throughout the previous decade precisely because they were taking the bigger risks with regard to funding and exposures. This fact alone should caution us against the assumption that he who dares wins.

A gripping new study by two British neuroscientists, John Coates and Joe Herbert, shows that at a deep biological level the masculine response to risk may well be implicated in boom-bust cycles. They investigated how men and women react physically to life on a trading floor. What they found is that trading decisions were not the dispassionate syntheses of all possible market data imagined by economics textbooks. Instead they are powerfully influenced by excitement, pressure, and levels of testosterone. Their conclusion was that, before the crash, we were 'doing what no society ever allows, permitting young males to behave in an unregulated way'.[32]

The research measured the effects of testosterone and cortisol in male traders in London. Testosterone mediates sexual behavior and competitive encounters. Cortisol is a stress hormone which takes over from adrenaline should a physical challenge or psychological stress turn out to be prolonged. Effectively it assumes command of the body's metabolic functions, ordering them to release emergency glucose into the blood for the duration of the perceived threat. Coates and Herbert tracked the levels of these steroids in the saliva of seventeen male traders as they went about their work, on a trading floor with four women out of 260 traders. Their findings are illuminating.

We know that persistently high levels of testosterone affect the brain, increasing confidence and risk appetite. Studies of male athletes have shown that the winners of each event emerge

32 J. M. Coates and J. Herbert, 'Endogenous steroids and financial risk taking on a London trading floor', *PNAS*, April 2008

with elevated levels of testosterone. As they proceed to the next round of the competition the extra oxygen-carrying capacity testosterone confers on the blood gives them a competitive edge, helping them to win again.[33] The positive feedback loop this generates may well explain the incredible winning streaks of athletes like Usain Bolt, particularly as over time testosterone also increases lean-muscle mass. Yet research has also found that if testosterone levels stay chronically high, we see a pathological reverse: impulsiveness, harmful risk-taking, even euphoria and mania if additional steroids are taken at the same time. Other mammals, which have been shown to experience the same feedback loop by repeatedly winning fights for territory or mates, have also been found to suffer increased levels of mortality, as they are likely to start more fights and venture into the open more often.[34] Cortisol has almost the opposite effect to testosterone. If exposure is short and sharp, it can increase motivation and concentration. But if exposure is prolonged, it will increase anxiety, promoting a tendency to perceive danger where none exists. This can create paranoia and irrational risk aversion.

In the Coates and Herbert study levels of testosterone were found to rise when the day's takings were higher, while cortisol increased in line with the male traders' risk exposures. The scientists concluded that if the 'acutely elevated' levels of testosterone and cortisol remained high as volatility increased, they could 'shift risk preferences and even affect a trader's ability to engage in rational choice'.[35] More importantly however, they realized they had discovered a biological basis for the split market behavior we associate with boom and bust cycles. The

---

33 John Coates, *The Hour Between Dog and Wolf: Risk-Taking, Gut Feelings and the Biology of Boom and Bust* (London: Fourth Estate, 2012), p. 25
34 Ibid.
35 J. M. Coates and J. Herbert, 'Endogenous steroids and financial risk taking on a London trading floor', *PNAS*, April 2008

easy profits to be had at the height of a boom create a glut of testosterone which feeds back into a bull market. With elevated levels of confidence and increased risk appetite, traders are more likely to borrow and lenders will demand smaller margins; the flood of credit drives asset prices far higher than economic fundamentals can ever justify until, in Coates's words, the chemical hit 'causes them to become every bit as delusional, overconfident and risk-seeking as those animals venturing into the open, oblivious to all danger'.[36] Once the bubble bursts, a rush of cortisol exaggerates risk aversion and financiers rush to dispense of their riskiest assets, creating a 'one-way' market where asset prices race downwards because no one wants to buy, so that what starts as a sell-off tips over into a crash.

All of this suggests, from a scientific perspective, that bubbles could in effect be a more male phenomenon. Women are likely to be less susceptible to bubble psychology because they have 10 to 20 percent of the testosterone levels of men. In conversation, both scientists have been explicit about this. Joe Herbert told the *New York Magazine* that 'anyone who studied neurobiology would have predicted disaster'. Coates argues that if women made up 50 percent on the trading floor, we would not see the volatile swings that we do.

John Coates was inspired to explore the effect of these steroids by his time running a trading desk for Deutsche Bank, where he noticed that 'male traders ... were delusional, euphoric, over-confident, had racing thoughts, a diminished need for sleep. The guys had their eyes rolling back in their heads, desperate to get involved in what some genius was up to, and the women just didn't buy into it.'[37]

---

36 John Coates, *The Hour Between Dog and Wolf: Risk-Taking, Gut Feelings and the Biology of Boom and Bust* (London: Fourth Estate, 2012), p. 25
37 'What if women ran Wall Street?', *New York Magazine*, 21 March 2010

If anything, the crash has done nothing to reduce this belief in the success of masculinity. In March 2012, *World Finance* reported that

> Many alpha-male Wall Street traders remain convinced that testosterone is behind their financial success (or lack thereof). One result of the crisis, according to a recent report, is that increasing numbers of traders are approaching clinics to have their testosterone levels artificially boosted, in the hope that this will restore their edge. Sales of testosterone injections and pills are booming.[38]

Personal testimony backs this up. Barbara Stcherbatcheff, author of *Confessions of a City Girl* and a trader in London, cites her old risk manager, who used to say that, in proprietary trading, women were often the best performers, not least because they take more precautions before entering trades. As a female trader herself, Stcherbatcheff makes the case succinctly: 'Trading thrives under caution, thoroughness, and the ability to admit you're wrong. Trading is ideal for a woman.'[39]

So even though appetite for risk is a more masculine trait, and even though some areas of finance could not function without risk-taking, the current gender imbalance seems to be contributing to the kind of market manias that cause financial crises. The Coates and Herbert study suggests that too many men on the trading floor are subconsciously increasing the very risks they're supposedly so well-equipped to handle.

So, on the grounds of financial stability, there would appear to be a powerful argument for more women in finance.

---

38 'Male Crisis', *World Finance*, March 2012
39 www.barbarastcherbatcheff.com, 'Trading – No Job for a Nice Girl', 19 October 2009

Evidence from that most high-stakes corner of the financial system, the hedge fund industry, also suggests that women are better equipped to handle risk than their male counterparts. The Rothstein Kass WAI Hedge Index is an index of sixty-seven hedge funds run or owned by women. For the last five years it has nimbly outperformed the HFRX Global Hedge Fund Index, which represents the male-dominated hedge fund industry as a whole.[40] According to the Chicago-based Hedge Fund Research consultancy, the value of women-run funds fell by half as much as male-run funds in the twelve months after the fall of Lehman.[41]

But as well as a compelling financial case, there's an equally pressing business case for having more women at the top. Evidence from outside finance shows that the more female executives boards have, the more successful their companies are likely to be. McKinsey analyzed the eighty-nine European listed companies with the highest levels of gender diversity and found they enjoyed operating returns of 11 percent – nearly double the average of 6 percent. Stock-price growth was also given a significant boost: over the two-year period surveyed, the most diverse companies saw their share price grow by 64 percent, compared to 47 percent for the male-dominated firms.[42] A Leeds University Business School study showed that having at least one female director on the board appears to cut a company's risk of insolvency by 20 percent, and that having two or three female directors lowers the chances of bankruptcy even further.[43]

40 Rothstein Kass, Second Annual Survey, December 2012
41 Quoted in *The Guardian*, 19 October 2009
42 McKinsey & Co., 'Women Matter: Gender Diversity, a Corporate Performance Driver', 2008, p. 14
43 Nick Wilson and Ali Altanlar, 'Director Characteristics, Gender Balance and Insolvency Risk: An Empirical Study', *Credit Management Research Centre*, 30 May 2009

A report by the Canadian research group Catalyst found in 2007 that companies in the Fortune 500 index with the highest percentages of women board directors significantly outperformed those with the lowest percentages. Their return on equity was over 50 percent higher, their return on sales was over 40 percent higher, and their return on invested capital was two-thirds higher.[44]

Some suggest attendance at board level also improves as soon as more women are on the board, both because they are more likely to attend and because male directors attend more meetings when women are present.[45] This is underpinned by survey data that shows women being more assertive on corporate-governance issues like evaluation of board performance, while boards with both men and women emphasize board accountability and authority more heavily.[46]

Research into top French firms listed on the CAC 40 index has linked the number of women at management level to share price. The share price of companies like Alcatel-Lucent and Renault, which have mainly male management, decreased more than the average CAC 40 company over 2008. Hermès, on the other hand, with 55 percent of the management made up by women, was the only large company whose share price rose, by 17 percent. With banks, BNP Paribas, with 39 percent of its management made up of women, best resisted the financial crisis and its share price fell by 39 percent. Compare it with Crédit Agricole, where the figures are 16 percent and 63 percent respectively.[47] The sample size of this research was small, and of

44 Catalyst Report, 'The Bottom Line: Corporate Performance and Women's Representation on Boards', October 2007
45 Daniel Ferreira, Treasury Select Committe oral evidence, 13 October 2009
46 Lord Davies of Abersoch, 'Women on Boards', February 2011, p. 10
47 Michel Ferrary, 'CAC 40: Les enterprises feminisées résistent-elles mieux a la crise boursière?', Ceram Busines School, 2008

course simply because there is a correlation does not prove there is a direct causal link. But take it with larger, thorough studies with the same conclusions and the emerging argument is strongly in favor of increased gender diversity.

So through a combination of the embedded cultural bias and a skewed framework, women are not progressing as they could. The numbers show they are not. The evidence shows that, for the sake of good business, they should. And the reasons why they are not need to be tackled.

Does this mean women should stage a coup and take over finance? No. Indeed, an entirely feminized financial culture would have its own problems, and women in positions of corporate leadership are quite capable of making their own mistakes. But the evidence does make the argument that finance is a man's world look tired.

Instead, the case is for diversity. Any good board needs different perspectives to make the organization as stable and effective as possible. John Last, HR Director at RBS, argues that 'it is diversity of thought you want on a board, which diversity itself and gender diversity should give you'.[48] Kat Banyard of the Fawcett Society agreed: 'When you have greater diversity and more women on boards you have less groupthink. Women and men lead very different lives at the moment. They bring different experiences with them.'[49] Finance theory extols the virtues of portfolio diversification. So why is there such reluctance to diversify in a way that could reduce risk?

Since social norms are such an important determinant of behavior, and people tend to reward people like them, it is clear that significant barriers exist to a meritocracy of sexes in finance. The evidence shows that these barriers not only risk

48 John Last, Treasury Select Committe oral evidence, 14 October 2009
49 Kat Banyard, Treasury Select Committe oral evidence, 14 October 2009

financial stability but also hold back corporate performance. So it is time to accept that finance is not full of men because it requires masculine behavior, but that finance is dominated by masculine behavior because it is full of men. That must change.

Chapter 6

REWARDS FOR FAILURE

The mega remuneration endemic in the banks undermines the principle of capitalism – which is to reward risk capital. Professional managers should be well rewarded but not on terms which give them equity risk-type returns, with little downside.
– John Nelson, Chair, Lloyds of London, July 2012

The meaning of fairness is one of the oldest debates in politics, and one of the most important. For the way in which a society defines the word has profound economic consequences.

For those on the Right, fairness has the sense of just rewards, the idea that you should get out what you put in. In other words it describes a system in which reward is directly proportionate to effort and talent. Properly laid out, capitalism makes that principle real. Free markets ensure that the people who prosper are those who work hard and risk their capital to succeed in making other people's lives – their customers' lives – better. In this sense the market is a deeply moral institution.

On the Left fairness is more aligned with the idea of equality of outcome, as in the Marxist slogan: 'From each according to his ability, to each according to his needs.' Since this definition arose in extremely unfair societies like pre-Revolutionary France, where wealth was largely determined by birth and connections, its modern exponents have inherited a great enthusiasm for 'corrective' government action to redress perceived imbalances.

Political economists have demonstrated that the two

definitions of fairness exert a self-fulfilling influence on policy.[1] Societies that regard income as the result of good luck or social position tend to have higher taxes and more redistribution. Societies that believe a person's income is an expression of individual effort are likely to have lower taxes and a smaller welfare state, meaning they offer greater incentives to work hard.

History has shown that the latter arrangement is more conducive to human flourishing. The twentieth century revealed state-enforced equality for what it was: one of history's dead ends, corrupt, totalitarian and grossly inefficient. As if the collapse of Soviet Communism in 1989 wasn't evidence enough, the last three decades of market reforms in China have lifted more people out of remorseless poverty than any other government policy in the history of the world.

Yet capitalism's turn of the century vindication was perhaps too complete for its own good. The fall of the Berlin Wall and the rise of China became the basis of an intoxicating story about the final global victory of free markets. From now on, all was for the best in the best of all possible economic systems. This narrative helped to screen financial markets from critical scrutiny, even when they started to behave in ways which violated the fundamental rules of capitalism. Nowhere can this be seen more clearly than in the field of bankers' pay.

High leverage at financial institutions massively amplifies both potential returns and potential losses. For this reason, bankers' pay is supposed to be carefully structured in a way that incentivizes success and disincentivizes failure. This is why financial services make greater use of variable pay, 'bonuses', than any other industry. So much for the theory. What actually happens is that senior bankers charge shareholders a huge premium to

---

1   See Alesina and Angeletos: 'Fairness and Redistribution: US versus Europe', *MIT*, 2002

offset the risks they take by tying their pay to company performance. The resulting 'heads I win, tails you lose' compensation deals have bred a corrosive culture of rewards for failure.

This culture is most visible at the very top. Fred Goodwin left Royal Bank of Scotland with a pension pot worth £8.4 million. Given that he'd posted the biggest loss in UK corporate history, the deal brought a new meaning to the phrase 'got off Scot-free'. But this pay-off was loose change compared to the rewards for failure bestowed on Goodwin's American counterparts. Joe Cassano, who made an estimated $300 million in salary and bonuses over the course of his career at AIG's Financial Products division, left the firm clutching a bonus package worth $34 million. The management of AIG, convinced that Cassano knew where the bodies were buried, retained him as a consultant with a monthly salary of $1 million until an outraged Congress put a stop to this arrangement.

Notoriously, AIG executives also spent $440,000 on a week-long vacation at the luxury St Regis spa resort in Monarch Beach, California, just days after the firm received an $85-billion government bailout. The US taxpayer would eventually spend $182 billion rescuing AIG. Dick Fuld managed to amass around $500 million as Lehman CEO. In 2007, the last year he was paid, he earned $34 million, $22 million as a cash bonus. In June 2008 G. Kennedy Thompson retired from Wachovia at the insistence of the board with $9 million worth of severance package. Jimmy Cayne, champion bridge enthusiast and disgraced Bear Stearns CEO, cashed out his stock in 2007, netting himself $61 million.

These are the most egregious examples of rewards for failure exposed in the crash, but this malign culture is not confined to the boardroom. Citigroup and Merrill Lynch suffered losses of more than $27 billion apiece during the crisis. Together they received TARP bailouts worth $55 billion. Yet in 2008,

Citigroup and Merrill paid their employees $5.3 billion and $3.6 billion in bonuses.[2] That same year three other firms also in receipt of TARP money, Goldman Sachs, Morgan Stanley and JPMorgan Chase, all paid out bonuses worth more than their net income. When the banks did well, their employees were paid well. As Governor Cuomo puts it: 'When the banks did poorly, their employees were paid well. And when the banks did very poorly, they were bailed out by taxpayers and their employees were still paid well.'[3]

For the Right, rewards for failure in banking are a serious problem. When the vital link between effort and reward is seen to be repeatedly broken it becomes harder for supporters of capitalism to defend free markets against those who wish to undermine them. Occupy Wall Street's arguments may be simplistic but they demand a response.

Our response has three parts: a moral, a behavioral and an economic case for tackling rewards for failure.

Socially Useless?

In the years leading up to the crash, many argued that finance and ethics belonged in separate spheres. When questions of ethical behavior made an appearance in public life it was usually in relation to issues like abortion, euthanasia, or minority rights – intensely emotive issues that cut right to the heart of most people's idea of what it is to be human. Finance, by contrast, seemed to exist on an amoral plane.

In 1970, the godfather of deregulated capitalism, Milton Friedman, wrote a wildly influential essay called 'The Social Responsibility of Business is to Increase its Profits'. The article

---

2 Andrew M. Cuomo, 'No Rhyme or Reason: the "Heads I Win, Tails You Lose" Bank Bonus Culture', State of New York, 2009
3 Ibid.

became a lodestar for those who wanted to believe that when they went into work they could leave their conscience at the door: that not only is there not, but that there ought not to be, any moral dimension to corporate behavior.

But the amoralists saw the headline and didn't read the argument. Friedman made a vital caveat. He understood the crucial role of the frameworks, rules and culture in which markets operate. What Friedman actually wrote was that it is the social responsibility of business to 'make as much money as possible, *while conforming to the basic rules of society, both those embodied in law and those embodied in ethical custom*' [emphasis added].[4] In Friedman's view the only entity with the moral authority to spend other people's money in ways which prejudiced their individual interests was government itself. Only government could suspend the principle of private property because it alone had a democratic mandate. As a result, managers who spent shareholders' money in ways which failed to maximize shareholder value were violating basic property rights. If Friedman had been around in late 2007, when Morgan Stanley announced it was writing off $9.4 billion worth of subprime debt while increasing its bonus pool by 18 percent, he would have been appalled.

In a similar vein, the British philosopher John Gray has written that 'market institutions will be politically legitimate only insofar as they respect and reflect the norms and traditions, including the sense of fairness of the cultures whose needs they exist to serve'.[5] In other words, unless financial markets regain the respect of the public by demonstrating that they do operate within the same moral framework as wider society then a

---

4   Milton Friedman, 'The Social Responsibility of Business is to Increase its Profits', *New York Times Magazine*, 13 September 1970

5   John Gray, 'After Social Democracy: Politics, Capitalism and the Common Life, (London: Demos, 1996), p. 11

government's room for maneuver will be severely tested in a future crisis.

This problem was foreshadowed by the TARP negotiations in the fall of 2008. On the day the House of Representatives rejected Hank Paulson's original bailout proposals, the S&P 500 share index recorded its largest one-day drop since 1987. The House initially repudiated the Paulson plan not on strictly economic grounds but because Democrat and Republican alike were outraged at the prospect of using public funds to replenish the bonus pools of greedy Wall Street bankers. In this they were echoing the views of the American people. Pew Research Center surveys taken at the time found that 86 percent of Americans disapproved of high bonuses given out by many financial institutions, with 62 percent saying they were angered by them.[6] In polling undertaken for this book, 56 percent of Americans agreed that the collapse of a large bank would hurt the overall economy 'a lot', yet 46 percent opposed government rescues of large banks at risk of failing, with only 26 percent in favor (the rest were undecided).[7] The anger over rewards for failure may explain this discrepancy.

With this in mind, we need to be clear that tackling rewards for failure is not about envy, or soaking the rich. No society can afford to call itself free if it imposes a cap on what people can aspire to, and not all high pay is undeserved, even in finance. Most people support wealth creation, and the polling suggests that Americans in particular prioritize economic growth over reducing inequality, but this comes with an important qualifier: they must be able to see the link between high pay and high performance. People don't object to the vast sums earned by entrepreneurs like the late Steve Jobs, or Google founders Larry

6 Pew President Andrew Kohut in the *New York Times*, 27 January 2012
7 YouGov survey of general population, conducted 28–31 January 2013

Page and Sergey Brin because they can see how they're adding value to the real economy we all live and work in. This is not just a crude dichotomy of manufacturing versus services. The Google search engine is intangible. Essentially it's a mathematical algorithm backed by a huge amount of processing power, yet we can all see how it allows for more efficient communication and sourcing of information. It makes our lives easier every day. So supporters of capitalism are just as concerned about what constitutes a 'fair' source of income as those who want to bury free markets. Indeed, the argument is a recurring theme in the history of capitalist thought.

At the dawn of the Industrial Age, the nineteenth-century economist David Ricardo produced a highly influential body of work on the rent income of landowners. Ricardo argued that rent was merely the difference between the values of the most and the least productive land, which had nonetheless been brought into cultivation as the population expanded. When the British population soared during the Industrial Revolution the surplus productivity of the more fertile land was not channeled into extra investment, instead it simply increased the rent landowners charged their tenant farmers. Landowners, like bankers, were adding little of value to the 'real economy', he argued, they were merely profiting from their position as the owners of a necessary utility. Ricardo's work gave rise to the concept of 'rent-seeking', defined by the economist John Kay as 'the accumulation of a fortune not by creating wealth through serving customers better but by the appropriation of such wealth after it has already been created by other people'.[8]

In August 2009, Britain's top regulator Lord Adair Turner updated Ricardo, causing a storm of controversy in financial

---

8 John Kay, 'The monumental folly of rent-seeking', *Financial Times*, 21 November 2012

circles when he suggested in an interview that some financial activities might be 'socially useless':

> It is hard to distinguish between valuable financial innovation and non-valuable. Clearly, not all innovation should be treated in the same category as the innovation of either a new pharmaceutical drug or a new retail format. I think that some of it is socially useless activity.[9]

Turner's language was not used by mistake. His argument was that banks were no longer performing their traditional function of looking after savings and allocating them to the businesses and capital projects which generate growth for the economy as a whole. In a 2010 lecture he pointed out that while the combined balance sheet of all British banks stood at 500 percent of British GDP in 2008, the country had little to show for it in terms of increased investment. For example, while mortgage credit had grown from 14 percent to 79 percent of GDP over the last fifty years, the amount actually invested in UK housing stock had barely changed.[10] The banks were simply pumping credit into existing properties and driving up their prices.

This situation was mirrored on the other side of the Atlantic. Historically, Wall Street has played a crucial role in helping to finance the growth of key American industries, from railroads and oil in the nineteenth century, to Hollywood and pharmaceuticals in the twentieth. As well as raising new funds for businesses, investment banks also make money from trading securities, either on behalf of clients, or on their own account (known as proprietary trading). To begin with, the banks traded

---

9 *Prospect Magazine*, 27 August 2009
10 Adair Turner, 'What do banks do, What should they do and what public policies are needed to ensure best results for the real economy?', lecture at Cass Business School, 17 March 2010

securities directly linked to the capital needs of businesses, such as equities and corporate bonds. The earliest derivatives were designed to stabilize annual crop prices. Turner's contention was that more recent trading innovations do not create value or hedge risk. Instead they generate their fees for banks by concealing risk or arbitraging the market. Complex mortgage securitization drove up US house prices; whether it ultimately improved the lives of American mortgage holders is another matter. It is certainly true that in recent years trading has gone from being one part of an investment bank's business to its driving engine. By 2006 trading accounted for 69 percent of net revenue at the big five, compared to 15 percent for traditional investment banking (i.e. M&A work and securities underwriting), and 16 percent for asset management.[11] At Lehman, Merrill and Bear, the three Wall Street firms which failed during the crash, the disparity between trading and investment banking was even greater.

In the short term, trading was the most profitable of the three activities because gains could be exaggerated through leverage – where traders borrow on margin to buy securities, hoping that the returns will outweigh the cost of servicing the debt. For the same reason it was also the most risky, because debt multiplies losses, particularly if, as Turner argues, certain securities were being created not because of their inherent economic usefulness but merely so they could be traded.

Accounting systems based on securitization have compounded the suspicion that certain traders are getting something for nothing. Old-fashioned retail banks used to make loans and gradually accumulated their profits as the loan

11 Robert Rhee, 'The Decline of Investment Banking: Preliminary Thoughts on the Evolution of the Industry 1996–2008', *Journal of Business and Technology Law*, vol. 5, no. 1, 2010, p. 81

was repaid. The bank and its managers were rewarded over time, according to outcomes. In the world of securitized lending, pay is determined by *expectations* rather than outcomes. Loans are made by mortgage companies, packaged up by Wall Street into mortgage-backed securities and sold on to investors at a profit. The value of the fee the MBS salesperson receives is determined by the expected future value of the loans being sold, not the value as actually realized over time. But this only makes sense if you believe you can predict the economic future.

In order to establish the value of a ten-year income stream from an MBS, for example, you would have to be able to predict the levels of repayments over the next ten years. This requires further predictions about where employment, inflation, interest rates and GDP growth will be over the coming decade. Economic models purported to be able to make these forecasts, but the models rested on false assumptions. As one hedge fund manager Mark Bathgate put it to us: 'It's like Toyota saying they know how many cars they'll sell over the next ten years and then booking the profits today.'[12] This system allowed bankers to make vast profits in upfront sales fees selling products whose value they could only guess at, some of which turned out to be worthless. Wall Street traders coined a term to describe this system, 'IBGYBG', which stood for 'I'll be gone, you'll be gone'.[13]

Greed and Fear
Given that pay and bonuses are all about making sure bankers have the right incentives, the behavioral literature might give us some clues as to how and why the wrong behavior has been incentivized.

---

12 Mark Bathgate, private interview
13 Financial Crisis Inquiry Commission Report, 2010, p. 8

In a landmark study conducted in 2000, a group of neurologists asked their subjects to play a card game.[14] They were given $2,000 each and told to choose cards from four decks. If they picked bad cards they would lose money. The decks were stacked. Two of them contained cards which produced more extreme wins and losses, but would set players back on average. The other two decks contained cards which produced less extreme wins and losses but a more favorable long-term average. Half the subjects in the test had suffered damage to their ventromedial prefrontal cortex (VM), the part of the brain implicated in the processing of risk and fear. The other half formed a representative sample of the population as a whole. Both groups were found to sweat when high-loss cards were first encountered: they both experienced the unconscious symptoms of fear. But compared to the control group, the subjects with VM damage were much more likely to return to the high-risk deck after suffering a loss. As a result they went 'bankrupt' more often.

What this group lacked was the ability to consciously experience fear. They unconsciously felt its effects, but they could not form the crucial emotive link between those effects and the external source of the fear. So they repeatedly took risks that cost them in the long term. The researchers concluded that their prefrontal cortices 'did not store the pain of remembered losses' as well as the control group.

The great economic historian J. K. Galbraith wrote that the 'pain of remembered losses' can restrain a society, as well as individuals, from excessive risk-taking. He characterized post-war financial stability in the United States in terms of a response to

---

14 Antoine Bechara, Daniel Tranel and Hanna Damasio, 'Characterization of the decision-making deficit of patients with ventromedial prefrontal cortex lesions', *Brain*, vol. 23, issue 11, July 2000, pp. 2189–2202

the trauma of the Great Crash: 'As a protection against financial illusion or insanity, memory is far better than law. When the memory of the 1929 disaster failed, law and regulation no longer sufficed.'[15] The experience of other countries bears this out. Sweden, which spent 4 percent of its GDP rescuing its banking system from a major crisis in 1992, fared remarkably well in 2008.

Colin Camerer, a behavioral economist commenting on the study's economic implications, has written that 'insufficient fear can produce nonmaximizing behavior when risky options have negative value'.[16] Negative value is a term familiar to poker players. It means a situation in which average losses outweigh average gains when all probable outcomes have been taken into account. Let's say we have a bet. If the next car that drives by is red then I pay you $10, if it's a different color then you have to pay me $15. That's a situation exhibiting negative value. 'Nonmaximizing behavior', on the other hand, is an economists' euphemism for screwing up. Dick Fuld's decision to ramp up Lehman's leverage and debt-to-equity ratios to ten-year highs during the crucial 2006–2008 period, when the housing market had peaked, reeked of negative value. But given the lavish pay deals outlined at the start of this chapter it's not surprising that Wall Street bosses felt 'insufficient fear' when it came to making firm-wide decisions on risk. As far as their personal finances were concerned, there really was nothing to fear.

This was a serious failure of corporate governance, which is all about ensuring that the interests of the owners of the business – shareholders – are aligned with the interests of those who

15 J. K. Galbraith, *The Great Crash 1929* (London: Hamish Hamilton, 1955)

16 Colin Camerer, George Lowenstein, Drazen Pralec, 'Neuroeconomics: How Neuroscience can Inform Economics' in the *Journal of Economic Literature*, vol. 43, March 2005

run the business on their behalf. Since the 1980s remuneration consultants have tried to realize this alignment by advising boards to pay managers shares or share options on top of their basic salary. The idea is if the value of the company declines through mismanagement then executives will experience the same loss as shareholders.

Some commentators, seeking to downplay the role executive pay played in goading risk-seeking, have made much of these manager–ownership deals. An oft-cited fact in this debate is that Dick Fuld held Lehman stock and stock options worth $1 billion in 2006, a holding which he sold for just $500,000 on the Friday before the bank filed for Chapter 11. But this is a one-dimensional way of looking at the issue, for the question is not how much Fuld lost in the crash, but how much Fuld lost relative to other Lehman shareholders during his time as CEO.

Lucian Bebchuk, Alma Cohen and Holger Spamann have made a detailed study of the compensation afforded to the five most highly paid executive officers at Bear Stearns and Lehman Brothers between 2000 and 2008.[17] They found that while shares in these companies were worth almost nothing by the end of 2008, over the same eight-year period the top five executives at Bear cashed out about $1.4 billion in Bear's case and $1 billion in Lehman's. Crucially, the vast majority of the cash resulted from the sale of share and share options, rather than from cash bonuses. Bear executives made $1.1 billion from selling shareholdings while Lehman bosses made $850 million. Indeed, the study finds that 'during the years preceding the firms' collapse, each of the teams sold more shares than they held when the music stopped in 2008.' With regard to the $950

17 Lucian Bebchuk, Alma Cohen and Holger Spamann, 'The Wages of Failure: Executive Compensation at Bear Stearns and Lehman 2000–2008', European Corporate Governance Institute Working Paper No. 287, June 2010

million that Fuld 'lost' when Lehman Brothers filed for bankruptcy, we need to remember that this sum was not in cash but equity which, in normal circumstances, the board would never have allowed him to dispose of in one swoop. The frequently quoted $1 billion figure refers to a purely nominal sum, rather than money in Fuld's wallet.

Obviously, if Bear and Lehman had not failed, these executives would have made even more money. It also goes without saying that no one on the board of Lehman woke up one morning and decided to trash an institution that had survived two world wars, the Great Depression, and 9/11. The point is that, even taking into account the effects of the crash the net pay-offs senior managers enjoyed were emphatically positive, whereas shareholder returns over the same period were negative, so in what sense could their interests be said to be aligned?

The ease with which senior managers could cash-out their shareholdings gave them an obvious incentive to push for short-term gains in the share price – such as by leveraging up or investing in volatile assets – even when this undermined the long-term financial health of the firm. This might go some way towards explaining why, in the fatal 2006–2008 period, leverage at the failing banks precipitously increased. As Robert Rhee, a former investment banker puts it, 'In proverbial gambling parlance, the failing firms were doubling down their bets at precisely the time probability favored the house'.[18] But for these executives there was no downside to the gamble. If they misjudged the risks, then at the very worst they would lose their jobs and have more time to spend with their money, or bridge, in Jimmy Cayne's case.

---

18 Robert Rhee, 'The Decline of Investment Banking: Preliminary Thoughts on the Evolution of the Industry 1996–2008', *Journal of Business and Technology Law*, vol. 5, no. 1, 2010, p. 91

Path-dependent Decision-making

Closely related to the lack of downside in bankers' pay is the problem of compensation structures which fail to reflect the uneven distribution of financial risk across time.

Historically, the core of an investment bank's business was agency work, where the firm would earn a fee by providing a service for clients. Typical activities included advising on M&A transactions and securities underwriting. As the Epicurean Dealmaker puts it: 'None of these businesses entailed any material amount of persistent or hidden financial risk to investment banks: we did the deal, we got paid, and we moved on.'[19] The problem arose when banks started to act less as agents and more as principals, bringing the tail risk associated with credit derivatives or mortgage-backed securities onto their own balance sheet. Traders continued to receive bonuses derived from profits booked in the previous year. But the old system made no allowance for the new risks blossoming on the balance sheet – risks which if they ever materialized could wipe out the very profits on which previous compensation was based. This is why the 'IBGYBG' attitude is so dangerous.

The perverse incentives latent in this system were supercharged by a powerful cognitive bias known as path-dependent decision-making. The academic study of behavioral economics has long rested on experiments with college students roped into a series of experiments into how they behave, usually involving colored marbles. Over the years these experiments have yielded many valuable insights into the way people behave in a market environment, often in marked contrast to the unthinking assumptions made by more traditional branches of economics. Some scenarios, however, are harder to simulate than others.

---

19 The Epicurean Dealmaker, 'The Root of Some Evil', www.epicureandealmaker@blogspot.co.uk, January 8 2012

Anything involving risk or gambling, for example, suffers from the budgetary constraints of an economics faculty. How do we know if someone will gamble in the same way if the stakes are $500,000, instead of $5?

Yet there are two areas of life which provide academics with a huge dataset of high stakes risk-taking: casinos and game shows. Big bets placed by both winners and losers are a phenomenon found in casinos across the world. Big losers suffer from the 'break-even effect'. This cognitive bias describes the situation where unlucky gamblers bet big in the hope they'll make good on their previous losses. The most notorious instance of this effect in the world of finance must be Nick Leeson's unauthorized trading on behalf of Barings Bank in 1995, and is supported by the new polling evidence detailed in Chapter 4. Winners suffer the so-called 'house-money effect', where high rollers continue to gamble even after a big win because they haven't internalized the gain. They think of the newly acquired chips as belonging to the 'house', rather than to themselves.

In 2008 a group of economists produced similar results by studying *Deal or No Deal*, a hugely popular game show that exists around the world (there's even a version airing in Afghanistan).[20] For those who haven't seen the show, the game is played with twenty-two sealed boxes, each one containing a hidden amount of prize money, ranging from a few cents to hundreds of thousands of dollars. Before an episode begins the boxes are sealed and one is randomly assigned to the contestant. That box and its contents are then owned by the player. The game consists of six rounds in which the player chooses three

20 Thierry Post, Martijn J. van den Assem, Guido Baltussen, and Richard H. Thaler, 'Deal or No Deal? Decision Making under Risk in a Large-Payoff Game Show', *American Economic Review*, 2008

boxes to open. The prizes they contain are then eliminated from the list of possible sums which could be in the player's box.

At the end of each round a shadowy figure called 'the Banker', who supposedly puts up the money for each show, phones the host on an old-fashioned Bakelite phone and offers to buy the player's box. The potential value of this box varies depending on which sums have already been revealed. The host conveys the Banker's offer to the player and then poses the question, 'Deal or No Deal?' If the player chooses to deal they win whatever the Banker has promised, their box is unsealed and the game ends. If the answer is 'No Deal' then the game continues until either the player agrees to a deal, or they reach the final round with only two boxes left in play. The Banker then offers one last chance to deal. If the offer is refused the player's own box is unsealed and they win whatever sum it contains.

The game works entirely according to chance. Neither the player, the Banker, nor the host knows which prizes are in any of the boxes. In theory the player estimates the value of his or her box based on which sums have already been removed from play and then makes a decision based on elementary probability. In practice the researchers discovered something very different was going on.

After studying hundreds of episodes they found that in later rounds the contestants' choices were being driven largely in response to previous outcomes in the game. Choices were 'path dependent'. Players did not calmly assess the situation on its merits, as conventional economic theory predicts they should, instead past outcomes were inscribed on decisions made in the present, *even when the odds had changed*. Not only did lucky contestants keep gambling as they felt 'in luck', unlucky contestants also took higher risks in an attempt to make up for their losses. Following a dramatic event in a previous round, both winners and losers, unlike the middling contestants, would routinely reject generous offers from the Banker, even if the offer was greater than the average remaining prize: a clear example of irrational risk-seeking behavior.

Some might sneer at the idea that sophisticated Wall Streeters could fall into the same cognitive trap as impulsive game show contestants, but one of the most startling aspects of the crisis is the extent to which the whole subprime mortgage machine depended on the belief that US house prices would keep rising in the future as they had done in the past. AIG's Financial Products division, where traders received a greater proportion of the profits than the average hedge fund manager, paid dearly for this path-dependent thinking. Before the crash, Goldman Sachs and others managed to convince Joe Cassano to post ruinous amounts of collateral against the risk that the subprime-backed bonds AIG was insuring would fall in value. Cassano was so confident that he'd got the better end of the deal that he famously told investors in an August 2007 conference call, 'It is hard for us, without being flippant, to even see a scenario within any kind of realm of reason that would see us losing \$1 on any of those transactions'.[21] When Wall Street came knocking for their collateral in the summer of 2008, AIG FP was wiped out in what Michael Lewis has described as an 'upmarket version of a run on a bank'.[22] What's curious is that when AIG refused to insure any more subprime mortgage-backed bonds after 2005, the same conscientious Wall Street firms that had required Cassano to post collateral continued to buy subprime bonds, uninsured, from the even more rotten vintage of 2006/2007. The people who traded these securities were making so much money that they continued to gamble,

---

21 Financial Crisis Inquiry Commission Report, 2011, p. 268
22 Michael Lewis, 'The Man who Crashed the World', *Vanity Fair*, August 2009

even when the odds had changed. It's no surprise that quantitative studies have shown that firms which adopted CEO compensation contracts with a heavier emphasis on annual cash bonuses (as opposed to deferred share-based compensation) experienced larger losses during the crisis.[23] These CEOs had come to associate risk-taking with immediate and certain financial gain. The result was a destructive feedback loop.

There's also the possibility of a chemical addiction to risk-taking, which could aggravate path-dependent decision-making. Neurologists have shown that a sudden financial gain lights up the same reward circuitry in the brain as a cocaine high.[24] Our bankers were hooked. In some cases literally: at the mortgage lender Ameriquest's Sacramento offices, loan officers reportedly took cocaine and methamphetamines so they could sell subprime loans for up to fourteen hours a day.[25]

All of this has led the prominent risk theorist and former trader Nassim Nicholas Taleb to propose that: 'Any person who works for a company that, regardless of its current financial health, would require a taxpayer-financed bailout if it failed should not get a bonus, ever.'[26] For Taleb, bonuses are dangerous because they encourage bankers to game the system by hiding the risks of 'unpredictable yet consequential blow-ups', or what Taleb has written of as 'black swan events'. For example, a proprietary trader who bought AAA-rated CDOs would generate returns of 5 or 6 basis points higher than an

---

23 David Erkens, Mingyi Hung, Pedro Matos, 'Corporate Governance in the 2007–2008 Financial Crisis: Evidence from Financial Institutions Worldwide', *Journal of Corporate Finance*, vol. 18, January 2012

24 Andrew Lo, 'Fear Greed and the Financial Crisis', in the *Handbook on Systemic Risk* (Cambridge: Cambridge University Press, 2011)

25 Bethany McLean and Joe Nocera *All the Devils are Here: The Hidden History of the Financial Crisis* (London: HarperCollins, 2010)

26 Nassim Nicholas Taleb, 'End Bonuses for Bankers', *New York Times*, 7 November 2011

AAA-rated corporate bond, and the additional return would mean a bigger bonus for the trader. But this extra return was merely compensation for the hidden risk that the CDO would default. Taleb concludes:

> Consider that we trust military and homeland security personnel with our lives, yet we don't give them lavish bonuses. They get promotions and the honor of a job well done if they succeed, and the severe disincentive of shame if they fail. For bankers, it is the opposite: a bonus if they make short-term profits and a bailout if they go bust.

The Broken Chain

So far we've looked at the moral arguments for tackling rewards for failure, as well as behavioral insights which suggest these deals undermine financial stability, but there is also a compelling business case for reform.

By now we've all heard the answer given by top earners when challenged on excessive pay: 'in a competitive global market you have to pay competitively to get the best talent'. After all, Steve Jobs was Apple, and Warren Buffett is Berkshire Hathaway: their behavior is imprinted on the DNA of their organizations. A CEO's ability to provide inspiring leadership or pursue a brilliant investment strategy will have a major impact on the profitability of the whole firm. In the depths of the crisis the CEOs of failing banks were able to cling to power for some time precisely because of this belief that they were irreplaceable.

This argument, while widespread, is flawed. Taken to its extreme, banks would pay staff all of their return to the company, which is absurd. Some economists have drawn a parallel between executive pay and the enormous sums commanded by famous musicians, actors and athletes, but this too is a bogus analogy. In these industries the economic value of talented individuals is easily deduced from box-office returns, ticket billings, or album sales: a relatively efficient market for top talent exists because talent itself is the product on sale. In finance, by contrast, individuals cannot make a profit without the supporting infrastructure of a bank's capital, back office, and brand. Productivity is a team concept.

It's strange that the same consultants who advise shareholders that competition forces pay upward at executive level also tend to argue that competition should exert a downward pressure on pay at all other levels of the firm. In a truly competitive market buyers make a trade-off between quality and price. We do this every time we go grocery shopping, choose a hotel room, or hire a lawyer. Yet this trade-off is rarely considered by company boards when it comes to choosing a new CEO. During the CEO selection process boards pick their next chief executive largely without reference to price (beyond what is considered generally affordable), and the incoming CEO's compensation package is only negotiated once they have accepted the position.[27] It's also difficult for defenders of the status quo to point to many instances where CEOs of an S&P 500 company have resigned because they are unhappy with their pay. CEOs certainly resign, but in practice this is almost always because of a clash with the board over company policy, or because of some perceived mistake. Indeed, during the crisis, several resignations were triggered at failing banks because they allowed CEOs to retain more generous pension entitlements than if they had been dismissed by their boards.

Much of the argument about the need to pay 'competitively' for mobile executive talent rests on the assumption that an

---

27 Charles M. Elson and Craig K. Ferrere, 'Executive Superstars, Peer Groups and Over-Compensation – Cause, Effect and Solution', available at SSRN, 7 August 2010

executive's skills and abilities are readily transferable from firm to firm, particularly as economies become more globalized. But there is little empirical evidence for this assertion. If skills are so transferable we would expect firms boasting successful, externally hired CEOs to outperform firms headed up by internal hires, but this does not happen. Far from favoring generalists who will leapfrog from firm to firm at the drop of a hat, greater access to global markets is more likely to reward corporate specialists who have mastered the art of doing one thing extremely well. We've already seen this in the case of the tech giants of Silicon Valley: Facebook does social media, Amazon retail, Apple consumer electronics and so on.

In finance, by contrast, 'universal banking' has been nothing short of a disaster. The big five Wall Street investment banks only ran into trouble when they marginalized their core business and took a sudden interest in the wholesale American mortgage market, while AIG's traumatic odyssey into the unfamiliar world of credit-default swaps speaks for itself. Tellingly, Dick Fuld has gone back to his investment-banking roots and now runs a company which performs advisory work for large corporations.

In a modern globalized economy, therefore, the most effective executives will tend to be those who have acquired the most knowledge and experience of a particular business, not CEOs, however charismatic and successful, poached from elsewhere. If we think of the 'star' CEOs like Jobs and Buffett, more often than not they have worked within the same firm for decades.

So the notion of a frenetic and cut-throat yet totally efficient global trade in banking executives who excel at every financial activity is a myth, and a dangerous myth as far as shareholders are concerned. Rewards-for-failure pay deals are not evidence of an efficient market but of market failure.

Where has this market failure come from? After all, shareholders are not stupid: it's not in their interests to see their investment capital diverted into the pockets of rent-seeking employees. We think it arises from misalignment of incentives, mostly in the form of what economists call a principal/agent problem. The interests of shareholders, 'the principal', are not properly aligned with the interests of the agents, i.e. the managers who act on their behalf. In plain English, the chain from ownership to control has been broken. As Lloyds of London CEO John Nelson argues in the quote at the start of this chapter, this has allowed managers to reward themselves as though they were the real owners.

This chain can be divided into three parts. The owners, mostly retail savers, often entrust their capital to a fund manager who owns the shares and technically appoints the board. The board holds the executive to account. And the executive runs the company. Let's take each in turn.

The Shareholders

Recent work in psychology suggests that people have a strong bias to choose 'the default option'. Below the level of conscious awareness our minds constantly usher us along mental shortcuts, allowing us to skip past sustained thought or difficult decision-making wherever possible. Studies have shown that when a company provides an automatic opt-in to their pension plan, employee enrolment shoots up.[28] Conversely, when an opt-out is the default option, take-up is significantly reduced, in direct contradiction to the employees' long-term self-interest. Just so in investment culture. In recent times shareholders have tended to choose the default option of non-interference with a bank's remuneration policies.

---

28 Shlomo Benartzi and Richard Thaler, 'Save more tomorrow: Using behavioral economics to increase employee savings', *Journal of Political Economy*, vol. 112, 2004

This problem has been catalyzed by the relative decline of individual investors. At the close of the Second World War, 90 percent of shareholders in the US were individuals, today the figure is closer 28 percent.[29] Direct ownership of shares by individuals has given way to ownership by institutions such as pension funds, insurance firms and corporations as well as overseas shareholders, who also tend to be institutions. This extra layer of intermediation puts the ultimate owners of the business at an even further remove from dealings in the boardroom, while the diffuse nature of modern share ownership conspires against concerted action. As anyone who has attended a bank's AGM in recent years will know, individual investors tend to be far more exercised about rewards-for-failure deals than institutions. This is hardly surprising as institutional investments are often managed by people who profit from the same rent-seeking culture. Other investors are quite open about the disengaged, transactional nature of their holdings. When the Financial Crisis Inquiry Commission asked Warren Buffett about his attitude to management failings at Moody's, of which Berkshire Hathaway owns half, Buffett replied: 'I had no idea. I'd never been at Moody's, I don't know where they are located.'[30] According to Buffett he only invested in the company because the rating agency business was 'a natural duopoly,' which gave it 'incredible pricing power'.

A further problem is that shareholders, particularly institutional investors, seem to be growing ever more addicted to short-term profits. In 1998 the average holding period for shares in UK and US banks was three years. Ten years later it was around

---

29 Roger Bootle, *The Trouble with Markets* (London: Nicholas Brealey Publishing, 2009), p. 70

30 Financial Crisis Inquiry Commission Report, 2011, p. 207

three months.[31] As any smoker trying to quit will confirm, short-termism is deeply ingrained in human nature. We discount the value of future gains in direct proportion to their distance from us in time. In other words, the longer you wait, the less it's worth. PwC surveyed top UK executives, asking them if they would prefer 75 percent chance of winning £250,000 tomorrow, or a 75 percent chance of winning £400,000 in three years time. The majority chose the first option, even though the second was worth more than its face value given the interest it would accrue. Some neurologists have argued that short-termism is a response to recent technological change, that our brains are adapting to greater volume and speed of information by contracting our attention spans.[32]

The Bank of England's Andrew Haldane has studied the impact of short-termism on investment markets. He finds that in the US and the UK, investors are discounting the value of cash-flows five years into the future at rates more appropriate to eight years, ten-year-ahead cash-flows are valued as if they are sixteen years ahead, and cash-flows which are realized more than thirty years into the future are barely valued at all.[33] Haldane concludes that this short-termism represents a serious market failure.

A consequence of this failure has been for shareholders to rubber-stamp any compensation package, no matter how indulgent, provided the management agrees to maintain a regular and immediate delivery of high returns. Preference

---

31 Andrew Haldane, 'Control rights (and wrongs)', Wincott Memorial Lecture, Westminster, London, 24 October 2011

32 Nicholas Carr, 'Is Google Making Us Stupid? What the Internet is doing to our brains', *Atlantic Magazine*, July/August 2008

33 Andrew Haldane, 'The Short Long', speech to the 29th Société Universitaire Européene de Recherches Financières Colloquium: New Paradigms in Money and Finance?, Brussels, May 2011

for short-term gains is most pronounced among institutional investors, most likely because fund managers have their own performance targets to meet. Yet short-term targets set by shareholders incite banking executives to gorge on risk. This is because banking performance is judged not in terms of return on assets (the income a bank gains from the loans it makes or the securities it trades), but in terms of its return on equity, which is return on assets multiplied by leverage. This system allows any manager to improve his return on equity without improving underlying performance simply by leveraging up to the hilt. As Haldane puts it, 'return on equity is skill multiplied by luck'.[34] In the boom the incentives to go forth and multiply were overwhelming.

It's not all bad news however. As banks reduce their balance sheets and return on equity is sluggish, there are welcome signs that attitudes among institutional shareholders are starting to change. In 2012, Citigroup shareholders took the unprecedented step of voting down CEO Vikram Pandit's $15-million pay package. Although the vote was non-binding, the loss of face led Pandit to relinquish his bonus. This kind of AGM has become a familiar scene: a packed auditorium, rebellious mutterings, onstage a row of stony-faced executives sipping mineral water and fiddling with their microphones, impassioned speeches, a rumble of assent, clapping, pleas from the management then scattered booing, shaking of heads, a journalist in the corner scribbling fast. If the sleeping giants that are the world's large institutional investors really have woken up to the need for change then we might be about to witness

---

34 Andrew Haldane, 'Small Lessons from a Big Crisis', Remarks at the Federal Reserve Bank of Chicago 45th Annual Conference 'Reforming Financial Regulation', 8 May 2009

a fundamental rebalancing from return on labor to return to shareholders.

The Board of Directors

Share-owning non-executive directors (NEDs), who represent the interests of outside shareholders on boards, ought to be leading the charge for more effective corporate governance. Unlike outside shareholders they should know how much risk a bank can bear, when to call the executives off and how to make the case for doing so. The economist Ruth Lea is an NED at Arbuthnot, an institution which weathered the credit freeze by imposing strict limits on its ratio of loans to deposits, and which, unlike Lehman Brothers, declined to fund itself from the wholesale money markets. Lea pointed out to us that an NED will never know as much about the business as a member of the executive directors, but Arbuthnot's fostered a culture where all members of the board were intimately involved in the bank's inner workings. The social norm is that questions are welcomed: 'I'm in the bank twice a week, I know what's going on. I can go up to any of my CEOs and say I want to know x.'[35]

Unfortunately, this culture seems to have been the exception rather than the rule. Before the crash there were few incentives for independent board members to restrain the management – in fact they may well have been cheering them on. One 2009 study of 306 financial firms in Europe and America found that boards with higher numbers of NEDs were actually *more* likely to invest in risky assets before 2006, more likely to experience shareholder losses and more likely to become insolvent during the crash.[36] The study's authors conclude that this is

---

35 Private interview

36 David Erkens, Mingyi Hung, Pedro Matos, 'Corporate Governance in the 2007–2008 Financial Crisis: Evidence from Financial Institutions Worldwide', *Journal of Corporate Finance*, vol. 18, January 2012

because share-owning board members are likely to be captivated by the same short-term impulses as outside shareholders. Another factor might be that independent directors are less likely to have specialist financial knowledge and so will find it harder to challenge their executives on the more technical aspects of risk management. As British regulators investigating the collapse of RBS found when they interrogated the board, 'Some of those interviewed said that, given the CEO's excellent grasp of detail and skill in forensic analysis, it was sometimes difficult to raise more general questions or concerns that were not readily supported by detailed, objective facts and evidence.'[37]

The best type of NED would be prepared to resign rather than sign off a proposal which he or she felt to be against the interests of the company. But how often does this actually happen? Unlike the executive directors, they are removed enough from the day to day operations of the bank to escape unfavorable comment when something goes wrong. And because NEDs typically hold several boardroom positions across the economy, when a financial institution blows up they can simply cross it off their resumé and find a replacement. Lord Stevenson, chairman of the British bank HBOS – an institution that effectively ran out of money in September 2008 – was typical of the disengaged independent director. Two days after the collapse of Bear Stearns, Stevenson assured British regulators that HBOS was in 'as safe a harbor as possible'. When Parliament later questioned Stevenson on his hands-off approach to risk management, he told MPs they had to bear in mind that he was a 'part-time' director. For the privilege of employing this occasional

---

37 Financial Services Authority, 'The Failure of the Royal Bank of Scotland: Financial Services Authority Board Report', December 2011, p. 234

chairman, HBOS shareholders stumped up an annual £703,000 in salary plus £113,000 in taxable benefits.[38]

Boards have ultimate responsibility for decisions on top pay because board members make up the compensation committees which devise executive compensation packages. In yet another layer of intermediation, compensation committees hire professional remuneration consultants to help them work out how much their executives are worth. Typically, the board's compensation committee asks these consultants to put the proposed package into perspective by constructing a 'peer group' of executives at similar companies. The level and structure of top pay at these other companies is then used as a benchmark against which proposed deals can be judged. Once this peer group analysis has been completed, the board will devise a package that is almost always targeted above the median average enjoyed by the comparison group.

This system makes life easy for boards, for it provides them with an apparently objective measure of an executive's worth. Yet it has serious shortcomings. For one, it is easily gamed, as managers are often allowed an input into choosing which companies should form the peer group. More seriously it is hugely wasteful. A widely quoted study of Stanford MBA students showed that 87 percent rated their academic performance as above average, a cognitive bias known as illusory superiority. Unsurprisingly, MBA-toting chief executives of major financial institutions are just as reluctant to self-identify as average when compared to their peer group. This means boards are nearly always obliged to pay them above the median, because to do otherwise would raise serious questions over the executive's position in the company. Yet if everyone in their peer group is paid above the median then average executive pay is guaranteed to ratchet up year on year. Do the math! In this way top pay becomes ever more disconnected from actual company performance. It also imposes rising demands on a bank's capital base because top pay has a knock-on effect further down the organization.

Instead of relying on these dubious peer-group comparisons, boards would be better advised to draw their own, independent conclusions about an executive's worth. This will be more difficult, because it involves a more subjective set of judgments. But it has the obvious attraction of encouraging directors to think more about their own firm and less about an arbitrary grouping of completely unrelated businesses. Boards of directors must start to take their fiduciary duty to shareholders more seriously, and this in turn requires shareholders to put more pressure on boards.

The Executives

Finally, we come to the executives themselves. The demutualization of Wall Street is arguably the ultimate source of the principal/agent problem. Until 1970, the New York Stock Exchange required its members to operate as private partnerships. Partners at the big broker–dealer firms were as amply rewarded as they are today, but they were also extremely careful because it was their own money on the line. Peter J. Solomon, a former partner at Lehman Brothers, explained to the Financial Crisis Inquiry Commission how the partnership structure shaped the bank's culture. Before Lehman went public, he and the other partners sat in a single room at headquarters, not to socialize but to 'overhear, interact, and monitor... Since they were personally liable as partners, they took risk very seriously'.[39] Brian Leach, a former executive at Morgan Stanley,

---

39 Financial Crisis Inquiry Crisis Report, 2011, p. 61

concurs: 'When I first started at Morgan Stanley, it was a private company. When you're a private company, you don't get paid until you retire. I mean, you get a good, you know, year-to-year "compensation". But the big payout was when you retired'.[40] When investment banks went public in the 1980s and 1990s they continued to pay out about half their revenues as compensation, even though the managers were no longer the owners. Compensation packages which include large amounts of equity, turning managers into major undiversified shareholders, have only entrenched the principal/agent confusion. This confusion goes a long way towards explaining why at Bear and Lehman returns were so skewed towards management. It also explains why at Bear, CEO Jimmy Cayne was responsible for setting his own compensation. According to Cayne, no one on the board ever questioned his decisions on pay.

If the link between executive pay and executive performance seems fairly tangential in modern banking, there is an ironclad link between the size of a CEO's compensation and company size. In 1989 the CEOs of the seven largest American banks earned $2.8 million on average, which was 100 times the median US household income. By 2007, CEO compensation at the largest banks had risen tenfold to $26 million, 500 times the median US household income.[41] It's no coincidence that this unprecedented growth spurt for CEO pay coincided with a period of major consolidation in the banking industry. The best known symbol of this was the merger of Citicorp with the insurance giant Travelers to form Citigroup in 1998, an event which marked the end of the post-Depression consensus on the need to restrain the size and scope of banking. From 1998 to

---

40 Ibid., p. 62
41 Andrew Haldane, 'Control rights (and wrongs)', Wincott Memorial Lecture, Westminster, London, 24 October 2011

2007, the combined assets of the five largest US banks – Bank of America, Citigroup, JPMorgan, Wachovia, and Wells Fargo – more than tripled, from $2.2. trillion to $ 6.8 trillion.[42] And with size came concentration: the top three US banks' share of assets rose from 10 percent in 1990 to 40 percent in 2007.[43]

The link between size and CEO pay persists because shareholders reason that the larger the company, the greater opportunity for the CEO to add value. This means the management almost always have a strong personal incentive to ensure that a takeover deal goes ahead. But this can create a conflict of interest as not all mergers add value for shareholders, and some may involve a huge transfer of risk to the bidding company. This is especially true in finance where risk can be hidden in credit default swaps or off-balance-sheet instruments. When G. Kennedy 'Ken' Thompson of Wachovia proposed the acquisition of the S&L Golden West in 2006 both he and Golden West CEO Herb Sandler had major incentives to ensure the deal went through. Sandler wanted to cash out at the top of the market and Thompson wanted to grow his empire: the acquisition would give Wachovia access to $125 billion in assets and 283 savings branches.[44] The incentives for Wachovia shareholders were less obvious. Seventy percent of Golden West's loans were Option ARMs, mortgages where the loan balance grew if you picked the minimum payment option. This business model only made sense as long as house prices kept rising, and they were falling by the time of the merger. Two years after the acquisition Wachovia's share price had fallen by 72 percent.

---

42 Financial Crisis Inquiry Crisis Report, 2011, p. 53

43 Andrew Haldane, 'The $100 Billion Question', comments given at the Institute of Regulation & Risk, Hong Kong, 30 March 2010, Bank of England

44 www.seekingaplha.com, 8 September 2008

Thompson later wrote to shareholders admitting that in hind-sight 'the timing was poor'.

Golden West and the ABN AMRO merger with RBS were extreme events but were far from atypical; the majority of recent financial mergers have resulted in the merged company under-performing the market.[45] But as well as providing rewards for failure for CEOs, there was a further consequence of the break-neck push for growth. As the large banks grew so too did their complexity and interconnectedness. This would have profound consequences for the way we regulated the financial system.

45 Andrew Haldane, 'The $100 Billion Question', comments given at the Institute of Regulation & Risk, Hong Kong, 30 March 2010

Chapter 7

TOO COMPLEX TO MANAGE
– WHY REGULATION FAILED

I knew a lot about financial regulation, but not nearly as much as I needed to know, and I knew very little about regulatory powers and authorities...

– Henry Paulson, CEO of Goldman Sachs 1999–2006, United States Secretary of the Treasury 2006–2009

In the 1920s the Chicago economist Frank Knight laid out a distinction between risk and what he called uncertainty. Uncertainty in Knight's sense refers to a risk that cannot be measured, in other words a situation where it is impossible to make a judgment about the probability of a given outcome.[1] The insurance industry recognizes this distinction by designating certain events 'Acts of God': events that occur so rarely their risks cannot be quantified. Nearly all the behavioral biases described in this book are human responses to uncertainty. As Knight's contemporary John Maynard Keynes recognized, because our knowledge of the future is limited we are forced to rely on 'conventions, stories, rules of thumb, habits, traditions in forming our expectations and deciding how to act'.[2]

Uncertainty and complexity are closely related. We saw in Chapter 2 that finance is an example of a complex system: a

---

1 Frank H. Knight, *Risk, Uncertainty and Profit* (1921)
2 Quoted in Robert Skidelsky, *Keynes: The Return of the Master* (London: Penguin Press, 2010)

category which embraces human societies, viral pandemics, the internet and the climate. The essential property of a complex system is that its behavior cannot be predicted by looking at the properties of its constituent parts. Instead the observer must study the interactions *between* each part to account for the behavior of the system as a whole. This means complex systems are inherently uncertain. Given the overwhelming number of variables involved, it is impossible to judge on the basis of probability how a complex system will develop. Meteorologists, for example, cannot forecast the weather any further than five days in advance. And who can judge *ex ante* which of the hundreds of millions of amateur videos on YouTube is destined to go viral?

As a complex system, finance is naturally shrouded in uncertainty. Despite the best efforts of financial theorists, there really is no way of knowing for sure what price an asset will trade for in the future. If it were otherwise there would be no such thing as financial speculation. Yet finance is unique among complex systems in that the system actively tries to suppress the uncertainty it generates. This is what financial regulation is all about. The weather doesn't aim to make itself easier to forecast, but the Fed sets an inflation target so banks can predict where interest rates will be in the future. Similarly, the Securities and Exchange Commission enforces disclosure rules so investors can make informed decisions about what they buy.

It's necessary for regulators to tackle uncertainty in this way because financial markets must have confidence in their assumptions about the future; if a bank cannot judge the likelihood a loan will be repaid it will not lend. It is also possible for markets to systematically mistake uncertainty for risk. This is what happens during bubbles.

By the 1990s it seemed to many as though risk had finally triumphed over uncertainty. In 1992 the American political scientist Francis Fukuyama published his famous book *The End of History*, which predicted the final global triumph of liberal democracy in the coming millennium. Caught up in the mood, many of Fukuyama's colleagues in the economics faculty began to confidently forecast the 'end of the business cycle'. Following the painful slumps and inflationary turbulence of the 1970s and early 1980s, the Fed under Greenspan had achieved the Great Moderation of steady, stable growth. The economic climate of today was now a steady guide to the economic climate of tomorrow. In a speech in 2004, then Fed Governor Ben Bernanke advised caution: 'Whether the dominant cause of the Great Moderation is structural change, improved monetary policy, *or simply good luck* [our emphasis] is an important question about which no consensus has yet formed.'[3] But few were listening by the time Bernanke arrived at his third option. Meanwhile, in the dealing rooms of Wall Street, computerized risk models had supplanted gut instinct and educated guesswork, transforming risk management into a precision science. In the housing market new quantitative credit-scoring techniques meant home loans could be extended to those whose credit risk had once been regarded as a black box. Financial markets congratulated themselves on attaining the power of prophecy. These developments called for a new style of regulation, one which the authorities called a 'risk-focused' approach.

As the Office of the Comptroller of the Currency (OCC), which regulates banks with national charters, explains in its handbook, 'Under this approach, examiners do not attempt to restrict risk-taking but rather determine whether banks identify, understand, and control the risks they assume'.[4]

In a world where all risks were known and quantifiable financial markets could always be relied upon to dexterously

---

3 Financial Crisis Inquiry Commission Report, 2011, p. 84
4 Ibid., p. 307

'self-correct' when a problem arose. If, for example, investors saw that a bank was dangerously overleveraged they would swiftly punish it by depressing its share price. As a result the heavy-handed bans and prohibitions of the 1930s were no longer necessary. This was the view of Alan Greenspan, who held that over time, 'market-stabilizing private regulatory forces should gradually displace many cumbersome, increasingly ineffective government structures'.[5]

But for this approach to work the authorities had to be sure that banks really did understand the risks they were taking. And this was a highly subjective judgment for regulators to make, in a system which demanded objectivity. The solution was to expand massively the size and complexity of the rulebook. If the banks could demonstrate in meticulous detail that they had complied with the rules then this amounted to objective proof that they understood the risks they were taking. It was no longer necessary to invoke the judgment of the regulator.

The risk-focused approach generated a vast and intricate bureaucracy to process the paperwork and ensure regulatory compliance across the board. Government spending on financial regulation has swollen from $725 million in 1980 to $2.07 billion in 2007.[6] In 1935 there were 4,500 banking regulators in the US; today the combined strength of the main government agencies is about 18,500.[7] On the eve of the crash Citibank alone had sixty full-time OCC examiners onsite.[8] The filing cabinets have also expanded. Since 1978, the Fed has required quarterly reporting by all bank holding companies. In 1986,

---

5 Financial Crisis Inquiry Commission Report, 2011, p. 28

6 *Forbes Magazine*, 11 December 2012

7 Andrew Haldane, 'The Dog and the Frisbee', speech given at the Federal Reserve Bank of Kansas City's 36th economic policy symposium, 'The Changing Policy Landscape', Jackson Hole, Wyoming, 31 August 2012

8 Financial Crisis Inquiry Commission Report, 2011, p. 153

the data required took up the equivalent of 547 columns in Microsoft Excel. By 1999, this had risen to 1,208 columns, and by 2011 it had reached 2,271.[9] And the sums have become harder. In 1988 the calculations to determine how much capital a bank should hold as a buffer against insolvency could be done on the back of envelope, but today several million calculations are required. This process has developed its own momentum. As more financial risks become known to the authorities, more rules and institutions are spawned to ensure the banks account for them.

If all this sounds complicated that's because it is. And that was the problem. If complex systems already generate uncertainty then a complex regulatory response will only exacerbate that uncertainty. This is what happened before the crash. At every level of the regulatory regime excessive complexity concealed risk, both from the markets and from the regulators themselves.

Complexity and Policymaking

As you might expect, Democratic and Republican accounts of the policy errors which contributed to the crisis are sharply divergent. Republicans tend to focus on government policies aimed at broadening homeownership among low-income groups, as well as the role of the government-chartered enterprises Fannie Mae and Freddie Mac. Democrats concentrate on the legacy of financial deregulation which began in 1987 when Alan Greenspan replaced Paul Volcker as Chairman of the Fed.

What's beyond argument is that the American mortgage market was out of control by the time of the crash. From at least the late 1990s state-level officials had noticed a suspicious pattern: sharply rising house prices in a low-income area followed by a wave of foreclosures. They began to hear reports of

---

9   Andrew Haldane, 'The Dog and the Frisbee', 2012

new kinds of loans that allowed people to buy homes and then refinance their mortgages with very small down payments and minimal documentation. The mortgage companies involved then sold bundles of these loans on to Wall Street.

These companies were known to employ questionable business models: extortionate fees and penalties, deliberate targeting of vulnerable groups, aggressive sales tactics such as salesmen turning up at homes uninvited and talking people into signing deals on the kitchen table, and high levels of fraud. In 2004 Chris Swecker, an assistant director of the FBI, held a press conference warning about a 'potential epidemic' of fraud in the US mortgage market.[10] According to one study, between 2000 and 2007, 10,500 people with criminal records entered the mortgage-brokering business in Florida alone.[11] But the market was warped in more subtle ways, in particular by a change in the terms of trade between those who originated the mortgages and those who purchased them to package up and sell on to investors. In the past Fannie and Freddie had set strict guidelines about what kind of mortgages they would buy. Since the two agencies traditionally accounted for about 70 percent of the secondary mortgage market, most originators were forced to comply. By 2006 the lion's share of the secondary market was dominated by Wall Street banks, who gave lenders a freer hand. Increasingly the banks molded their terms and conditions around the demands of lenders who had no stake in the quality of their loans. Since the strategy was to maximize volume, quantity predominated over quality.

For those who tend towards the conservative end of the political spectrum it is customary to cast Fannie and Freddie as the

10 Chris Swecker, statement before the House Financial Services Subcommittee on Housing and Community Opportunity, 7 October 2004

11 Financial Crisis Inquiry Commission Report, 2011, p. 14

instigators of this race to the bottom. Detractors point out that successive administrations ramped up the agencies' low-income lending requirements in an effort to extend homeownership. It is suggested that the pressure to meet these obligations caused a ripple effect of declining lending standards across the board. But this interpretation does not square easily with the facts. In 2006 and 2007, mortgage default rates reached 13.2 and 14.9 percent at the two government-sponsored enterprises.[12] This was shockingly high, but less devastating than the rate of failure in the private market: 45.1 percent in 2006 and 42.3 in 2007. Wall Street was clearly leading the charge. Sheila Bair, the current chair of the Federal Deposit Insurance Corporation (FDIC), notes that 75 percent of all subprime mortgages were for refinancing – where homeowners tap equity against rising house prices – rather than for home *purchase*.[13] If subprime lending was merely a government scheme to grow homeownership then it wasn't a very efficient one.

But liberals who blame 'deregulation' for the government's failure to intervene don't have it all their own way either. For a start, the necessary powers were on the books before the crash. In 1994, President Clinton signed the Homeowners Equity Protection Act (HOEPA) into law. HOEPA gave the Fed broad authority to ban unfair and abusive lending practices in the mortgage market.

Bair, who as a Treasury official lobbied the Fed to press its prerogatives, has argued that failure to use HOEPA on subprime lending was the 'one bullet' that could have prevented the crisis:

I think nipping this in the bud in 2000 and 2001 with some

---

12 *New York Times*, 13 July 2011
13 Quoted in David Faber, *And then the Roof Caved In: How Wall Street's Greed and Stupidity Brought Capitalism to its Knees* (New York: John Wiley & Sons, 2009), p. 54

strong consumer rules applying across the board that just simply
said you've got to document a customer's income to make sure
they can repay the loan, you've got to make sure the income
is sufficient to pay the loans when the interest rate resets, just
simple rules like that ... could have done a lot to stop this.[14]

Fed Chairman Ben Bernanke finally imposed rules along these
lines in July 2008. They only came into effect in October
2009, by which time it was far too late. So why didn't the Fed
act earlier?

In June 2002 President Bush made a speech to the
Department of Housing and Urban Development. He began
by imaginatively linking the War on Terror to the administration's housing policies. 'Let me first talk about how to make
sure America is secure from a group of killers, people who hate
– you know what they hate? They hate the idea that somebody
can go buy a home.'[15]

Bush concluded that 'part of the cornerstone of America is the
ability for somebody, regardless of where they're from, regardless of where they were born, to say, this is my home; I own this
home, it is my piece of property, it is my part of the American
experience.'[16] This charged rhetorical climate presented a major
obstacle for regulators. As Greenspan put it to CBS journalist
David Faber:

Had we tried to suppress the expansion of the subprime mortgage market, do you think that would have gone over very well
with the Congress, when it looked as though we were dealing

---

14 Financial Crisis Inquiry Commission Report, 2011, p. 79
15 US Department of Housing and Urban Development, 'George Bush speaks
   to HUD employees on National Homeownership Month', Washington
   DC, 18 June 2002
16 Ibid.

with a major increase in homeownership, which is of unquestioned value to this society?[17]

Former Fed Governor Susan Bies recalls testifying to Congress
about a proposal to tighten up lending rules: 'members of
Congress [said] that we were going to deny the dream of homeownership to Americans if we put this new stronger standard
in place'.[18]

In other words, the real significance of the government's
promotion of homeownership was not economic but political.
Effectively it shut down serious debate about how to regulate
the mortgage market. One form of interventionism barred the
way for another. The lesson is that in a complex system policy
decisions have unexpected effects, effects quite divorced from
the intent of policymakers. Few predicted that a commitment to
the American Dream of homeownership would shield predatory
lenders from effective scrutiny. A secondary lesson for economists is that the distinction between politics and economics is
an artificial one: political rhetoric may have a direct bearing
on financial stability. In the nineteenth century economics was
known as 'political economy'. Both subjects, like matter and
energy, were regarded as aspects of the other. Perhaps it is time
to revive that notion.

But the policy framework itself can also be too complex.
The United States Government requires the Fed to pursue
two monetary policy objectives at once: stable prices and
maximum sustainable employment. The recovery which
followed the bursting of the dot-com bubble in 2001 was
'jobless'. This meant growth returned without a corresponding
increase in employment. At that time a tide of money from the

---

17 David Faber, *And then the Roof Caved In*, p. 53
18 Financial Crisis Inquiry Commission Report, 2011, p. 21

high-saving economies of the East were holding down prices, which left the Fed free to pursue its other main policy objective. By stimulating the US economy with low interest rates Greenspan hoped to encourage job creation, and for him to have done otherwise would have invited serious questions on Capitol Hill. Unfortunately, the historically low interest rates set by the Fed between 2001 and 2004 also fueled a credit bubble which beguiled everyone – homeowners, investors and banks – into borrowing against illusionary wealth.

It's possible to argue that the Fed's interest rate decisions were trying to achieve too much at once. (For an even more disastrous example of where this can lead, take the example of the European Central Bank, which is required to set a single interest rate for the seventeen wildly disparate economies of the eurozone.) What is certain is that the Fed pursued its monetary policy objectives without any real reference to its third objective: the preservation of financial stability.

This was perverse because, as the crisis has shown, monetary policy and financial stability are inextricably linked. Monetary policy works through the financial system, banks create money, and transmit interest rates to the wider economy. Loose monetary policy encourages borrowing as the price of debt – the interest rate – falls. If debt is too cheap, people will borrow to buy assets.

When most prices are held down by a combination of cheaper imports and low expectations of future inflation, excess lending finds a home in asset price inflation. Asset prices are unlike the price of most goods, because when asset prices rise, they appear more, not less, attractive. So as we have seen, rising asset prices can swell into a bubble. Eventually it dawns on people that assets aren't really worth the market price and the bubble bursts. The assets lose value, but if people have borrowed against them their debts remain, putting financial stability at risk. At this point the Fed steps in as 'lender of last resort', allowing troubled banks to borrow federal funds at a specially discounted rate, known as the 'discount window'.

But as we have seen, in spite of this unique role within the financial system, and notwithstanding Greenspan's occasional misgivings about the 'irrational exuberance' of markets, the Fed explicitly disclaimed any responsibility for acting against the formation of financial bubbles. As the man himself put it in 2004: 'Instead of trying to contain a putative bubble by drastic actions with largely unpredictable consequences we chose ... to focus on policies to mitigate the fallout when it occurs.'[19]

Commentators generally describe this encouragement of moral hazard as flawed economic dogma and leave it at that. But dogma doesn't arise out of thin air. Keynes saw that in a complex world we make use of 'conventions, stories, rules of thumb, habits, traditions' to guide our decision-making. Behavioral psychologists call these rules of thumb 'heuristics'. Often heuristics can be useful, but sometimes they lead us up a blind alley. Consider this example from a famous paper by Kahneman and Tversky:

> A certain town is served by two hospitals. In the larger hospital about forty-five babies are born each day, and in the smaller hospital about fifteen babies are born each day. As you know, about 50 percent of all babies are boys. However, the exact percentage varies from day to day. Sometimes it may be higher than 50 percent, sometimes lower. For a period of one year, each hospital recorded the days on which more than 60 percent of the babies born were boys. Which hospital do you think recorded more such days?
> – The larger hospital?

---

19 Financial Crisis Inquiry Commission Report, p. 61

– The smaller hospital?

– About the same? (i.e. within 5 percent of each other)[20]

Kahneman and Tversky recorded that the majority would pick option C. In fact the correct answer is B because smaller samples are more likely to deviate from the statistical average of 50 percent. The heuristic in this case is representativeness: because both hospitals incorporate the same statistic (50 percent of babies are boys), people assume that they are equally representative samples of the general population. In this and many other experiments Kahneman and Tversky showed that, faced with uncertainty, most people will take irrational, or at least non-rational, cognitive shortcuts to arrive at their judgments.

Large institutions also make use of heuristics. In the previous chapter we saw how company boards rely on peer-group benchmarking when making decisions on executive pay. This is an example of an institutional heuristic. Target-hitting is another. When asked to perform a complex role under conditions of uncertainty institutions are strongly biased towards actions which deliver easily measurable outcomes. Pointing to a past record of targets met partially absolves them of the need to confront a vague and uncertain future.

In this, the FBI in the 1990s provides a useful analogy with the pre-crisis Fed. Before the creation of the Department of Homeland Security in October 2001, the main US agency with responsibility for counterterrorism was the FBI. Like the Fed, the FBI was responsible for averting high impact yet rare events, while at the same time dealing with more common ongoing problems, in the FBI's case serious crime. In a pre-9/11 world

---

20 Amos Tversky and Daniel Kahneman, 'Judgment under Uncertainty: Heuristics and Biases', *Science, New Series*, vol. 185, no. 4157, 27 September 1974, p. 1125

where do you think the bulk of the Bureau's time, talent and resources ended up? As the 9/11 Commission found in its report, 'performance in the Bureau was generally measured against statistics such as numbers of arrests, indictments, prosecutions, and convictions. Counterterrorism and counterintelligence work, often involving lengthy intelligence investigations that might never have positive or quantifiable results, was not career-enhancing.'[21] The Fed suffered from the same problem: the Fed Board's performance was measured against employment growth and by its record on inflation, not in terms of its ability to prevent a financial crisis.

Complexity and Structure

One puzzle for those who argue that 'deregulation' was the prime cause of the crash is that the institutions at the heart of this crisis, the banks, were regulated by a multitude of government agencies including the Fed, the Office of the Comptroller of the Currency (OCC), the Federal Deposit Insurance Corporation (FDIC), the Office of Thrift Supervision (OTS) and the SEC, as well as by regulators at the state level. By contrast the hedge fund industry – lightly regulated and on a voluntary basis – played a peripheral role. Indeed, by making large bets *against* the subprime mortgage sector in 2005, 2006 and 2007 several hedge funds actually exposed the bubble in the housing market.

Once again complexity is key. The Hank Paulson quote at the start of this chapter: 'I knew a lot about financial regulation, *but not nearly as much as I needed to know*',[22] is a fitting indict-ment of the system he presided over. Here was one of the most experienced bankers in the world, and a US Treasury Secretary

---

21 9/11 Commission Report, 26 July 2004, p. 74

22 Quoted in *The Great Hangover: 21 Tales of the New Recession*, ed. Graydon Carter (New York: Harper Perennial, 2010), p. 192

to boot, who felt that the regulatory system was too intricate to get his head around.

The structure of the American financial system is itself uniquely complex. The reasons for this go right back to the earliest years of the Republic. The US Constitution gives the federal government authority to regulate the currency but makes no mention of banking. This meant that central banking, along the lines of the Bank of England, founded in 1694, never really took off in America. (The decentralized Federal Reserve System, with its twelve regional Reserve Banks, only came into being in 1913.) It also meant that the right to charter banks was reserved exclusively for the states. To protect their own bank-chartering powers, states prevented branches of banks chartered in other states from intruding on their territory, to create a banking system fragmented along state lines. Even when a federal chartering system was introduced during the Civil War, national banks could still not branch across state lines. This compromise condemned the US financial system to perpetual fragility, resulting in large numbers of small, poorly diversified banks which were vulnerable to runs and panics – during the Great Depression 9,000 US banks suspended operations. It also introduced a competitive dynamic into the regulatory system. If national banks didn't like the way they were regulated by the OCC they could always switch to a state charter and be regulated by the state instead. And vice versa.

Officials at state level were among the first to identify the delinquent character of the subprime mortgage companies. In late 2003, Prentiss Cox, then a Minnesota assistant attorney general, ordered one of these companies, Ameriquest, to hand over information about its loans. Ten boxes of files arrived at his office. He pulled one out at random and found the borrower was listed as an 'antiques dealer'. Then he pulled out another, and another. File after file said the same thing. Either Minnesota had become a global hub for the antiques trade, or the applications were fraudulent. Cox later recalled another Ameriquest loan application form where a disabled man in his eighties had been described as working in 'light construction'.[23]

But when the states tried to act against the banks that provided a market for these 'liar loans' they were blocked by national regulators. In 2003, Wachovia informed state regulators it would no longer abide by state lending laws because it was a nationally chartered bank and fell under the jurisdiction of the OCC. When the State of Michigan protested this announcement Wachovia sued Michigan. The OCC weighed in on Wachovia's side and the ensuing legal battle dragged on until April 2007, ending when the Supreme Court found in Wachovia's favor.

The ease with which financial institutions could shop around for more lenient regulation undermined the comprehensiveness of the system. In December 2006 the mortgage lender Countrywide applied to switch from being supervised by the Fed and the OCC to the Office of Thrift Supervision. In an internal briefing note circulated at the time Countrywide remarked that 'the OTS is generally considered a less sophisticated regulator than the Federal Reserve'.[24] The OTS was also left in charge of supervising the insurance giant AIG, a situation one OTS director later compared to a 'gnat on an elephant'.[25] OTS supervisors only got round to examining AIG's massive portfolio of derivatives contracts ten days before AIG applied to the Fed for a bailout. This situation was mirrored on Wall Street, where the 'pure' investment banks had opted to be supervised by the SEC rather than the Fed in 2004. The SEC assigned just

---

23 Financial Crisis Inquiry Commission Report, 2011, p. 12
24 Ibid., p. 174
25 Ibid., p. 351

ten monitors to the big five, meaning that Bear Stearns missed its annual examination in 2006 because the Commission was busy with a staffing reorganization.

To complicate matters even further, not only did the regulatory system resemble a competitive market but private companies were also given a major role in assisting with regulation. Ratings agencies are private companies paid to assess the creditworthiness of big firms or governments wishing to borrow. The agency analyzes the bond-issuer and then publishes a grade from AAA through to D expressing the likelihood it will meet its obligation to the creditor. The AAA rating is most coveted by bond-issuers because it classifies the bond as an unimpeachably sound investment. For most of their history the agencies were minor players in the US financial system, their income derived from dour manuals of bond statistics which investors paid for by subscription, their existence largely unsuspected by the public. Their big break came in 1975, when the Securities and Exchange Commission drew up rules designating the largest agencies Nationally Recognized Statistical Rating Organizations (NRSROs). The SEC then permitted the Wall Street firms under its supervision to use NRSRO ratings to calculate their capital requirements. Assets on their books with higher credit ratings would incur a lower capital charge. In 2001 the Fed confirmed the agencies' power. It adopted a measure known as the 'Recourse Rule', which permitted all American banks to lower their capital against assets with high credit ratings.

Leaving the agencies to define what safe assets were (for regulatory purposes) blurred the distinction between public and private. On the one hand the three agencies had a fiercely commercial agenda. From about 1970 onward they abandoned their old subscription model of funding, moving instead to a system where the bond-issuer paid to have their product rated. This was more profitable, but it compromised the impartiality of the agencies. They now had every incentive to gratify their clients by offering them high ratings. At the same time they were no longer subject to market discipline – if their ratings proved faulty they wouldn't lose out on business since ratings were now part of the plumbing of the financial system. Notoriously, Moody's, S&P and Fitch rated Enron bonds 'investment grade' until four days before it filed for bankruptcy in December 2001. This complex system of private–public risk management created a malign reflexivity. In order to work, the regulatory framework demanded accurate ratings, yet by stimulating demand for high credit scores the same framework gave the agencies an incentive to lower the quality of these ratings.

As we saw in Chapter 2, collateralized debt obligations were investment products that structured subprime mortgage-backed securities in a way which disguised their inherent risk. Credit ratings were the essential ingredient in this process, for they relieved buyers of the need to perform their own due diligence. The agencies used mathematical models to show that even the riskiest homeowners in the CDO couldn't all default at once. This cleared the way for higher ratings than the underlying quality of the assets could strictly justify. Around 80 percent of asset-backed CDOs issued before 2007 would receive AAA ratings.

In spite of self-serving claims that 'no one could have predicted the housing bust' it's been shown that the agencies' models were seriously defective. For instance, Moody's MBS model assumed that even in a time of rocketing house prices underwriting standards would remain high across the board. As we have seen, there were good reasons to reserve skepticism on this point. But what's worse is that agency employees were well aware of the flaws in their rating procedures. In a candid online conversation dating from April 2007 an analyst on S&P's structured finance committee admitted to a colleague that the model used to rate the MBS deal they were working on did 'not capture half the risk'.

'We should not be rating it,' agreed his colleague. But theirs was not to reason why. 'We rate every deal,' she continued, 'it could be structured by cows and we would rate it.' This was herd behavior indeed. Yet the first analyst was uneasy: 'There's a lot of risk associated with it – I personally don't feel comfy signing this off as a committee member.'[26] In all likelihood he had little choice. In another email exchange between S&P analysts, concern was expressed about the lack of data on loans underlying a different CDO. The scalding response from their manager is worth quoting in full:

> Any request for loan level tapes is TOTALLY UNREASONABLE!!! Investors don't have it and can't provide it... It is your responsibility to provide those credit estimates and your responsibility to devise some method for doing so. Please provide the credit estimates requested![27]

The 'loan tapes' he referred to were computer scans of mortgage documents – essential for gauging the true value of the CDO. But lenders in the subprime mortgage market weren't exactly sticklers for paperwork and in many cases such documentation did not exist. As a result the true risks in the housing market weren't captured at all. Between mid-2007 and mid-2008 the ratings agencies were forced to downgrade $1.9 trillion worth of mortgage-backed securities. The scale of revision was huge: 76 percent of the mortgage-backed securities Moody's rated 'investment grade' in 2006 were downgraded to junk, rising to

26 House Oversight Committee hearing, 22 October 2008
27 Ibid.

89 percent of the 2007 crop.[28] In an echo of the Enron debacle, the agencies continued to issue investment-grade ratings for Lehman securities until the day Dick Fuld filed for Chapter 11 bankruptcy.

The uniquely complex structure of the American financial system also informs the context in which the hotly debated repeal of the Depression-era Glass–Steagall Act should be viewed. The fragmented nature of America's commercial-banking system explains why Wall Street and the securities market it manages is so powerful and sophisticated. Since a banking system historically fragmented along state lines could not easily move funds across the country this created a strong incentive to move funds around in the form of financial assets traded on the securities market.

Senator Carter Glass and Congressman Henry Steagall's 1934 Banking Act was a model of brevity, standing at just thirty-seven pages long. Its aim was simple: to prevent a repetition of the Great Depression. This was achieved by imposing diversity on the US financial system as a whole. By separating commercial banking from securities-dealing risk was compartmentalized. This is why, for example, the wider US economy was unaffected by the 1987 stock-market crash.

Those who argue that the 1999 repeal of the Glass–Steagall Act was superficial to the unfolding of the crisis point out that Lehman, Bear, Merrill and AIG – the four institutions that failed most comprehensively – were never covered by this legislation as they were 'non-banks' and did not take deposits. Quite apart from the fact that Citigroup and Bank of America would also have failed without a $45-billion cash infusion apiece, courtesy of the US taxpayer, this interpretation is flawed because it treats finance as a simple system where the interrelations between institutions do not matter.

---

28 Financial Crisis Inquiry Commission Report, 2011, p. 223

The purpose of the repeal was to allow commercial banks to directly compete with an overmighty Wall Street. In the 1970s and 1980s, Wall Street investment firms had adopted distinctly bank-like funding structures, using the money markets to fund long-term asset purchases with the equivalent of short-term deposits. This system, known as 'shadow banking', allowed Wall Street to greatly expand the size and complexity of its collective balance sheet, threatening the traditional role of retail banks. The repeal of Glass–Steagall was an attempt to level the playing field. The new 'universal banks', like Citigroup, which ventured into investment banking would be subject to more regulatory scrutiny than Wall Street, but this was more than offset by the fact that they had access to government-insured deposits. This government guarantee effectively subsidized the universal banks' borrowing costs, tipping the balance back in their favor.

The subsequent competition between the banking and shadow-banking sectors assumed the character of an arms race, or as Haldane puts it, a 'return on equity race'. Balance sheets ballooned and investment banks developed large in-house hedge funds to trade securities on the firm's own account. At one point in 2006 Dick Fuld even floated the idea of a merger to Martin Sullivan of AIG. This would have given Lehman access to a trillion-dollar balance sheet, funded by AIG's steady stream of insurance premiums. Fortunately for the world, Sullivan declined the offer. Meanwhile, Wall Street eyed up a part of the financial system that had traditionally been the preserve of commercial banks: the mortgage market. The Street dived in, acquiring mortgage lenders and, in Lehman's case, ramping up exposure to commercial real estate.

This race created a new species of vast, ultra-diversified, dizzyingly complex and completely unmanageable financial institutions. As Thomas Hoenig, a director of the FDIC puts it, 'In the end, nobody – not managements, the market or regulators – could adequately assess and control the risks of these firms.'[29] Chuck Prince told the Financial Crisis Inquiry Commission that a $40-billion position in highly rated mortgage securities would 'not in any way have excited my attention'.[30] The co-head of Citigroup's investment bank adds that he spent 'a small fraction of 1 percent' of his time on those securities. It's not surprising that their attention was scattered: this was an organization which kept $1.2 trillion off balance sheet in its 2,000 operating subsidiaries. Lehman Brothers controlled around 3,000 subsidiaries and had over a million derivatives contracts on its books by the time of its demise. Institutions that were Too Big to Fail had also become Too Complex to Manage.

Complexity and Rules

In a famous essay entitled 'Rationalism in Politics', the British conservative philosopher Michael Oakeshott distinguished between two different types of knowledge: the technical and the practical.[31] Technical knowledge is 'capable of precise formulation' and consists of 'rules, principles, direction and maxims – comprehensively in propositions.' It's the kind of knowledge you might find in an economic forecast, the traffic code, or even a political manifesto. Then there is practical knowledge, which 'exists only in use, and cannot be formulated in rules'. Practical knowledge can 'neither be taught or learned, only imparted or acquired' and yet it is essential to the mastery of any skill. To demonstrate the distinction, Oakeshott gave the example of a talented chef. When preparing a dish the chef will, to a greater or lesser extent, be following a recipe. The instructions contained

29 *Wall Street Journal*, 6 November 2012

30 Financial Crisis Inquiry Commission Report, 2011, Conclusions, p.xix

31 Michael Oakeshott, *Rationalism in Politics and Other Essays* (London: Methuen, 1962)

in the recipe are technical knowledge. Practical knowledge is whatever it is that makes her a great cook – imagination, intuition and sensitivity.

Both kinds of knowledge are vital, yet Oakeshott argued that modern politicians of all parties had come to believe 'practical knowledge was not knowledge at all, that the only kind of knowledge was technical'. Because technical knowledge is self-contained, people also think it is self-sufficient. Politicians convinced themselves that they could solve any problem, provided they gathered enough formal information about it first. More recently Daniel Kahneman has confirmed Oakeshott's insights with his dual-process model of the brain. Kahneman finds that our cognitive processes consist of two types: System 1 thinking, which is fast, intuitive and automatic and System 2 thinking, which is slow, deliberate and conscious. System 1 thinking includes 'expert intuition', the ability to spot patterns in a fraction of a second so that we 'automatically produce adequate solutions to challenges'.[32] A classic example of this is a firefighting captain who, without being able to explain why, correctly predicts that a house on fire is about to explode and gets his team out on time.

In regulatory terms technical knowledge/System 2 corresponds to the rulebook and practical knowledge/System 1 to the professional judgment of the regulator. The risk-focused approach relied exclusively on the first, however, which stymied the growth of the second. Where rules are few and broad, regulators tend to rely on their professional experience when a problem arises. Where rules are many and detailed, as under the 'risk-focused approach', they look to the rulebook. This explains why the SEC was such an ineffective banking supervisor. 'Above all the SEC is a law enforcement agency', Christopher Cox told

---

32 Daniel Kahneman, *Thinking Fast and Slow* (London: Allen Lane, 2011)

the Senate Oversight Committee when asked to defend the Commission's record.[33] Ever since its founding in 1934 the SEC had operated on the principle that it only has a mandate to act if it suspects a clear breach of the securities laws. So while SEC officials were aware that Bear Stearns was dangerously overleveraged and had a high concentration of mortgage securities on its books, they did not challenge the business model or ask it to increase its capital beyond minimum regulatory requirements.

One investment banker we spoke to told us a story which illustrates how the obsession with formal rules and technical compliance distorted his bank's priorities. Securities rules require that the font used to write 'warning: this document contains important disclaimers and disclosures' on an investment prospectus must be bigger than the body of the text. Because space on the front page of a prospectus is at a premium, it being the page the client is most likely to read, on one occasion he decided to shrink the disclaimer so that it was the same size as the rest of the text, at which point his compliance department went ballistic. After a couple of weeks, and two separate legal opinions, compliance agreed that the disclaimer was not in breach of the regulations provided the font was 0.5 bigger than the body of the text, a difference which happens to be invisible to the naked eye. This whole process involved six people from the compliance department and two lawyers from outside. Meanwhile, in other parts of the bank, risk limits rose as house prices fell.

The rulebook had been designed to cover every foreseeable eventuality. Unfortunately, the regulators had failed to foresee

---

33 Christopher Cox, 'Testimony Concerning the Role of Federal Regulators: Lessons from the Credit Crisis for the Future of Regulation', 23 October 2008

a system-wide financial meltdown, so the complex rules went out the window once the crisis actually hit. Managers of small regional banks recall their astonishment when the application documents for TARP bailout money landed on their desks. The TARP application form was only two pages long and contained just twenty questions. Remarking on this fact, Graydon Carter points out that an application to open a basic savings account at Citibank is six pages long and requires the applicant to answer forty-six questions.[34]

Recent changes to the regulations surrounding bank capital provide the best illustration of how rapidly the rules have multiplied. In 1988 the Fed approached the Bank of England and proposed the creation of internationally recognized capital requirements. This resulted in the landmark Basel Accord, known as Basel I. The first Basel Accord employed a relatively simple method with which to calculate capital ratios. It divided up the many risks a bank could take into five broad asset classes – mortgages, consumer lending, corporate loans and so on – which were 'risk weighted' from 0 percent to 100 percent. In this way capital ratios could be easily calculated using a pen and paper. Despite its huge scope, there were only thirty pages in the Basel I agreement.

In 1996 the Basel Accord was updated. For the first time banks were allowed to use their own internal models for calibrating regulatory capital against individual assets. As a result, the number of different categories of risk exploded from just five to 200,000. The number of calculations needed to determine a bank's regulatory capital rose from the single figures to several million.[35] The number of pages in the new Basel agreement was 347.

---

34 Graydon Carter, *Vanity Fair* editorial, August 2009
35 Andrew Haldane, 'Capital Discipline', speech to the American Economic Association, 9 January 2011

The shift towards more complex capital rules had profound consequences. Capital is supposed to provide a signal of a firm's financial stability to the market. But the new system was so opaque that it became impossible for investors to make this judgment, or to compare stability across firms. Haldane finds that more than half of investors do not trust or understand banks' risk weightings. This takes us back to the problem of risk versus uncertainty. If the market does not have confidence in a bank's reported solvency levels, if it cannot make a fair assessment of the risks a bank is taking, then it will be unable to exert market discipline. When the crisis actually hit, capital ratios were equally useless at signaling to regulators which institutions were in danger. A survey of thirty-three large international banks finds that, in the six months before the fall of Lehman, reported capital ratios of those banks which eventually required government bailouts were virtually identical to the ratios of those banks which did not.[36] There is also evidence that banks were gaming the rules by configuring their models to produce lower risk weightings for certain assets. When, in 2009, the US Treasury conducted stress tests at major banks using independent models, it revealed major capital shortfalls despite the fact that banks were meeting their minimum capital requirements.[37] Most important of all, the new rules took responsibility for the safety and soundness of a firm out of the boardroom and turned it into an esoteric 'science', intelligible only to an elite group of model-equipped technical experts. With senior managers no longer personally accountable for risk management, there was a greater incentive to be reckless.

36 Andrew Haldane, 'Capital Discipline', speech to the American Economic Association, 9 January 2011, Chart 5

37 Harry Huizinga and Luc Laeven, 'Bank Valuation and Regulatory Forbearance during a Financial Crisis', European Banking Center Discussion Paper No. 2009–17, March 2011

Finally, there is a cultural consequence to a regulatory system based on excessively complex rules. If you replace people's moral obligations with an all-encompassing rulebook they'll stop asking 'is this right?' and instead ask 'is this ok with the lawyers?' From there it's a short mental journey to 'can we get away with this?'

We can see this process at work in the creative accounting techniques employed by Lehman Brothers staff from 2001 onwards. Repo 105 transactions were, in the words of one Lehman executive, 'an accounting gimmick'[38] used to camouflage the health of the bank's balance sheet. In the final days of each accounting period, Lehman staff would shift tens of billions of dollars worth of problematic assets off the balance sheet, classifying these transactions as 'sales' in its public accounts. Lehman then used the cash from these transactions to pay down debts and reduce the leverage ratio it reported to the market. What investors, regulators and rating agencies weren't told however is that Lehman was obliged to purchase these assets back a week later. Repo 105 'sales' were just a covert form of borrowing. In 2007–2008, as Lehman ramped up its exposure to mortgage-backed securities, its use of Repo 105 increased too, breaching the firm's own internally agreed limits. In an email, Bart McDade, Lehman's chief operating officer, referred to the repo scam as 'another drug we rely on'.[39]

The Case for a Ring-Fence

Research from a number of different fields suggests that in a complex environment simple rules result in more effective decision-making than more complex ones. Simple location rules help the police catch more hardened criminals than

---

38 Financial Crisis Inquiry Commission Report, 2011, p. 177
39 Ibid.

sophisticated psychological-profiling techniques. Relatively passive investment strategies consistently outperform the most active ones. Physicians report that simple decision trees are better predictors of heart attacks than complex models.[40] Before the Battle of Trafalgar in 1805 Admiral Nelson advised his captains that if, in the confusion of battle, his flag signals could neither be 'seen or perfectly understood, no captain can do very wrong if he places his ship alongside that of the enemy'. The British navy routed Napoleon's invasion fleet.

Simple rules hold up better against an uncertain world because they make fewer assumptions about what we can't know. As Haldane puts it, they are more 'robust to ignorance'. In finance – that most uncertain of worlds – this argument is especially compelling. For the past thirty years, regulators have attempted to regulate bankers through a 'risk-based' system. But there is little sense in a regulator trying to determine whether a banker understands the risks he assumes if the regulator himself does not understand them, and recent history puts that in doubt. Instead of regulating individual bankers with narrow, complex rules, regulators would be better advised to regulate banks themselves with a broad simple rule which takes it as given that we cannot predict the future. This means acting directly on the structure of financial institutions to create a system where banks can suffer the consequences of their risk-taking without causing harm to the wider economy.

Modern 'universal banks' are large, complex, opaque and highly interconnected. Although they are controlled by a single point of management, the bank holding company, their numerous subsidiaries are separate legal entities. This is important because, pre-crash, the Federal Deposit Insurance Corporation, which guarantees savers' deposits, only had the power to put

---

40 Andrew Haldane, 'The Dog and the Frisbee', Bank of England, 2012

deposit-taking institutions into receivership, whereby it seizes the institution's assets to pay off the bank's debts. In the crisis however, it wasn't the deposit-taking part of the bank holding company that posed systemic risk but the company as a whole, as losses faced by its investment bank and mortgage lending subsidiaries put severe pressure on the holding company's underlying capital. Because the FDIC lacked the legal authority to wind down the holding company safely, the only tools at the authorities' disposal were emergency bailouts. And we are all familiar with the consequences for the taxpayer and the specter of moral hazard that TARP entailed.

The Dodd–Frank Act has attempted to address this problem by granting the FDIC powers to resolve failing banks through an orderly liquidation process. In 2012 the FDIC published a joint paper with the Bank of England explaining how these resolution procedures would work in the case of large multinational financial conglomerates.[41] This is an important collaboration because the banks most likely to cause systemic effects if they fail are also likely to have operations in London and New York.

The plan goes like this: depending on whether the bank is headquartered in the UK or the US, either the Bank of England or the FDIC will take control of the parent-bank holding company. The resolution authority will then fire the management and divide the bank's losses between the shareholders, and then bondholders if the write-down in equity is not big enough to cover the loss. This ensures that owners and creditors, and not the taxpayer, suffer the consequences of the bank's failure. The resolution authority will then employ a new power

41 Federal Deposit Insurance Corporation and the Bank of England, 'Resolving Globally Active Systemically Important Financial Institutions', 10 December 2012

to convert the remaining unsecured debt into equity, which would recapitalize the holding company's surviving subsidiaries, known as a 'bail-in'. Crucially, while this resolution process is underway, the holding company's retail subsidiaries are kept operational to prevent panic and bank runs. This is achieved by transferring the subsidiaries to a 'bridge' holding company controlled by the resolution authority and then selling them off into private hands. Losses and insolvency proceedings are therefore quarantined at the level of the parent company.

These resolution powers represent real progress. But in Britain we are going much further however, with a plan for a simple rule to ring-fence retail banking from investment banking.

A ring-fence works by erecting legal and financial barriers between the 'utility', a bank's customer savings accounts, and the 'casino', its investment-banking activities – also known as a 'Chinese wall'. The ring-fenced utility has a separate capital base from the non-ring-fenced casino arm, and its own independent management, and is barred from lending or transferring capital to support the activities of the investment bank. This ensures that depositors are protected from any losses should the investment bank's bets go wrong. Before the crisis, the investment-banking arms of banks like Citigroup, UBS and RBS were able to attain the stupendous leverage that they did by using their customer-savings base as effective collateral. The market was prepared to lend to the investment arm at artificially low rates because it knew that the financial group as a whole, the 'bank holding company', could not be allowed to fail. The experience of Greece in the eurozone is an example of this problem writ large. Successive Greek governments were able to run bigger deficits than their tax base allowed because the market anticipated that Germany would never allow Greece to exit the single currency.

As we have observed, this cross-subsidization also had implications for the 'pure' investment banks of Wall Street. To compete with the heavily subsidized investment firms like Citibank, Barclays Capital, Bear Stearn, Lehman et al. expanded their highly profitable proprietary trading activities and pursued ever more reckless leverage strategies. Ring-fencing the utility from the casino means that if the riskier investment arm experiences losses, it cannot replenish itself with capital from the retail arm. Knowing this, the market will then be much more cautious when it lends to the investment bank. In the United States the cross-subsidization problem is now even more pronounced than it was before the crisis because JPMorgan has acquired Bear Stearns and Bank of America owns Merrill Lynch.

In this respect the Dodd–Frank's Volcker Rule, which bars FDIC-insured banks from trading on their own account rather than on behalf of clients, will not have the same impact as a ring-fence, as it does not enforce a financial separation between retail and investment banking. Instead, under Volcker, certain types of investment deemed 'proprietary' are prohibited by the authorities. Yet this is a complex judgment for a regulator to make. A bank may inadvertently make a profit for itself when holding securities as inventory in anticipation of client demand, or when hedging its balance sheet against risk, for example. A ring-fence, by contrast, is unequivocal: the capital backing retail deposits may not be used for any other purpose. Regulators can judge what banks actually do rather than try and puzzle out their intentions.

When it comes to dealing with banking failures, the ring-fenced approach has two further attractions. First, it prevents investment banks from taking dangerous risks in the first place because managers know they will not be bailed out by the retail arm and ultimately the taxpayer if those risks do not bear fruit. Second, it makes the resolution process smoother and more flexible. Because there will already be a financial separation in place between the retail bank and the bank holding the company's other subsidiaries under a ring-fence system, the retail bank can continue operating the payments system and maintaining the supply of credit to the real economy, even while it is being transferred to a bridge bank or sold to a purchaser. The independent management of the ring-fenced entity will also be able to ensure continuity while other parts of the group are being resolved.

The alternative, of course, is to do what former Citigroup CEO Sandy Weill has advocated and go for a full Glass–Steagall, with a forcible separation of investment and retail banking. The ring-fencing option appears more attractive to us however because, while often exaggerated by the big banks, there are a number of benefits conferred by diversification. Many large non-financial corporations will want to make use of both retail and investment-banking services, for instance, so it makes sense to keep them in one place. It's also possible that capital from the investment bank could be used to bail out the retail bank if it ever got into trouble. Indeed, we should not fall into the trap of assuming that only investment banks fail. Northern Rock, the British bank that experienced a nineteenth-century-style run, was a retail bank which simply lent too many mortgages and couldn't access short-term funding when the money markets froze. In the US, Wachovia got into trouble and was ultimately absorbed by Wells Fargo because of its exposure to mortgage subsidiary Golden West. The damage that can be done, actual and psychological, by an interruption to the payments system is why it is vital to ensure that retail banks are well capitalized.

Ultimately, it is impossible to design a perfect regulatory system. However well-intentioned the rules, a minority of market participants will break them. However competent the regulators, people are flawed and regulators will fail. To mitigate this we also need rules that the banks can internalize, rules that people will adhere to even when no one is looking. In other words: culture. It is to this that we turn to in the next chapter.

Chapter 6

THE IMPORTANCE OF CULTURE AND THE DANGERS OF BUSINESS AS USUAL

Dick Fuld is very conscious of risk. He's created a culture that's enabled us to do fine.
– Thomas A. Russo, vice-chairman of Lehman Brothers, Bloomberg TV interview, January 2008

This was the worst crisis for seventy years – indeed potentially it could have been the worst in the history of market capitalism... A crisis cooked up in trading rooms where not just a few but many people earned annual bonuses equal to a lifetime's earnings of some of those now suffering the consequences. We cannot go back to business as usual and accept the risk that a similar crisis occurs again in ten or twenty years' time.
– Adair Turner, September 2009

In the fall of 2008, as the lights went out over Wall Street, Seamus Smith, the head of American Express's European division, was in New York on business. Smith was a man of routine. He always stayed at the Millennium Hilton, five minutes away from Wall Street. As a keen marathon runner, he'd rise early and train at the hotel gym. Situated on the fifth floor with a goldfish bowl view of the city, it's a quiet place from which the so-called Masters of the Universe can ponder their creation.

But this day was different. As Smith was changing in the locker room, a muscular Wall Streeter next to him suddenly broke down in tears, sobbing loudly into his BlackBerry. Public displays of vulnerability are virtually unheard of in finance, so Smith was unsure how to respond.

'Are you alright?' he asked hesitantly.

There was no response.

'Do you need help?' This worked. Between great gasping sobs, the man pieced together a reply.

'I've ... lost ... everything.'[1]

The broken banker had been caught up in a grand Wall Street tradition. Eighty years before the invention of the BlackBerry the instrument of torture was the ticker tape: a telegraphic machine which punched out stock market data onto a thin strip of paper. In that fatal week of October 1929, when the New York Stock Market crashed and ultimately lost 89 percent of its value, the volume of trading was so large that the ticker tape couldn't cope. Once the markets had closed, brokers would sit in agonized suspense while the machines caught up with their last transactions. The delay allowed for the occasional pocket of hope.

Digital technology now allows market movements to be tracked second by second, but the human impact is the same. As we saw in Chapter 2, the maddening complexity of global finance meant it took well over a year before a turn in the housing market revealed the system for what it was: a house of cards. In the final weeks before the fall of Lehman, staff remained convinced that the bank would find a buyer.

And then, as now, people thought they had lost everything. As trillions were wiped from balance sheets around the world the markets tipped from irrational exuberance to cold hysteria. Traders screamed sell, but there was no longer any credit with which to buy. Lines on stock-index charts formed themselves into jagged cliffs as assets plummeted in value. In New York,

---

1   Seamus Smith, private interview

grown men sobbed in gyms. At Goldman Sachs bankers bought guns, ready to bed down in bunkers if civil society collapsed.[2] No one was old enough to remember the last Wall Street crash, but plenty could recall the CNN pictures of food riots during the East Asian financial crisis of the 1990s. At the time they'd told themselves 'it couldn't happen here'. But now they asked: 'what if it could?'

There's a happy ending to this story. In 2010 Seamus Smith was staying at his favorite hotel, exercising at the same gym, at the same time in the morning. The same square-jawed Wall Streeter appeared. Gone were the tears, the swagger was back. His only comment?

'Thank God that's all over.'

At the tipping point, the bankers were finally afraid. Their worldview, that rock-solid belief in the invincibility of the system, had cracked. Many reports from that time stress the emotional trauma of the crisis. As we saw in Chapter 1, Alan Greenspan was 'shocked' and 'distressed' by the paradox the crash had exposed: self-destruction in the pursuit of rational self-interest. As far as the public is concerned, that other paradox: 'risk-based regulation' was also shattered.

After the crash, in a period of relative financial calm, for many the trauma is forgotten. We've witnessed a mass act of that mental brushing under the carpet termed 'sublimation' by Freud. Although the consequences of the banking collapse are all around us, those consequences are at one remove from finance. In Europe, the banking crisis has rolled over into a sovereign-debt crisis; at home people struggle with falling real incomes and tight credit as a consequence of deleveraging. But while government has stepped in to pick up the pieces, many on Wall Street carry on with business as usual. Polling undertaken

for this book found that over 60 percent of financial sector
workers said that their colleagues would behave no differently if
the crisis happened again today.

What's most shocking to an outside observer is that it is hard
to see evidence of changed behavior as a result of the personal
trauma people went through. Few at the top of those institutions which received taxpayer bailouts have expressed any sense
of personal responsibility or even remorse for what happened.
The former CEO of Countrywide Angelo Mozilo, who
famously described one of his company's loan products as 'the
most dangerous product in existence ... there can be nothing
more toxic',[3] maintains that Countrywide was 'one of the greatest companies in the history of this country and probably made
more difference to society, to the integrity of our society, than
any company in the history of America'. Joe Cassano continues
to blame the auditors for overstating AIG's losses; worse, his
boss Hank Greenberg is currently suing the US Government
for what he claims was the 'unconstitutional' takeover of AIG.
Dick Fuld ruefully told a reporter who had managed to track
him down on the 2009 anniversary of Lehman's collapse that
'good guys do win in the end'.[4]

Senior policymakers at the time of the crash have also
failed to acknowledge any mistakes. In an interview with the
US Government's Financial Inquiry Crisis Commission, Alan
Greenspan contended that under his leadership the Fed developed a set of mortgage-lending rules which have 'held up to
this day'.[5] Hank Paulson, defending his decision to let Lehman
go bust, has said 'it is absolutely a fiction that Lehman was
anything more than a symptom'.[6] He also told the *New York*

---

3 *New York Times*, 25 February 2011
4 *Daily Telegraph*, 8 September 2009
5 Financial Crisis Inquiry Commission Report, 2011, p. 94
6 *New York Times*, 18 May 2009

Times that if he could have his time again he wouldn't have done anything differently.

Because the bailouts have had their desired effect and the crisis appears to have passed, the sector seems to think it can make as few adjustments as necessary and move on. We see this most clearly at the top, but it was also the message coming from almost everyone we spoke to: they wanted to be left in peace to get on with their jobs. It's also telling that when we asked bankers what they thought were the most important causes of the financial crisis, with very few exceptions, they pointed to the monetary policies pursued by the Fed.

This reluctance to face up to facts is unfortunate. If we fail to associate unwelcome outcomes with our own decision-making then our behavior is unlikely to change. Cognitive behavioral therapy (CBT) has shown that by consciously changing our habits of thought we can influence the emotional stimuli which drive dysfunctional behavior. In a 2012 study, psychologists at the University of Melbourne found that people who believe that what happens in life stems mainly from their own actions eat more healthily and exercise more regularly than people who believe life's outcomes are determined by external factors, such as luck, fate, and other people. This result holds true even when you control for other factors such as more future-oriented thinking.[7] With this in mind, it's telling that Dick Fuld told the Financial Crisis Inquiry Commission that 'Lehman's demise was caused by uncontrollable market forces and the incorrect perception and accompanying rumors that Lehman did not

---

7   Deborah A. Cobb-Clark, Sonja K. Kassenboehmer and Stefanie Schurer, 'Healthy Habits: The Connection between Diet, Exercise and the Locus of Control', Melbourne Institute Working Paper No. 15, available at SSRN, August 2012

have sufficient capital to support its investments'.[8] In doing so he was locating what psychologists call 'the locus of control' outside of himself, just like those who lead unhealthy lifestyles. If the CEO really believed he was in no way responsible for the company's fate then perhaps we should not be surprised that Lehman would end up gorging itself to death on finance's equivalent of fast food: subprime bonds and borrowing from the short-term money markets.

Too Big to Jail?

As it currently stands, company law is a major impediment to instilling a greater sense of individual responsibility at the top in finance. In spite of the efforts of the regulatory agencies, and a number of high-profile class action lawsuits from shareholders, not a single senior Wall Street figure has ever been successfully prosecuted for the devastating consequences of their business decisions.

Where the regulatory authorities suspect a material breach of the securities laws (as opposed to a poor business decision) that cannot be proven without a long and costly lawsuit, and there exists a well established system of 'deferred prosecution', which allows executives to agree to an out-of-court fine to settle the charges. In October 2010, for example, Angelo Mozilo agreed to pay the SEC $67.5 million to settle a civil case involving charges of insider trading and misleading investors. The US Justice Department later tried to bring a criminal prosecution against Mozilo, but this was abandoned after prosecutors concluded that his actions 'did not amount to criminal wrongdoing'.[9]

Critics of deferred prosecutions argue that they undermine

---

8 Richard S. Fuld, testimony to the Financial Crisis Inquiry Commission, 1 September 2010

9 *New York Times*, 25 February 2011

the principle of equality under the law, allowing exceptionally wealthy lawbreakers to evade responsibility in exchange for a fee and a slap on the wrist. The SEC proudly boasts of Mozilo's 'record fine' on its website, but it's worth noting that the settlement amounted to half the $132 million he took home in 2007 and that $20 million was picked up by his former employer, Countrywide. William Black, a former executive director of the National Institute for Fraud Prevention, points out that the S&L crisis yielded more than 1,000 felony convictions, including hundreds of executives. He puts this success down to a strong political will to bring the perpetrators to justice, with a special taskforce and over a thousand FBI agents involved in the investigation.[10] Given that the FBI's responsibilities are now dominated by counterterrorism Black thinks a repeat of the S&L haul unlikely.

There can be no doubt that criminal behavior, above all mortgage fraud, played a significant role in this crisis, particularly at the lower end of the food chain. What this analysis overlooks, however, is that the most cataclysmic decisions made by Wall Street are not indictable offences. There is no 'crime' of taking on excessive leverage or recklessly investing in risky assets. Nor can the law adequately account for the important yet diffuse issue of culture. The veteran business journalist Joe Nocera neatly summarizes the dilemma: 'The problem is that Mr. Mozilo, though he helped create the culture that made such predatory lending acceptable, never made the fraudulent loans himself.'[11]

This problem has been well tested in law. Where cases have been brought against banking directors the courts have affirmed

10 William K. Black, 'Why nobody went to jail during the credit crisis', speech to Financial Sense Newshour, 14 September 2011

11 Joe Nocera, 'Biggest Fish Face Little Risk of Being Caught', *New York Times*, 25 February 2011

the protection of the business judgment rule (BJR). The BJR is a longstanding precedent in US case law which presumes that a director shall not be held personally liable for company losses provided it can be shown that he did not have a financial interest in the judgment, that he took reasonable steps to ensure he was properly informed, and that he rationally believed the judgment was in the best interests of the corporation. As the Colorado Supreme Court puts it: 'The business judgment doctrine bars judicial inquiry into the actions of [a manager] taken in good faith and in the exercise of honest judgment in furtherance of a lawful and legitimate corporate purpose.'[12] The principle was upheld in February 2009 when the Delaware Court of Chancery threw out a class action lawsuit by Citigroup shareholders alleging that directors were in breach of their fiduciary duty by failing to properly manage and monitor the risks the bank faced from exposure to the subprime mortgage market.

The BJR arose in the mid-twentieth century out of a need to protect directors from vindictive shareholders who refused to accept the reality that investing is an inherently risky business. It also ensured that managers did not have to worry about having their business decisions second-guessed by the courts.

However, modern compensation structures in banking mean that at very senior level it is increasingly hard to show that a business decision is financially disinterested – the first test of the business judgment rule. As we saw in Chapter 6, executive compensation has been set according to narrow, return-on-equity performance targets. This gives managers an incentive to push for short-term gains in the share price, either by gearing up or investing in volatile assets. More than in any other industry, in banking a managerial decision over strategy can result in real and immediate gains for the decision-maker. Further, the crisis has shown that the

---

12 Hirsch v. Jones Intercable, Inc. 984 P.2d 629, Colorado 1999

consequences of poor decision-making in Systemically Important Financial Institutions (SIFIs) extend far beyond losses experienced by shareholders or bondholders. If a bank goes down it has serious consequences for the wider economy. This fact already results in special treatment for banks in other parts of the law. A bank director, for example, has to be approved by the regulator as a 'fit and proper person' to discharge a director's duties.

Accountability could be restored to finance and Wall Street safeguarded against a return to 'business as usual', were banking executives subject to a stricter form of liability. For centuries the maritime industry has operated on an unwritten but universally acknowledged principle of strict liability, where the captain is held accountable for everything that happens on his ship. As John Kay puts it, 'the corollary of unquestioned authority is unquestioned responsibility'.[13] In January 2012 Captain Francesco Schettino ignominiously abandoned the cruise liner Costa Concordia after crashing it into rocks off the Italian island of Giorgio. He was excoriated by his peer group and will probably never command a ship again. Commenting on the case, the Chairman of the Swedish Maritime Officers Association said: 'It's a matter of honor that the master is the last to leave. Nothing less will do in this profession.'[14] It's hard to imagine senior banking executives appealing to the same standards of honor and integrity in their profession, and yet for the sake of our economy it's vital that they do.

Kay suggests personal liability could be established by introducing a legal duty for directors of retail banks to protect their deposits.[15] Other commentators have argued that a stricter form

---

13 John Kay, '"Not on my watch" applies to banks and the navy', *Financial Times*, 3 July 2012

14 *Associated Press*, 20 January 2012

15 John Kay, 'Why banks' ring-fences risk being Chinese walls', *Financial Times*, 14 June 2011

of liability could be built on tougher disclosure rules. Frank Partnoy and Jesse Eisinger argue that the annual and quarterly reports banks file with the SEC are deliberately engineered to be as opaque and misleading as possible, while remaining within the letter of the law. In a Wells Fargo report they sampled, large derivatives bets, for example, are euphemistically recorded as 'customer-accommodation trades' and the reader must cross-reference several footnotes to puzzle out what kind of exposures they entail. Partnoy and Eisinger suggest that the way forward is a broad law which requires banks to

> describe risks in commonsense terms that an investor can understand... The idea would be to require banks to disclose all material facts, without specifying how. Bankers would know that whatever they chose to put in their annual reports might be assessed at some future date by a judge who would ask one simple question: was the report complete, clear, and accurate?[16]

Failure to properly disclose this information would then constitute criminal fraud.

This is a valuable suggestion. But we have also proposed a new offence of criminal negligence over valuation, where directors of SIFIs requiring government intervention failed to take reasonable steps to establish the true value of an asset or an acquisition. Before the crash, bankers had too much discretion when it came to judging the value of the assets on their books, while too little due diligence was performed when it came to valuing major acquisitions. The so-called 'liar loans' which proliferated from 2005 would be a fruitful area of investigation under our hypothetical law. These stated income mortgages,

---

16 Frank Partnoy and Jesse Eisinger, 'What's Inside America's Banks?', *Atlantic Magazine*, January/February 2013

which required no independent verification of a borrower's income, allowed banks leeway when it came to interpreting their value. If it could be shown that company policy was reckless in this regard then the senior managers would face serious consequences. Like a nuclear deterrent, one might hope such a law would never have to be used, but it could help concentrate the minds of those entrusted with institutions of national economic importance.

The One Percent

In Brett Easton Ellis's 1991 novel *American Psycho*, the reader is cast adrift in the murderous delusions of Patrick Bateman, a deranged investment banker who may or may not be a serial killer. He's both the predator and victim of an emotionally void Wall Street, where reality is made up of surface appearance and no one looks beyond the haircut, the handshake and the business card. When the novel first appeared it was generally greeted with unfavorable reviews – too few critics understood what it was Easton Ellis was satirizing. In the wake of Enron, Bernie Madoff and the global financial crisis, it's now considered a modern classic.

Like all the best satires, the novel grasps an element of truth that even the author may have been unaware of. Since its publication, the pathology of the modern business executive has become a popular subject of academic research.

Individual psychopathic traits – the inability to empathize, lack of remorse, stimulation-seeking, impulsiveness, and poor behavioral control, among others – are diffused among the population at large. Psychopaths are people with abnormally high concentrations of these traits. Studies estimate that 1 percent of the population might be considered psychopaths in the strict psychiatric sense, but this percentage rises within the corporate world.

In 2006, Paul Babiak and Robert Hare found that of 200 high-profile executives sampled, 3.5 percent matched the psychopathic profile.[17] Research from Babiak and Hare, and others, suggests that highly functioning 'industrial psychopaths' tend to thrive in transitional organizations. One example of such an organization might be a company undergoing aggressive expansion. The rapidly changing business environment provides the psychopath within it with the constant stimulation he needs while diverting critical attention away from his personal failings. There is also a clear correlation between psychopathic tendencies and risk appetite. As Holly Andrews of Worcester Business School puts it, 'Studies have shown that once focused on a goal, psychopaths are not good at attending to cues that suggest their current course of action is likely to lead to failure.'[18] Brian Basham, a veteran Wall Street PR man, recalls a conversation he had with an investment banker who wished to remain anonymous. According to the banker, 'At one major investment bank for which I worked, we used psychometric testing to recruit social psychopaths because their characteristics exactly suited them to senior corporate finance roles.'[19]

We are not accusing anyone in this book of being a psychopath. Our point is that the culture of modern finance encourages and rewards the kind of behavior that would be completely unacceptable in most other walks of life.

Let's look at this culture in more detail.

---

17 Paul Babiak and Robert D. Hare, *Snakes in Suits: When Psychopaths go to Work* (New York: HarperCollins, 2007)

18 Holly Andrews, 'Snakes in Suits: Dealing with Psychopaths in the Workplace and Boardroom', speech to the Institute of Risk Management, 19 November 2010

19 Brian Basham, 'Beware Corporate Psychopaths – They are Still Occupying Positions of Power', *Independent*, 29 December 2011

Duty and Trust

Experience of life tells us there are two kinds of rules. The first are explicitly stated and often have the full force of the law behind them. Take speed limits, for example, or the ban on doping in international sport, or the Basel rules which stipulate how much and what type of capital banks should hold. The second kind are unwritten, deriving their authority not from the law or the rulebook but from powerful social obligations: shaking hands, observing two minutes silence on Memorial Day, saying thank you, queuing. Each of these unwritten rules is an incremental expression of our values as a society, of our sense of decency, respect, fair play and what's reasonable. This second type of rule is what we are referring to when we talk about culture or 'frameworks'.

Both types of rules, the official and the unwritten, are interdependent. We can see this most clearly in sport. The official rules of play, as codified by bodies like the NFL, give the game a structure, but the spirit of the game arises from a culture of good sportsmanship. Where that culture is lacking the rules of play offer little protection against systematic attempts to distort the game: questionable tackles, diving, and at worst, match-fixing.

Adam Smith, the father of capitalist thought, knew well that markets too must operate within a strong moral framework. In his 1759 work *The Theory of Moral Sentiments*, Smith observed that

> How selfish soever man may be supposed, there are evidently some principles in his nature which interest him in the fortune of others, and render their happiness necessary to him, though he derives nothing from it but the pleasure of seeing it.[20]

---

20 Adam Smith, *The Theory of Moral Sentiments* (1759)

Smith believed that the basis of all ethical reflection was 'fellow-feeling': our instinctive urge to recreate, or mimic another's feelings in ourselves, what we would call empathy. But he was realistic enough about human nature to know that most of us won't be able to empathize with the same degree of sensitivity in every situation. This is where duty comes in. 'Duty', for Smith, is our regard for 'the established rules of behavior'. It's the social pressure which binds us to a certain standard of conduct, even when we're not really considering the people our actions might affect.

There is no contradiction between Smith's *Theory of Moral Sentiments* and his later and more famous *Wealth of Nations*: Smith later published both works together, as a double edition. This is because self-interest is only one side of the coin. Markets are sustained by values which can't be captured on a P+L sheet: values like trust, fairness and reciprocity. Banks in particular need greater empathy among individuals and a sense of duty ingrained in the culture of the firm.

When the values of bankers seem so wildly out of kilter with those of wider society then public trust in the financial system is damaged. In polling for this book we asked a general sample of the American population how much they now trusted the financial system to look after their money. Sixty-two percent answered either 'not much' or 'not at all'.[21]

Loss of trust can also demoralize employees. After all, they are the ones who have to confront public attitudes towards their profession on a daily basis: in bars, at parties and in the morning papers over breakfast. In May 2010 it was reported that Fred Goodwin's successor Stephen Hester had invited RBS employees to post comments reflecting on their jobs on the bank's internal website. 'I used to be proud to work for this bank after

---

21 YouGov survey of general population, conducted 28–31 January 2013

twenty-plus years of service,' said one, 'now I'm embarrassed by who I work for. I tell people I'm an accountant, you get less abuse.' Another replied: 'I would love to say I love my job, I love coming into work and I'm proud to tell people I work for RBS – but I'd be lying.' The breakdown in trust between a major sector of the economy and the wider public cannot, in the end, be good for business. Professional investors have certainly made their feelings known. Five years after the crash, America's largest banks continue to trade below 'book value', meaning these institutions are worth less in the eyes of the stock market than the stated value of the assets on their books.

Raghuram Rajan, the economist encountered in Chapter 1, argues that it is comparatively harder for financial professionals to consider the social consequences of their actions, because those consequences are themselves less visible. Securitization in particular worked to stifle empathy. Of the subprime mortgage brokers of small town America he asks:

> Should the broker have counseled the debt-ridden homeowners they were working with to cut back on consumption, pay off credit cards and move to a smaller, more affordable home? Perhaps some would have done so had they thought they would see their clients again. Knowing, however, that the mortgages they originated would be packaged and sold, they had little stake in the relationship, other than the fee...[22]

Economists who study corruption in the developing world are all too familiar with this dynamic. It might be both rational and profitable for an individual to take a bribe, but if enough officials choose to behave the same way this creates a destructive

---

22 Raghuram G. Rajan, *Fault Lines: How Hidden Fractures Still Threaten the World Economy* (Princeton: Princeton University Press, 2010), p. 130

herding effect whereby corruption is normalized and development stalls as the cost of doing business becomes intolerably high. As John Kay has written,

> Market economies are always vulnerable to chancers and spivs who sell overpriced goods to ill-informed customers and seem to promise things they do not intend to deliver. If such behavior becomes a dominant business style, you end up with the economies of Nigeria and Haiti, where rampant opportunism makes it almost prohibitively difficult for honest people to do business.[23]

On the question of what Smith called duty, the unique role banks play in our economy means they have a special responsibility to wider society. First, because deposit insurance means they enjoy an effective public subsidy, directly in the case of commercial banks and indirectly in the case of their counterparties. Second, because unlike a non-financial company, when a bank becomes insolvent its assets – our savings – go up in smoke. And third, because we all rely on a bank's powers of credit creation – whether for business loans, mortgages or overdrafts – financial institutions cannot fail without causing serious harm to the wider economy. For these three reasons a bank's culture, not ought but *must* be built around the core duties of risk management: regard to capital, regard to liquidity and regard to asset quality. We want to be able to trust banks to look after our money and give it back to us when we need it. Sustaining that trust must be their immediate priority. Income, growth, and earnings per share should always come second.

This point has long been accepted with regard to the medical profession. Nobody expects doctors to work for free. Indeed,

---

23 John Kay, 'Cautionary Lessons on Ethics from Yet Another Bank Fiasco', *Financial Times*, 11 May 2011

until about 1980, a top surgeon's annual salary was equal to that enjoyed by most investment bankers. But a doctor's duty of care, as embodied in the Hippocratic Oath, always trumps the profit motive. That's why the medical profession, quite rightly, regulates the number of operations a surgeon can perform in a single day. In finance we need to return to the idea that bankers too have a duty of care because they are stewards of other people's money. Those who don't want to accept this responsibility are very welcome to go and work for the many thousands of small, highly competitive, entrepreneurial firms in the asset management industry that thrive without subsidy and fail without bailouts.

The Cult of the CEO

As statisticians are fond of saying, the plural of anecdote is not data, but with this caveat in mind we believe it is well worth looking for common patterns in the managerial cultures of the most dysfunctional firms. One recurring theme in the testimony of former employees is that certain executives had a gift for intimidation, coupled with a low tolerance for dissenting subordinates.

The most senior tier of the Lehman Brothers management was known by staff as Club 31, after the location of Fuld's office on the thirty-first floor of Lehman's Times Square headquarters. By all accounts, Fuld was personally as well as physically aloof – locked in his cabin with a few trusted subordinates while the storm raged outside. 'Quite simply, people were afraid of him, even though they couldn't see him,' reports Larry McDonald, a former trader at Lehman, 'and this was a fear based upon reputation, because through the years Fuld had fired many, many people, for a thousand different reasons.'[24] Like Fred Goodwin,

---

24 Larry McDonald, *A Colossal Failure of Common Sense: The Inside Story of the Collapse of Lehman Brothers* (New York: Crown Business, 2010)

the Lehman CEO was rarely seen on the trading floor, apart from one memorable occasion in the summer of 2008 when he took to the stage to deliver a bizarre rant about predatory speculators, explaining to a bemused workforce that he wanted to 'reach in, rip out their heart and then eat it before they die'!

The style of leadership practiced by senior Lehman executives has been described by former employees as authoritarian. According to one person who was present when the executive committee reviewed budgets for 2007, a committee member dared to question the performance of a particular unit. Fuld fixed him with a dead stare, paused, then said: 'You've got some balls to say that, knowing how much I hate that topic.'[25] After the meeting, the committee member was given another going over by the Lehman COO Joe Gregory, then informed that any future objections be brought to the COO directly and not voiced in committee.

After Fred Goodwin's downfall at RBS, stories of his dictatorial behavior and its effect on his staff also came tumbling out. 'Most people in the bank were absolutely terrified of him,' said corporate financier Peter de Vink, managing director of Edinburgh Financial & General Holdings. 'He treated anyone who had a different view from his own with contempt.'[26] Staff 'went into panic mode' after a window cleaner fell off a ladder in Goodwin's office and broke a small model airplane. Apparently staff were more worried about Goodwin's broken toy than the unfortunate window cleaner. In another incident, catering staff were threatened with disciplinary action in an email entitled 'Rogue Biscuits' after someone had the audacity to include pink wafer biscuits in the executives' afternoon tea.

---

25 'Fuld Sought Buffett Offer He Refused as Lehman Sank', *Bloomberg News*, 10 November 2008
26 *Daily Telegraph*, 25 August 2011

This behavior had consequences. In a memorandum sent to the RBS Chairman on 15 July 2008, RBS's Head of Group Internal Audit had the following observations to make about the group executive management committee, RBS's senior management team:

1. GEMC are not operating as team.
2. Conversations are typically bilateral.
3. Performance targets consume too much of the agenda.
4. Discussions often seem bullying in nature.
5. The atmosphere is often negative and is at a low point currently.[27]

The memo also noted a lack of meaningful discussion of strategy and risk at executive level.

Meanwhile, at AIG, Joe Cassano was a more immediate presence in the life of his employees. 'One day he got me on the phone and was pissed off about a trade that had lost money,' says a former AIG FP trader. 'He said, "When you lose money it's my fucking money. Say it." I said, "What?" "Say 'Joe, it's your fucking money!'" So I said, "It's your fucking money, Joe."'[28]

Cassano laid personal claim to other AIG assets too, as another AIG man reports: 'Joe always said, "This is my company. You work for my company." He'd see you with a bottle of water. He'd come over and say, "That's my water."' In the words of another, 'The fear level was so high that when we had these morning meetings you presented what you did so as not to

27 Financial Services Authority, 'The Failure of the Royal Bank of Scotland: Financial Services Authority Board Report', December 2011, p. 233
28 Michael Lewis, 'The Man who Crashed the World', *Vanity Fair*, August 2009

upset him. And if you were critical of the organization, all hell would break loose.'[29]

At Moody's, chief operating officer Brian Clarkson adopted a similarly robust approach to management. According to Gary Witt, a former Moody's managing director, if he asked an employee to do something, 'either you comply with his request or you start looking for another job'.[30] In 2001, Clarkson had circulated a spreadsheet that listed forty-nine ratings analysts and the bonds each had 'rated', or 'NOT rated'. His instruction to subordinates was clear: 'You should be using this in PEs [performance evaluations] and to give people a heads up on where they stand relative to their peers.'[31]

The hell-bent fixation with growth created a culture which marginalized those in the risk-management side of these firms. Lehman's former European head of communications recalls that, 'there was risk management, but the prevailing atmosphere was for fast growth and special fast-track treatment for what we now know were toxic deals'.[32] In September 2007 Lehman's chief risk officer, Madelyn Antoncic, found herself shunted off to a peripheral government relations job. Though correlation does not imply causation, the court-appointed bankruptcy examiner's report notes that Antoncic had counseled against the firm's decision to raise its agreed risk limit by 50 percent in 2006. The new ceiling was breached in any event as Fuld and Gregory took to waving through risk limits on individual deals. The Lehman Brothers risk committee only met twice in 2006 and 2007.[33]

---

29 Ibid.

30 Financial Crisis Inquiry Commission Report, 2011, p. 208

31 Ibid., p. 209

32 'Banking's Big Question: Why didn't Anyone Stop Them?', *The Observer*, Sunday 15 February 2009

33 G. Kirkpatrick, 'The Corporate Governance Lessons from the Financial Crisis', OECD, 11 February 2009, p. 19

Scott McCleskey, a former chief compliance officer at Moody's, told the Financial Crisis Inquiry Commission a story about a dinner he and Clarkson had with the board of directors. The dinner had been held just after the company had announced strong earnings, particularly in the CDO rating part of the business:

> So Brian Clarkson comes up to me, in front of everybody at the table, including board members, and says literally, 'How much revenue did Compliance bring in this quarter? Nothing. Nothing.' ... For him to say that in front of the board, that's just so telling of how he felt that he was bulletproof... For him, it was all about revenue.[34]

At RBS, the board never formally approved a firm-wide liquidity policy, and the group chief risk officer was not invited to join the senior management team until April 2008. In their investigation UK regulators concluded that by the time of the crash the bank's risk committee had become 'a forum where the bias of discussion was to approve policies [...] rather than to ensure that emerging risks were understood and addressed'.[35]

Bear Stearns did not even have a full risk committee until shortly before it failed.[36]

My Bank's Bigger than Yours

Yet profit was not the only value to which the bankers subscribed. Money isn't the *only* measure of worth. Success is also about status. As the philosopher Alain de Botton has written:

---

34 Financial Crisis Inquiry Commission Report, 2011, p. 208
35 Financial Services Authority, 'The Failure of the Royal Bank of Scotland: Financial Services Authority Board Report', December 2011, p. 237
36 G. Kirkpatrick, 'The Corporate Governance Lessons from the Financial Crisis', OECD, 11 February 2009, p. 19

'We may seek a fortune for no greater reason than to secure the respect and attention of people who would otherwise look straight through us.'[37]

A former head of derivatives at a major Wall Street firm emphasized to us that being the number one financial institution in terms of size or sales didn't necessarily equate to being the most profitable, and yet executives still craved that position at the top of the list in *Bloomberg Businessweek*. An ex-employee of Merrill Lynch who worked in the M&A department told us how the management required all business presentations to include a league table showing that Merrill was number one, irrespective of the subject at hand. If it turned out the bank didn't top the league in any given area, researchers were made to pore through pages of statistics until they invented a definition by which it did.[38] Stan O'Neal, Merrill Lynch's CEO from 2002 to 2007, was constantly goading his staff into taking on more risk, with the aim of beating Goldman Sachs. According to one of his lieutenants, 'You didn't want to be in Stan's office on the day Goldman reported earnings'.[39]

We can also see this dynamic at work in the ABN AMRO transaction that brought RBS to its knees. No fewer than nineteen investment banks advised the competing banks on the deal: 'I cannot recall a deal that has so many advisors,' said Scott Moeller, a professor of mergers and acquisitions at Cass Business School in London and a former banker at Morgan Stanley. 'The most significant issue is bragging rights. It's more important to the bank than the client.'[40]

---

37 Alain de Botton *Status Anxiety* (London: Hamish Hamilton, 2004)

38 Private interview

39 Quoted in Hersh Shefrin and Meir Statman, 'Behavioral Finance in the Financial Crisis: Market Efficiency, Minsky, and Keynes', Santa Clara University, November 2011, p. 4

40 *Independent*, 20 January 2009

For all Goodwin's ambitions to create a world-class banking conglomerate, at the point of collapse RBS had critical internal flaws and shambolic risk controls. After a decade of nonstop takeovers, the bank was operating over twenty different computer systems, which did not easily interact, so it was impossible to get an overall picture of the position of the bank. Despite having over 2,500 risk managers, not one considered liquidity a risk. The seeds of the bank's collapse were sown in its poor management. As David Buik, a partner at BGC Partners, has said: 'Fred Goodwin is a megalomaniac. RBS never had a chance to digest anything they bought and so they've never delivered shareholder value. It's a combination of relentless greed and an inability to deliver shareholder value.'[41]

In retail banking, executives competed on size. At the British bank HBOS, for example, the chief executive Andy Hornby was overwhelmingly concerned with expansion. For a non-financial institution like Asda, the British supermarket chain where Hornby had previously been CEO, expansion is constrained by market share of sales. Financing is important of course, but because leverage is so much lower, the liability side of the balance sheet matters much less. But banks are different. Both sides of the balance sheet matter, as their core business is to take deposits to make loans. Market share matters, but so does the origin of the loans.

The free-market Cobden Centre think tank estimates that for most high-street retail firms, a healthy solvency ratio is around 20 percent. Anything below that exposes the firm to the risk of bankruptcy. But when six high street banks were surveyed, they found the average solvency ratio was just 0.18 percent. So while the finance was available, banks had an apparently infinite capacity to borrow and expand market share in their lending.

---

41 *Daily Telegraph*, 20 January 2009

But in the lending business, market share is not king. It's easy to expand market share by making cheaper loans to less solid borrowers. Easy but not prudent, as Hornby and others like him discovered. In the short term they captured market share and the status that went with it, but they reaped what they sowed.

There is something primal about the modern financial fixation with size and growth. The idea of gaining validation from the sheer size of one's financial empire recalls the monarchs of early-modern Europe, who would compete among themselves to build the biggest and most splendid palaces, much to the dismay of their taxpaying subjects. In Chapter 3 we drew a comparison between Fred Goodwin and John Law, the eighteenth-century Scottish gambler turned economist who became master of Bourbon France's finances. But there also seems to have been something of a Louis XIV complex among the senior management of RBS.

They even built a palace. In 2005 RBS completed a state-of-the-art £350-million headquarters outside Edinburgh. Goodwin had been intimately involved with the planning process. As the project manager put it, 'he has strong opinions... He wanted high-quality finishes, a timeless, understated quality.' His executive office overlooked a landscaped woodland area, featuring the stately residence of his eighteenth-century predecessor. The mansion may have reflected a glorious past, but during the twentieth century it was converted into an asylum.

Diamonds aren't Forever

Some in the industry have begun to recognize the need for cultural change. In a letter to the *Financial Times*, co-signed by senior executives from nearly all the major London firms, Marcus Agius, Chairman of Barclays, publicly admitted excesses in the sector and called for a new, 'enlightened culture'.

Ultimately, it is the responsibility of the leaders of financial institutions – not their regulators, shareholders or other stakeholders – to create, oversee and imbue their organizations with an enlightened culture based on professionalism and integrity.[42]

This was a welcome first step. But shortly afterwards, the Board of Barclays appointed Bob Diamond as CEO. Diamond had no experience of running a retail bank and before taking up the post had managed Barclays own internal investment bank. In January 2011 Diamond was hauled up in front of the Treasury Committee of the House of Commons to answer questions about the state of the industry. During the session he remarked of the public: 'I think they recognize that there was a period of remorse and apology for banks. I think that period needs to be over'.[43] This was a surprising line for Diamond to take, for at that very moment his bank was under investigation by US and UK regulators for systematic attempts to rig the Libor rate.

Libor, the London InterBank Offered Rate, is the daily average of the eighteen largest banks' reported borrowing costs. It's

---

42 'Financial Leaders pledge excellence and integrity', *Financial Times*, 28 September 2010, signed by: Marcus Agius, Chairman, Barclays. Sir Winfried Bischoff, Chairman, Lloyds Banking Group. Mark Garvin, Chairman, JPMorgan UK. Chris Gibson-Smith, Chairman, London Stock Exchange. Richard Gnodde, Co-Chief Executive Officer, Goldman Sachs. Colin Grassie, Chief Executive Officer UK, Deutsche Bank. Stephen Green, Group Chairman, HSBC. John Griffith-Jones, Managing Partner, KPMG. Sir Philip Hampton, Chairman, Royal Bank of Scotland Group. Lord Levene of Portsoken, Chairman, Lloyd's of London. Harvey McGrath, Chairman, Prudential. Mark Otty, Managing Partner, Ernst & Young. Stuart Popham, Senior Partner, Clifford Chance. Ian Powell, Managing Partner, PricewaterhouseCoopers. Lord Sharman of Redlynch, Chairman, Aviva. John Stewart, Chairman, Legal and General. Sir David Walker, Senior Advisor, Morgan Stanley

43 Robert Diamond, Treasury Select Committee, oral evidence, 11 January 2011

one of the most important benchmarks in the global financial system – used to price trillions of dollars worth of derivatives contracts, loans and mortgages. From 2005 to 2009 dozens of derivatives traders at Barclays breached the 'Chinese wall' which was supposed to separate their department from those submitting the bank's borrowing costs. Every week these traders would ask the submitter to post fraudulent submissions, in the hope of benefitting their trading positions. There was big money at stake. If Libor could be moved by just one basis point (0.01 percent) each day, the value of the contracts would shift by as much as $80 million. At Barclays the corruption seems to have been routine, as though these requests were no different from asking a colleague to pick up a coffee on the way back from lunch. One trader even posted reminders in his email calendar so he'd remember to fiddle the figures the following week. 'Ask for High 6M Fix,'[44] the note said.

This scandal is not restricted to Barclays. At least twenty other banks have been named in investigations related to alleged Libor manipulations, and at the time of writing the Swiss bank UBS had just admitted to 'widespread and routine' attempts to fiddle Libor, settling with UK, US and Swiss regulators for $1.5 billion. But Barclays's immediate response to the revelations is a useful case study in how little the banking industry seems to have learned from the crash.

In a move intended to protect Diamond, Barclays's chairman Marcus Agius resigned as soon as the news broke. Yet the chairman's job is to hold the chief executive to account, not to take a bullet for him. Worse, until he became Group CEO in October 2010 Diamond had been in charge of Barclays Capital, the very part of the bank where these traders had worked. In July 2012 he was summoned once again to Parliament and gave

---

44 *The Economist*, 7 July 2012

a thoroughly evasive account, blaming the scandal first on a few 'jerks' who no longer worked at Barclays, then trying to implicate the Bank of England.

Twenty-four hours later Diamond resigned and Agius was reinstated. But the damage had been done. In his thwarted attempt to duck the blame, Diamond had made a mockery of Agius's letter to the *Financial Times* eighteen months earlier, in which he had argued that leaders of financial institutions were responsible for 'setting an enlightened culture based on professionalism and integrity'. Whether or not Diamond knowingly acquiesced to Libor-rigging, those at the top of our largest banks play a major role in shaping the value systems which govern the behavior of their staff. They set the tone. Former Citigroup CEO Vikram Pandit notes that banking is an apprenticeship industry: 'People learn from the people above them, and they copy the actions of the people above them. If you start from the top by acting responsibly, people will see and learn.'[45] The Libor scandal exposed a rotten culture that still existed at the top of Barclays in 2012, five years after the crisis broke. The former chair of Barclays' compensation committee later revealed that she had recommended to the board that Diamond forgo his bonus in 2011.

'My determination was quite straightforward, return to shareholders had been poor and Mr Diamond needed to set an example to all stakeholders that remuneration policies had to change to reflect the low return environment,' she told MPs.[46] The recommendation was politely refused.

Broken Windows, Broken Bank
All this talk of culture, norms and 'setting the right tone' makes

---

45 *New Yorker*, 29 November 2010
46 *BBC News*, 30 January 2013

for good rhetoric, for CEOs and politicians alike. But is there an empirical basis for any of it?

In the mid-1990s the Mayor of New York City, Rudy Giuliani, and his police commissioner, Bill Bratton, adopted a 'Quality of Life' campaign, which targeted police resources at signs of disorder and petty crime. This was based on the now famous 'Broken Windows theory', first popularized by James Q. Wilson and George L. Kelling, which holds that visible signs of disorder like broken windows and graffiti will tend to encourage the spread of criminal behavior. 'If a window in a building is broken and is left unrepaired,' Wilson and Kelling observed, 'all the rest of the windows will soon be broken.'[47] The idea is that once people observe that others have violated a social norm they are more likely to do so themselves.

The Broken Windows approach has always been controversial among academics because even though Giuliani's campaign was followed by an impressive fall in crime – by 2010, for example, violent crime rates had plunged 75 percent from their mid-90s peak – it was difficult to screen out other factors such as an increase in police numbers or broad demographic trends. In 2008 however, a team of Dutch social psychologists conducted a series of controlled experiments that put the theory on an empirical footing.[48]

One experiment took place in an alleyway next to a nearby shopping mall commonly used to park bicycles. While cyclists were out doing their shopping the researchers attached leaflets to the handlebars of their bikes with elastic bands. They then counted the number of times cyclists threw the leaflets on the ground, or stuck them on other peoples' bikes. Littering like

---

this was taken as a violation of a common social norm. The researchers repeated the experiment again, in the same area, with the same number of bikes, but with one important difference. This time the alleyway had been daubed with graffiti. Nearly twice as many participants in the second experiment (69 percent) violated the social norm of littering.

In another experiment the researchers wanted to see if the violation of more minor social norms could induce people to transgress a major ethical norm: not stealing. First they left an envelope sticking out of a mailbox with a five-dollar note clearly visible in the address window. Then they counted the number of people who opened the envelope or removed it from the mailbox. As with the bike experiment they repeated the process, but this time the mailbox was covered in graffiti and surrounded by litter. In the first experiment 13 percent of people stole the money, in the second this figure rose to 27 percent.

This study of the violation of social norms provides empirical proof of what most of us already know: that culture matters. In a bank where senior management are thinking only of the next acquisition, where self-worth is something most people find in their wallets, and where traders deride their clients and boast openly of selling 'toxic waste', it's almost inevitable that some people will cross the line – some quite considerably – as the money laundering scandals at Wachovia, HSBC, and Standard Chartered illustrate. Greg Smith, Goldman Sachs's head of US Equity Derivatives in Europe, Africa and the Middle East until March 2012, put the case most eloquently when he published an open letter of resignation in the *New York Times*:

> It might sound surprising to a skeptical public, but culture was always a vital part of Goldman Sachs's success. It revolved around teamwork, integrity, a spirit of humility, and always doing right by our clients. The culture was the secret sauce that

made this place great and allowed us to earn our clients' trust for 143 years. It wasn't just about making money; this alone will not sustain a firm for so long. It had something to do with pride and belief in the organization.[49]

Smith says he felt compelled to resign because he could 'no longer in good conscience identify with what Goldman Sachs stood for'. He describes the rise of a business model which had all but filleted out the interests of the client, referred to by senior staff as 'muppets', a culture in which the ability to push unsuitable products on unwitting investors had become sufficient grounds for promotion, and where the only measure of success was the audacity of the rip-off.

According to Smith, leadership at Goldman used to be about 'ideas, setting an example and doing the right thing'. But after a decade of excess, the only demand made of a Goldman manager is the ability to extract maximum fees from clients ('ripping out their eyeballs' in Goldman lingo). It is no surprise then that the more irresponsible elements in finance rise to the top, or that junior staff hearing this language 'don't turn out to be model citizens'.

The Epicurean Dealmaker, himself a senior investment banker, takes a more nuanced view, suggesting that the industry strives to cultivate a creative tension between the more anonymous transactional side of the business, i.e. trading, and the long-term relationship-building approach.

For him, the problem

arises from the fact that it is often more profitable to rip a customer's face off in the short term than to defer potentially

---

49 Greg Smith, 'Why I am Leaving Goldman Sachs', Open letter to the *New York Times*, 14 March 2012

larger profit opportunities with the same client in the long term. When bankers whose personal franchises, careers, and compensation depend on the former are evenly balanced with bankers whose interests are aligned with the latter, an investment bank perches profitably if precariously on the knife's edge of sustainable profitability.[50]

Incessant industry-wide growth may have been what tipped the balance. Culture is a delicate ecosystem, and after too many changes, restructurings and indigestible acquisitions, 'the glue which binds colleagues and potential rivals into a cohesive whole dissolves, and the mantra becomes every man for himself'.[51]

Moral Hazard

Looking to the future, if we want to see long-term changes in the culture of finance we need to confront the problem of moral hazard.

Moral hazard is the idea that if someone is protected from a risk they will behave more recklessly than if they were fully exposed. The term was coined by the insurance industry, which faced the conundrum that if it insured people against risks, it would encourage people to behave more dangerously. In the 1960s one resident of Vernon, Florida, reportedly claimed over $1 million from dozens of separate insurance companies after he lost his foot in a farming accident. Curiously, he happened to have a tourniquet in his pocket at the very time of the incident.[52]

---

50 The Epicurean Dealmaker, 'Three's a Crowd', www.epicureandealmaker. blogspot.co.uk, 19 March 2012

51 The Epicurean Dealmaker, 'The Fish Stinks from the Head', www.epicure-andealmaker.blogspot.co.uk, 30 July 2009

52 Tim Harford, *The Undercover Economist* (Oxford: Oxford University Press, 2012), p. 130

Whether you like it or not, moral hazard is a crucial concept in finance. We see it around us all the time. Sometimes it's useful, sometimes not. You wouldn't go on a high-rise assault course unless you were protected from falling by a safety harness. But equally, if a child knows their parents will always take their side over anyone else's, they will misbehave much more with everyone else – every babysitter's nightmare. If you are protected from a risk, you will change your behavior.

Back in the world of Wall Street, the golden age of moral hazard in banking lasted for Alan Greenspan's uninterrupted eighteen-year tenure at the Federal Reserve. He implicitly reassured the market that he would intervene to stabilize when the going got tough – as he did in the 1987 stock market crash, the recession in the early 1990s, when LTCM collapsed in 1998, after the Asian crash, at the end of the dot-com bubble, and in response to the 9/11 attacks. After each shock, he cut interest rates to stabilize the economy and encourage recovery. For three UK-based economists watching in 2001, the boom resembled 'not so much "irrational exuberance" as exaggerated faith in the stabilizing power of Mr Greenspan and the Fed.[53] As these economists delved into the guts of the US and UK investment markets, they found that investors seemed to expect the Fed to intervene to prevent failure but to stand aside to let growth burgeon.

This can be clearly observed in the behavior of the credit default swap market. If the market was accurately pricing in a bank's risks then as the crash approached we would expect to see rising premiums on the CDSs insuring the bank's default risk. Yet CDS premiums for all banks fell dramatically between

---

53 Marcus Miller, Paul Weller, and Lei Zhang, 'Moral Hazard and the US Stock Market: Analyzing the Greenspan Put', *Royal Economic Society Journal*, vol. 112, 2002, p. 3

2002 and 2007, by around three quarters on average.[54] Nor did the market distinguish between debt issued by failing and non-failing banks. Knowing the authorities would shoulder the risk on their behalf, debt-holders were lulled into a false sense of security that their world would never be left to fail.

And then came the collapse of Lehman Brothers. Treasury's decision not to bail out Lehman Brothers was part motivated by a realization that 'moral hazard' had built up in the system. By rescuing the bank, a message would be sent to the sector that it could carry on its business even more secure in the knowledge that there was a safety net. Ultimately, Lehman was allowed to fail and US Treasury Secretary Hank Paulson briefly boasted a 'badge of honor' for having the courage to let it go down.[55] That was the idea. Except that, as the crisis spread, it became very clear that this decision was the wrong one. The bailing out of the banks became necessary to prevent the system from collapse, and an international rescue strategy was implemented.

The rescue was clearly necessary, but had dire consequences for moral hazard. In a perverse way it confirmed what the banking elite had always secretly believed: that they were infallible. The FDIC's ostensible $100,000 limit on deposit insurance was rendered meaningless by the scale of government support, which is why the emergency 2008 rise to $250,000 was made permanent by Dodd–Frank. Martin Wolf, one of the world's leading financial journalists, observed in the aftermath of the crisis: 'the financial sector that is emerging from the crisis is even more riddled with moral hazard than the one that went into it'.[56]

---

54 Andrew Haldane, 'Control rights (and wrongs)', Wincott Memorial Lecture, Westminster, London, 24 October 2011

55 Anthony Seldon and Guy Lodge, *Brown at 10* (London: Biteback Publishing, 2010), p. 141

56 Martin Wolf, 'After the Storm Comes a Hard Climb', *Financial Times*, 14 July 2009

A survey in 2009 asked investors, fund managers, asset owners and others in the financial world if they agreed with Wolf's statement. Over 90 percent of respondents answered yes.[57] The results are not surprising. Underpinned by the knowledge that when push came to shove the banks were deemed too important to fail, swathes of Wall Street are acting as if the events of 2007 and 2008 simply haven't happened. With characteristically vivid Street language, one trader told us: 'Being too big to fail is the best of all worlds for banks... Now they're all thinking you might as well get your cock in the custard completely!'[58]

Moral hazard compounds a uniquely human ability to believe in what we want to believe. This observation from psychology and sociology can be useful – indeed necessary. The American political scientist Larry Bartels points to the way political beliefs can filter the perception of economic reality. At the end of the Reagan administration, US voters were asked whether they thought inflation had fallen – which it had, by nearly 10 percent. But only 8 percent of those who identified as strong Democrats agreed. By contrast, 47 percent of the Republicans surveyed thought it had fallen. At the end of Clinton's presidency the study was repeated. The results, of course, were reversed. Republicans were scathing and Democrats upbeat about the administration's economic management.[59]

Belief encourages us to act, to create, to live life to the full. When you marry, you believe that it will last. If you didn't, you wouldn't get married in the first place. You need that belief to allow you to marry. When you give money to charity, you need to believe it will go towards the new well in some parched African village, not a box of paperclips for the company office

---

57 AQ Research
58 Private interview
59 Quoted in David Brooks, *The Social Animal* (New York: Random House, 2011), p. 303

in New Jersey. If you believed otherwise you wouldn't donate. Now, we all want to believe that recovery is inevitable – the alternative is grim. We have to believe in order to be able to get on with our lives. In that vein, it is understandable that banks work on the assumption they would be bailed out.

Changing that assumption is essential for the long-term safety of our financial system. The recent introduction of macro-prudential regulation and enhanced-resolution powers point in the right direction. They are important for slowing a boom, and dealing in an orderly way with a bust. But alone they are by no means enough.

The mechanisms put in place to deal with a bank failure must be credible and expected to work, otherwise banks' management will know that in the inevitably difficult circumstances of a crisis, they cannot be used. Further, to reduce moral hazard for management as well as shareholders, the consequences of the failure of a bank should be severe. Spelt out in advance, the downside cost of failure for bank management will help make incentives more balanced, reduce moral hazard, and ultimately reduce the chances of such a failure in the first place.

This is crucial for the future.

Journalists write of the 'Financial Crisis of 2007–2008', attempting to seal away these events into the history books. Dick Fuld, Joe Cassano and Fred Goodwin have already assumed the aspect of historical characters, joining the likes of John Law or Irving Fisher, the American economist who declared that stocks had reached 'a permanently high plateau' three days before the Wall Street Crash, as instructive personifications of vice and folly in the long annals of financial misadventure. But this crisis is not yet over.

In the eurozone, the banking crisis has rolled into a highly contagious sovereign-debt crisis. While governments could stand behind over-indebted banks when they collapsed, there is no higher authority to stand behind over-indebted governments, save for other governments. In the eurozone the problem is compounded by the need to coordinate disparate democratic governments. Democratic governments are the only institutions with the legitimacy to spend taxpayers' money. Yet we have seen how complex the dynamics of group behavior are.

As the crisis has moved from banks to governments in the eurozone, so too has the question of moral hazard. Monetary union was supposed to curb the fiscal delinquency of southern European states like Greece, which has spent a total of fifty years since gaining independence in 1832 either in default or rescheduling its debt. The rules set out in the Maastricht Treaty were based on the principle that governments should always find it less painful to make difficult and unpopular spending decisions than risk defaulting on their debts. But as many a financial regulator could testify, unless such rules are anchored in institutions strong enough to enforce them they will be ducked when the crunch comes. In the absence of legal challenge, some countries borrowed to excess. Financial markets allowed them to do so in the expectation that Germany would never permit a default from within the eurozone.

And so, when faced with the damaging economic consequences of a default, Greece has been presented with lower borrowing costs and more time to repay; it has also received funds from the rest of the EU to recapitalize its banks and stimulate growth. Moral hazard applies just as much to countries as to banks. It is critical in the midst of this crisis that the lessons from the crash are learned: that the fool in the corner that no one wants to listen to might have a point; that behavior is not always rational; and herding, loss aversion, and leadership matter.

The Governor's Eyebrows

Older British bankers are prone to romanticize the old City of London – a world of merchant banks, bowler hats and gentlemanly capitalism – where the motto of the London Stock Exchange: *dictum meum pactum* (my word is my bond), was a business principle rather than a quaint verbal ornament. But every legend has a kernel of truth. Until the 1980s all banks in the City's Square Mile had to be situated no more than ten minutes' walking distance away from the Bank of England on Threadneedle Street. This was so that, in times of crisis, the Governor of the Bank of England could summon bank bosses to his office within half an hour's notice. Older City bankers still reminisce about regulation by 'the Governor's eyebrows', where a mere twitch of displeasure from the eyebrow of the Governor was enough to compel a senior banker's resignation.

The style of regulation represented by the 'Governor's eyebrows' metaphor never caught on in the United States for much the same reason that it was abandoned in Britain. It was too clubby and unaccountable. And yet discretionary, culture-based regulation seems to have worked more effectively than the system of explicit rules which followed. In the century between 1878 and 1984 not a single bank in the United Kingdom failed.

This is not as archaic as it sounds. The vast majority of economic activity that takes place every day depends not on formal rules but on a people choosing to do the right thing. When we pay a restaurant at the end of a meal it's not because we're scared of being arrested by the police or sued by the restaurant, but because it's simply the right thing to do: it's a social, reciprocal relationship. Most of us will normally do more than just fulfill our contract: we'll leave a tip.

During the Barclays Libor scandal the Governor's eyebrows made a welcome comeback. Diamond had managed to weather castigation in the media and a very public dressing down before Parliament. To many it seemed as though he would survive the storm. According to senior Barclays sources, the tipping point was a quiet phone call from the Bank of England, in which it was made clear that the Governor, Sir Mervyn King, would be 'happy if he resigned'.[60] This reassertion of regulatory authority over the banking system was hugely significant. The Governor's decision to oust the sitting CEO of an outwardly successful bank which not only survived but thrived in the crisis (Barclays was able to grow by successfully gobbling up the remains of Lehman), sent a long overdue message from the nation's central bank to other executives: the culture of your organization is as much our business as leverage ratios or capital adequacy.

There are encouraging signs that change is also coming from within business itself. In 2012 a series of high-profile investor revolts over rewards-for-failure pay packages at some of Britain's largest companies were dubbed the 'Shareholder Spring' by journalists. Credit Suisse and Barclays in particular were humiliated when over a third of shareholders failed to back their compensation reports. In addition, the number of FTSE 100 companies with clawback arrangements for executive compensation nearly doubled in 2012 from 36 percent of companies to 61 percent.[61]

Following Diamond's departure the board of Barclays appointed Antony Jenkins as CEO. As a former head of retail and business banking at Barclays, Jenkins is steeped in the heritage and culture of serving customers. One of his first acts as CEO was to send an email to all of Barclays 140,000 employees warning that from now on performance and reward would be judged against a set of core values including integrity, respect and quality of customer service. Jenkins wrote:

> There might be some who don't feel they can fully buy into an approach which so squarely links performance to the upholding

60 Robert Peston, 'Bank of England "Eased" Diamond Out', *BBC News*, 3 July 2012
61 Deloitte Executive Directors Remuneration Report, 2012

of our values. My message for those people is simple: Barclays is not the place for you. The rules have changed. You won't feel comfortable at Barclays and, to be frank, we won't feel comfortable with you as colleagues.[62]

This is a step in the right direction.

Finally, if culture is the best regulator of all, how do policymakers ensure we get the right culture? This is the subject to which we will turn in the last chapter of this book.

---

62 Quote in the *Financial Times*, 17 January 2013

Chapter 9

SO WHAT DO WE DO?

When the so-called masters of the universe discovered they were masters of nothing we all realized the frightening truth: they had built a machine they did not understand and could not fix. We are still living with the consequences. The banking-debt crisis has become a sovereign-debt crisis, raging in the eurozone. When the banks failed, governments stepped in. When governments fail, only other governments remain. This crisis is not yet over.

What's at Stake?

Since 2008 about four million Americans have lost their homes to foreclosure, another four and a half million have drifted into the foreclosure process and nearly $11 trillion in household wealth has evaporated.[1] The United States Government has spent $645 billion of the $700 billion allocated by Congress in the TARP program. A trillion and a half more has been expended on other forms of financial assistance such as buying mortgage-backed securities from Fannie and Freddie. During the crisis itself temporary support for the financial system from governments around the world peaked at a quarter of global GDP.[2]

But the costs of intervention were not merely financial.

---

1   Financial Crisis Inquiry Commission Report, 2011, p. xv
2   Andrew Haldane, 'Control rights (and wrongs)' Wincott Memorial Lecture, Westminster, London, 24 October 2011

The taxpayer's cash was intended to strengthen the banking system's collective balance sheet. The sight of bankers diverting it towards their bonus pools after such failure shattered public trust in the financial system.

For this book, YouGov asked members of the public in July 2011 'how much, if at all, do you trust the finance industry to look after your money?' Nearly 70 percent answered 'not much' or 'not at all'. Only two percent replied 'a great deal'. Yet the financial system is built on trust: trust that if you save for the future, your thrift will be rewarded.

After the financial crises of the 1930s, several nations turned against free-market capitalism. They uprooted the liberal institutions necessary to sustain a free society, and transferred their loyalties to an all-powerful State. The result was the Second World War.

Today the democratic tradition is rooted deeper, but we cannot afford to be complacent. Free-market capitalism can only work effectively if it enjoys public trust. That trust is undermined if the finance industry, which for better or worse has become a metaphor for capitalism at large, shows it is founded on the values to which our society subscribes – above all, the value of fairness. But in recent times banking has profited in a moral vacuum.

The ramifications of this are making themselves felt. In southern Europe, where whole economies are propped up on rotten stilts of bad debt, respect for the discipline of the market has been ground down. Large swathes of the population simply do not care about the international bond market's verdict on their government's creditworthiness. Attempts at economic reform are willfully sabotaged by vested interests hitched to a current of popular feeling. In one May 2011 poll, 33 percent of Greeks agreed that society must change radically through revolution, up from 11 percent in 1999.[3] The rhetorical question constantly posed by populists: 'why should we pay for bankers' mistakes?' is as difficult as it is necessary for politicians to answer.

In the countries of the former Eastern Bloc, support for capitalism is also in decline. According to a 2009 survey 'the prevailing view in Russia, Ukraine, Lithuania, Slovakia, Bulgaria and Hungary is that people were better off economically under Communism'. In Ukraine, Russia, Lithuania and Hungary only half or fewer of those polled approved of the transition to capitalism.[4] Even in the great citadel of capitalism, America itself, there are rumblings of protest. In 2011, 40 percent of Americans surveyed by Pew said they had a negative reaction to the term 'capitalism'.[5] Ex-Federal Reserve Chairman Paul Volcker has asked for 'some shred of evidence linking financial innovation with a benefit to the economy'. As far as he's concerned, the only socially useful banking invention of the last twenty-five years has been the ATM.[6] Meanwhile factions within the Tea Party movement agitate for a retrograde return to the gold standard.

Yet capitalism is the most successful economic system that has ever been tried. In China, India, Indonesia and Brazil the last thirty years of market reforms have lifted billions of people out of poverty, feeding the fastest rise in living standards in the history of the world. No amount of aid can replace the increased prosperity that such an expansion of commerce and trade can bring. But the system is discredited when the spoils of capitalism go to a small few who in turn are supported by the taxpayer.

So we face a task no less profound than to save capitalism

---

3 Public Issue, 'Memorandum and Debt: One Year After', survey published 20 May 2011

4 Pew Research Global Attitudes Project 2009

5 Pew Research, December 2011 Political Survey

6 *Wall Street Journal*, 8 December 2009

from itself. Central to this task is to restore public trust in the financial system.

Other professions enjoy widespread public trust in their ability to advise us while keeping our best interests at heart. One 2011 poll found that 88 percent trusted doctors to tell the truth, compared to 29 percent for bankers.[7] In 2012, after the news of the Libor scandal had broken, another survey found the stock of public trust in bankers had dwindled to just 10 percent.[8] In the pharmaceutical industry we trust pharmaceutical companies to create safe products where the possible side effects are clearly labeled. This allows us to make informed choices about the kind of treatment we want. Usually we won't understand the complex biochemical properties of a particular drug, so we rely on doctors or pharmacists to advise us. If the product turns out to be dangerous then liability rests squarely with the manufacturer. By contrast, financial services advisors insist that responsibility for gauging risk and sieving through deliberately opaque fine print lies with the consumer. From the sale of Alt-A mortgages to the trade in structured-credit products, the finance industry employed an opaque language to bamboozle both high-street customer and professional investor alike. All too often customers were led to believe they were dealing with disinterested advisors when in fact they were dealing with salespeople with targets to meet.

A leading asset manager described a fellow fund manager with a hugely successful career in the City of London who recently moved with his family to Geneva. His friend was not a banker, nor had he caused the crisis. Colleagues asked him why he'd chosen to emigrate. Was it lighter regulation, or a more lenient tax regime? No. It was because he didn't want his child

---

7 IPSOS Mori, *Trust in Professions 2011*, June 2011
8 ITV Cuts Index Survey, July 2012

growing up in a society where people like him were regarded as little better than pedophiles. This man was probably worth about half a billion pounds to the UK Treasury.

Occasional examples defy this trend. Handelsbanken, the Swedish bank, has devolved responsibility to branch managers, so that tailored customer service is at the heart of the bank's business model. It boasts top rankings for customer satisfaction and has shown higher profitability than its average competitors. Empowered local bank managers use their discretion and judgment to deal with clients that they know, while clients are able to deal with bankers they trust. But organizations like this are few and far between and, as we have seen from new polling data, public confidence in the finance sector is extremely low.

In banking, a new culture is required to ingrain the truth that public trust is as essential to finance as it is to medicine. For those who argue that banks are private businesses we reply that the banking system cannot exist without taxpayer support. Furthermore, banks are utilities which provide an essential service, just like water companies, energy firms and railways. The IMF estimates that a government guarantee against insolvency shaves 0.8 percent off the borrowing costs of banks regarded by governments as Too Big to Fail. This works out at a subsidy worth an annual $76 billion for America's eighteen largest banks, the equivalent of a year's profits. Of course the largest banks can always choose to divest themselves of the responsibilities that a public subsidy implies by breaking themselves up. But as long as they benefit from explicit or implicit taxpayer support, they should be expected to behave in a spirit of gratitude and reciprocity to their subsidizers.

This book has examined the crisis from a human perspective, whether the behavior of the fools in the corner who warned of an impending crisis; or the powerfully destructive relationship between debt and asset values built on a flawed modeling culture that would eventually cause a financial calamity; or the behavior of those who shaped the flawed culture that held people to be rational and markets efficient, or those who thought the authorities should not stop the build-up of a bubble, but merely clean up the debris afterwards.

This flawed culture needs to change. Human nature being what it is, that change will not be easy. But a more responsible, ethical, and trustworthy financial industry is vital, and can only be achieved through a change in culture. There have been encouraging steps to implement this shift at the heart of the government, with a behavioral insight team in the Cabinet Office producing important work on how best to shape policy to understand human behavior. We need to take these insights and apply them to the financial world.

What, then, can we do to bring this understanding of human behavior to bear to stop the crash happening again?

The Economics Profession

The problems stem from a deep-rooted error in the economics profession. At its base, the assumptions that underpin economic analysis must be more sophisticated. They must recognize how people behave. The forefront of the profession has already realized this. But there is a danger that the new strands of behavioral economics do not go far enough. We need also to recognize the dynamics of human behavior, and how policy and regulation itself is part of a complex adaptive system. So our first recommendation is that the significant resources of the economics profession must do more to understand the dynamics of human behavior, and that policymakers should take note.

To make this change we should understand how economists behaved as the world moved into the computer age. The economics profession, which was largely funded by the financial industry, harnessed the great silicone beast in pursuit of their models. Simple assumptions were made to explain human behavior, so complex algorithms based on these simple assumptions could produce numerical results. The fatal flaw was that throughout the economics ecosystem, economics students at universities around the world, graduate economists at banks and inside the regulatory bodies, all built models based on the same assumption: that we are all rational human beings and will behave rationally. In computing this is known as 'Garbage in, garbage out'. Much of the output of economics was garbage. The models delivered a false 'objectivity' that provided false comfort in decision-making. This obsession with 'objectivity' in decision-making would be fine, if it were not for the flaw in the assumptions.

It is a strength to accept we are all flawed, to accept the frailty of our knowledge, and to protect ourselves from hubris. Those who defend these flawed assumptions argue that they are the best we can do. In terms of observing the system, this may have some merit. But to insert a flawed model into the system, and then rest the system on its output as if gospel, is to undermine the system itself. As Warren Buffett puts it, 'Observing that markets were 90 percent efficient, they concluded that markets were always efficient. The difference between the two propositions is night and day.' The same arguments that determine this broad plea for change in economics apply equally to finance.

What does this mean in practice?

Reforming Banking Regulation
Given the complex role that banks play in the economy, there needs to be a new approach to regulation, one that relies less on complex rules and more on judgments about the big picture.

The Dodd–Frank Wall Street Reform and Consumer Protection Act that was signed into law by President Obama on 21 July 2010 has been billed as the most radical shake-up of Wall Street regulation since Roosevelt. Standing at 848 pages long it is certainly the wordiest. By way of comparison, the Glass–Steagall Act, which served the system well for nearly seventy years, was just thirty-seven pages long. At the time of writing, Dodd–Frank had spawned a further 9,000 pages as the various regulatory agencies translated the Act into new rules, and it's estimated that by the time all its many clauses and sub-clauses have been turned into regulation Dodd–Frank could comprise 30,000 pages of new rulemaking. Some of the detail is mind-bending. For example, the SEC recently released a 667-page proposed amendment to rules governing disclosure requirements for the issue of asset-backed securities.

In the aftermath of a crisis, major regulatory reforms run the perennial danger of fighting the last war. If we look back at recent financial scandals they all differ sharply on the who, the what, and the how. Enron was about accounting fraud, the dot-com bust was caused by the bursting of a speculative bubble in tech stocks, the S&L crisis involved thousands of small thrifts and so on. True, LTCM was brought down by its derivative exposures, but LTCM was a hedge fund not a bank, and those derivatives related to government bonds, not residential property. If there is one thing we can say for certain, the next big financial crisis will not be born from a surfeit of toxic mortgage-backed securities.

What does link these crises are recurrent patterns of human behavior: from herding instincts and short-termism, to path-dependent thinking and an overreliance on heuristics. Any regulation which can get to grips with these is likely to have a more lasting impact. In this respect there is much to recommend in Dodd–Frank.

The recent crises demonstrate that financial institutions go wrong when they make systematic misjudgments about the macroeconomic situation. This points to the timely need for monitoring of the important features of systemically important financial institutions, and a regulator that has enough oversight and authority to implement counter-cyclical policy, in other words, a regulator that has the clout it needs to intervene during a boom when intervention is likely to be at its least popular and most effective.

Such regulation should distinguish clearly between those banks which cannot fail without causing spill-over effects which threaten the entire financial system and the thousands of smaller institutions that pose no risk to the wider economy.

Dodd–Frank creates a new Financial Stability Oversight Council (FSOC) to operate a panoramic view of the economy. Chaired by the Treasury Secretary, the FSOC is a committee of the ten most powerful federal regulators, including the chairman of the Fed, the Comptroller of the Currency, and the heads of the SEC, FDIC and the Federal Housing Finance Authority. This body is charged with monitoring the stability of the financial system and controlling the build-up of systemic risks. By combining the regulatory perspectives of its members with a large-scale, macroeconomic view, the FSOC will be in a far better position to identify instability as and when it begins to contaminate the system and to assess the impact of regulatory decisions on the system as a whole.

Crucially, the FSOC also creates a single unequivocal point of responsibility where there was none before. In the past, regulatory authority was diffused between the Fed, the President's Working Group on Financial Markets, and numerous competing federal agencies. Not only did this make it harder for Congress to hold officials to account, as regulators could always locate the problem in an area beyond their remit, but at the start of the crisis it contributed to the very damaging sense that no one was in charge.

On the question of 'who watches the watchmen', it's

encouraging that a private, non-partisan group called the Systemic Risk Council has been set up by former regulators to monitor and issue reports on the performance of the FSOC. The group is chaired by former FDIC head Sheila Bair and advised by former Fed Chairman Paul Volcker, two heavyweights who tried to warn their colleagues of the risks they were running. We have just emerged from an era where too many of the big debates about financial policy happened behind closed doors. Expert policy scrutiny from outside government (and Wall Street), is a welcome innovation.

On the theme of scrutiny, note that Dodd–Frank also creates a new data-analysis arm called the Office of Financial Research to give regulators and the market more information. It is hoped this information will be used by investors to keep pace with risk as it emerges within banks, asset management firms, insurers and other financial institutions. Given the central role the ratings agencies played in this crisis and others, it would be a sign of real progress if regulators and investors alike could learn to rely more on independent analysis and less on the opinions of Moody's, Standard & Poor's, and Fitch.

It is significant that Dodd–Frank removes the agencies' protection under the First Amendment. Previously the Supreme Court had defined ratings as free speech, meaning investors could not sue the agencies for providing false or misleading information. Now that this privilege has been abolished, and the agencies are on the same legal footing as other financial advisors, some proper accountability might be restored to the credit rating industry. It is a sign of the law of unintended consequences that the agencies are now refusing to publicly disclose the ratings they give to private bonds. This forced the SEC to abolish rules allowing only rated bonds to trade, not necessarily a bad thing if it reduces the market's reliance on ratings.

Dodd–Frank also includes measures to tackle the problem

of complex systems incubating dangerous uncertainty. These include the creation of a new central clearing house for derivatives so that regulators can keep an eye on the swaps market (in the past derivatives were traded privately 'over the counter' rather than on a public exchange, meaning that exposures were hidden from prying eyes). Just as important, a new Bureau of Consumer Financial Protection has also been established to ban unfair lending practices, such as the hidden teaser rates and Alt-A loans which did so much to inflate the housing bubble.

In the UK we have decided that reforming the rules and addressing the regulatory blind spots is not enough. Regulators too will be flawed. In a complex world, unforeseen and hidden risks are inevitable. We need a banking system which can withstand myopic regulation. For us this means tackling the structure of the biggest banks.

The so-called Vickers reforms in the UK ensure that banks are not able to cross-subsidize by siphoning off the capital they hold to protect the deposits of millions of retail savers up and down the country to fund their investment-banking operations. Banks hold capital for a purpose: to mitigate against losses, so that when things go badly they do not go bust. Banks that hold savings and use those savings to fund loans to businesses and mortgages for homeowners are an important utility in any economy. They are the plumbing of the economic system. Running these banks is an act of stewardship, not entrepreneurship. So the capital put aside to support utility operations should be kept within the utility operations. To use that capital to support investment banking amounts to a subsidy. This change will not just increase the likelihood of the utilities surviving tough economic times, but also make it easier to protect savers if a bank collapses. The ring-fence should be designed to include deposits that are given this protection, and exclude everything else.

Big banks may not like the idea of removing these subsidies from their investment-banking operations, but until such subsidies are removed, they cannot claim to compete in a free market.

Reforming Corporate Governance

But reform of the regulatory rules and the structure of banks alone will not be enough. One consequence of recognizing that humans are not always rational is that we must recognize that regulators will fail. Recent experience confirms this, in spades.

So we must put in place systems to ensure that finance can survive regulatory failure. So far, the focus in global agreements and Dodd–Frank has rightly been on resolution regimes, the so-called 'living wills'.

These are very important. A 'living will' is a battle-plan for bankruptcy. As Sir Andrew Large foresaw, the crisis was exacerbated by the labyrinthine complexity of the failed banks' exposures. There were so many counterparties occupying positions both on- and off-balance sheet that it was impossible for other players to know where the write-downs would fall. Panic rapidly overtook the system and the result was a credit crunch. Resolution regimes attempt to head this problem off in advance by requiring the bank, in cooperation with the regulators, to detail all its exposures and plan for liquidation. If a plan is found to be deficient and adequate revisions are not made, under Dodd–Frank the FDIC and the Federal Reserve have the power jointly to impose more onerous capital, leverage, or liquidity requirements, or place restrictions on a company's growth. Drawing up living wills may be a morbid exercise for CEOs, but it is a healthy corrective to the hubris to which some of them are prone.

For living wills to work, the market must be confident that a large bank holding company really could be wound down within the space of a weekend. It is hard to see how this can be possible for a bank with a balance sheet larger than the annual GDP of a country the size of France. Indeed, during the crash, banks didn't even know their own positions, and the quality of management information in the biggest banks was shocking. This points to the need for banks to be smaller, on the grounds of financial stability.

The case for smaller banks is strengthened by the fact that the collapse of a large bank has a disproportionately greater impact on the economy, when rescuing or resolving a bank risks increasing the government's own borrowing costs. There is little evidence that recent mergers have improved efficiencies through economies of scale. Beyond a certain point it is clear that the gains of financial gigantism are more than offset by the inherent difficulty of managing so many risks and counter-party relationships.

The human analysis of the crash has shown that culture, self-responsibility, and social context are as necessary as the formal rules that surround banks.

These can be changed through leadership at the level of the firm. The father of modern conservatism Edmund Burke is believed to have said that all that is necessary for the triumph of evil is that good men do nothing. Leadership matters in finance as much as in any other area of life, particularly in shaping the boundaries of acceptable behavior. Such cultural boundaries can provide an important bulwark against some of the extremes that we have seen.

The rules of corporate governance can be used to strengthen a culture of responsibility, and shape incentives.

Punishment for Failure
The existing system of deferred prosecutions for directors who incur losses has not proven a deterrent to irresponsible behavior.

Even in the rare instances where wrongdoing has been proven beyond reasonable doubt, regulators are reluctant to impose truly punitive fines on institutions because to do so could hurt their balance sheets and provoke financial instability. Fines for individuals are also likely to be modest deterrents because most large companies typically indemnify directors against regulatory fines if the board agrees they acted in good faith to increase profits.

The deferred prosecution system relies on the authorities' ability to prove active fraud at the highest level. But after the hundreds of scalps claimed in the S&L crisis few executives would be foolish enough to compromise themselves so directly. Numerous regulatory investigations into the banks that failed found that since poor decision-making and incompetence did not amount to criminal wrongdoing, no action should be taken.

Even taken at face value this is a dubious assertion. There are still serious questions as to whether clients and investors were misled by the banks both before and during the crisis. No one at Lehman Brothers has ever been held responsible for the Repo 105 transactions that were used to camouflage the state of the bank's balance sheet. According to the court-appointed examiner of the Lehman bankruptcy, at least one witness testified that he discussed these transactions with Dick Fuld and that there were documents sent to him which mentioned the transactions.[9] There is no doubt that some in the industry were aware of the dangers posed by their products. In a 2006 email sent by Bear Stearn deal manager Nicolas Smith to a colleague on a trading desk, he referred to a subprime mortgage bond designated

---

9 Anton R. Valukas, Chapter 11 Case No. 08-13555, re: Lehman Brothers Holdings Inc., United States Bankruptcy Court Southern District of New York, 11 March 2010, pp. 914–19

SACO 2006–08 as 'SACK OF SHIT [2006–08]'.[10] The question usually asked of those ensconced in the boardroom, or in Club 31, is did they know about this kind of behavior? The more important question is: why did they not?

Joe Cassano of AIG FP was never prosecuted because the Justice Department could not show that he lied to shareholders or his bosses about AIG's exposure to the subprime mortgage market. This illustrates well the shortcomings of the current legal framework. For a criminal prosecution the law requires prosecutors to demonstrate criminal intent. Yet most senior banking executives will not put their careers on the line to knowingly commit fraud. What the law does not take into account is the concept of financial recklessness: failing to behave in a way which a reasonable person in their position would have done. The business judgment rule gives directors enormous discretion provided they acted within the rules of their company, but what if the rules of the company and the culture underpinning them are themselves flawed?

In 2005 Cassano hired Gene Park to be AIG's CDS sales ambassador to Wall Street's securitization desks. Before he took the job Park wanted to get a feel for the business by examining the loans AIG had insured. Park was shocked to discover that 95 percent of the loan bundles for which they were writing CDSs consisted of subprime mortgages. As Michael Lewis explains in his essay on the fall of AIG:

'Park then conducted a little survey, asking the people around AIG FP most directly involved in insuring them how much subprime was in them. He asked Gary Gorton, a Yale professor who had helped build the model Cassano used to price the credit-default swaps. Gorton guessed that the piles were no more than 10 percent subprime. He asked a risk analyst in

London, who guessed 20 percent. He asked Al Frost [a managing director], who had no clue, but then, his job was to sell, not to trade.'[11]

It is not surprising then that prosecutors were unable to show that Cassano had lied about AIG's subprime exposure: until Park's investigation the management of AIG FP were barely aware this exposure existed. It was only when they pondered its implications that Cassano agreed to stop writing CDS contracts, by which time it was too late.

Other industries know that public trust in their business model is too important to make skimping on safety worthwhile. What would we think of a pharmaceutical company which put a new drug on the shelves without testing it for side effects? Would we accept 'all the other companies are doing it' as an excuse? And what would we think of an airline which fired its chief engineer because of his concerns about the level of fuel the planes were carrying? A banking crash may not directly result in the loss of human life but its effects on society as a whole are deep and long-lasting.

For the future, in order to build a culture of responsibility and mitigate against rewards for failure, we should end the legal immunity which seems to surround the senior management of failed banks. For this reason we have proposed the establishment of a new recklessness test for the directors of any financial institution which availed itself of public funds in a future crisis. To prove financial recklessness prosecutors would have to show that the managers had failed to take reasonable steps to ensure the assets on their books were accurately valued. This could be done with reference to biased internal models, abuse of the credit-rating system, attitudes to the views of risk managers,

---

11 Michael Lewis, 'The Man who Crashed the World', *Vanity Fair*, August 2009

a breach of internal risk limits, or inadequate due diligence performed during an acquisition. A recklessness test would act as a check on aggressive boom-driven growth, as managers would be obliged to consider the value of a company more carefully before embarking on a leveraged buyout. It would also tackle the problem of excessively complex management structures, giving managers an incentive to ensure the asset side of their balance sheet was readily comprehensible. Fifty-seven percent of the Americans we surveyed agreed that the chief executives of banks that fail should face criminal prosecution, with only 12 percent opposed.[12]

We should not forget that professional negligence can be prosecuted in other walks of life. Drivers face criminal charges for driving without due care and attention. Doctors can be prosecuted for medical malpractice. A negligent doctor can harm our health, but negligent bankers poison the whole economy. There is much merit in HSBC Chairman Douglas Flint's proposal that bankers be made to take a financial version of the Hippocratic Oath. Even the threat of prison for some of the more egregious acts of greed would help change the culture of finance.

Stronger Boards

The second strand of improving corporate governance is to strengthen boards. Before the crash, too many boards were weak. The crisis refuted the Sarbanes–Oxley dogma that the presence of independent directors translates into better corporate governance. If NEDs do not understand the business they are dealing with, are captured by short-termism, or are too fixated on their own interests as shareholders rather than the interests of shareholders as a whole, then the benefits of independence

---

12 YouGov general population survey, conducted on 28–31 January 2013

are negated. It is telling that in 2009 both Citibank and UBS announced the departure of board members to make way for new directors with 'finance and investment experience'.[13]

While independent board members undoubtedly bring outside experience to bear, if they fail to understand the unique risks of this business they will not be able to hold their executives to account. Yet as we have seen, mismanagement of the biggest banks can have critical consequences for our whole economy. The non-executive directors of these large banks should put their full focus on their direction and strategy. It's a full-time job. And to deal with rewards for failure, the sanctions for failure should be significant.

As the crisis unfolded, non-executive directors successfully evaded much of the criticism leveled at the management. There needs to be a more proportionate distribution of responsibility, with boards collectively bearing the repercussions of their failure. Recent research into the psychology of gang culture yields crucial insights. In Cincinnati, a new approach to tackling gang-related violence has proven effective. If a member of a known gang kills someone, the entire gang will be targeted for other offences like drug activities, weapon possession and parole violation. Assigning guilt by association provides groups with a powerful incentive to re-fashion their social norms. Punishment is replicated in the same way as the delinquent behavior, through the social norm of gang membership. In Cincinnati gang-related homicides fell by 35 percent following the implementation of the program.[14] This research suggests that if a bank blows up, everyone on the board should be hauled up

---

13 G. Kirkpatrick., 'The Corporate Governance Lessons from the Financial Crisis,' OECD, 11 February 2009 , p. 18
14 Robin S. Engel, Nicholas Corsaro and Marie Skubak Tillyer, 'Evaluation of the Cincinnati Initiative to Reduce Violence (CIRV)', University of Cincinnati Policing Institute, 20 October 2010, p. 3

in front of the Senate Banking Committee, not just the CEO and Chairman. This would act as an incentive for boards to regulate their own behavior.

We need non-executive directors (NEDs) to treat their positions less like a pension plan and more like a job. Four of the ten directors on the Lehman Brothers board were over the age of seventy-five. The Walker Review, a government commissioned report on the state of corporate governance in the UK financial services industry, found that the typical time commitment of an NED at a major British bank was just twenty-five days a year.[15] Sir David Walker recommended an increased time commitment. Should not NEDs be in the bank several times a month, asking the executive management difficult questions and demanding answers? This demands both time and focus. Take a quick glance at the résumés of RBS's independent directors in 2007 and it seems unlikely that they could have had their mind fully on the job. Bob Scott, for example, was Chairman of Yell, a director of both Swiss Re and Jardine Lloyd Thompson, a trustee of the Crimestoppers Trust, and an advisor to Duke Street Capital Private Equity, all the while sitting on the board of Pension Insurance Corporate Holdings. To tackle this, we have suggested that non-executive directors of deposit-taking banks should spend more time in the institutions they govern and only be allowed to hold one such directorship. Audit committees and risk committees should not be one and the same, as is often the case with American banks. This prevents either job being done properly. Risk management should command the full attention of directors.

Public companies' compensation committees are also too often drawn from a small group if people who directly and

---

15 Sir David Walker, *The Walker Review of Corporate Governance of the UK Banking Industry* (HM Treasury 2009), p. 45

indirectly end up setting each others' pay. The conflicts of interest are obvious and unacceptable, and should be ended.

These changes would make the task of being a non-executive director more onerous. But this will not lead to a shortage of applications. In other professions, those in a position of trust are held accountable for their actions. If doctors are found guilty of serious malpractice then they are struck off the medical register. Would anyone seriously suggest that this system of punishing professional failure has resulted in the mass exodus of the best medical talent? The boards of systemically important financial institutions are placed in a similar position of social responsibility. If we want them to behave like professionals they must be treated as such. This means professional negligence should be met with serious sanction.

Co-CEOs

Ken Thompson's acquisition of Golden West and Fred Goodwin's purchase of ABN AMRO are now seen as strategic and tactical mistakes: 'the wrong price, the wrong way to pay, at the wrong time and the wrong deal,' in the words of the current RBS Chairman. Unless the minutes of RBS's board meetings are published, we will never know how open to challenge Goodwin's decisions were. But evidence and anecdote seem to suggest that the cult of personality surrounding most bank chief executives and the culture of the average boardroom mean that there is little opportunity for non-executives to challenge.

A simple solution to resolve this is to shift the role of the chief executive. When Nadhim Zahawi launched YouGov, it was a partnership. He and Stephan Shakespeare began the company in a shed, and together built it into a company ready to be listed on the stock exchange. The title on their business cards read co-chief executive and there was both a formal and informal recognition that the business was managed by two equals. There was no jostling for position or authority between either man, but there were at times disagreements and challenges. All of these were played out openly through their joint, glass-walled office.

However, when they first talked to investment banks about their listing, the first unanimous piece of advice they received was to pick a chief executive. 'The City won't like it,' they were told. 'Institutional investors want to know that a company has strong leadership. Without a single chief executive, how will they know who to listen to?' was the view in another meeting. They were given an ultimatum: choose one of you or we'll find you a new one.

In the end, Zahawi took on the role. But he feels strongly that the co-CEO approach to management was beneficial to the challenge-friendly culture of both the business and the board. If board members are used to seeing the co-chief executives challenged by their counterparts, then there is an unspoken authority for others in the business and boardroom to do the same.

YouGov wasn't the only business to be co-founded and come across this problem. Google, the business that was doing things differently, was co-founded by Larry Page and Sergey Brin. But as the business began to head towards flotation it hired Eric Schmidt, a tech industry insider, first as executive chairman and then as CEO. While the company's SEC filings stated that Schmidt, Page and Brin ran Google as a triumvirate, it was clear that it was Schmidt who had the legal responsibilities of CEO.

But having co-CEOs is a successful model where it has been allowed to remain. Goldman Sachs has adopted a co-senior partner approach to its corporate governance structure. Even as a public company, it continues to have a number of co-heads of department at board level and retains co-CEOs for its international business.

YouGov is still reaping the benefits of its original co-CEO structure. In 2008, three years after YouGov's flotation, Zahawi was pursuing a £160-million acquisition of a US research and polling firm. He was challenged by the board to ensure that the deal made financial sense. Eventually, he aborted it. It may have cost over a million pounds in fees, but Zahawi maintains it is one of the best business decisions the company ever made. The target is now worth a mere fraction of that its value. The freedom of the YouGov board to challenge its CEO has its roots in the original co-CEO structure.

For real change in boardroom and organizational culture, Wall Street and its institutional investors need to change their views on the suitability of co-chief executives.

Reforming Pay and Incentives

The culture of an organization is affected by its leadership, but the wider incentive structure is also crucial. Far from being an expression of robust, globalized competition, the system of pay incentives cushioned senior executives against the effects of poor decision-making and encouraged careers in certain parts of finance over others. At its worst it resembled the world of monopolies and cartels which Adam Smith wrote the *Wealth of Nations* in protest against. To foster a culture of more responsible risk management these systems of rewards for failure had to be unwound.

One very direct means of re-introducing the concept of personal liability would be to abolish limited liability. It's worth remembering that it was only relatively recently in the history of finance that the principle of limited liability was introduced for shareholders and directors. When the City of Glasgow Bank collapsed in 1878 depositors did not lose a single penny, but 80 percent of the shareholders were made bankrupt as they were liable beyond the value of their holdings.[16] Turning back the clock in this way is not very practical however. Limited

---

16 Andrew Haldane, 'Control rights (and wrongs)', Wincott Memorial Lecture, Westminster, London, 24 October 2011

liability was originally established because it made owners a bit too risk averse, reluctant to lend to a capital-hungry industrializing economy.

When it comes to shareholder engagement on this issue it's encouraging that the Dodd–Frank Act introduces a new 'say on pay' requirement for all public companies. The measure gives shareholders an advisory vote, to be held at least once every three years, on whether the board should approve executive compensation deals or golden parachute arrangements. In the first year of the new law operation 37 companies failed the new say on pay votes, eight of which were S&P 500 firms. A study of the failed votes prepared by the Council of Institutional Investors found that shareholder concerns of a disconnect between pay and performance accounted for 'no' votes 92 percent of the time.[17] In countries like the UK, which pioneered say on pay laws before the crisis, there is evidence that these votes have started to concentrate minds in the boardroom, spurred on greater engagement with shareholders and stimulated more shareholder activism. Some have suggested that the rules could be made even tougher, and the British government recently consulted on making these votes legally binding, or even imposing a minimum voting threshold for the resolution to pass.

Using behavioral insights, it is possible to bring loss aversion and path dependency to bear. Most people fear loss more than they seek gain. A steady stream of gains can induce people to keep gambling, even when the odds have changed. Both of these things point to the need for compensation clawback provisions. The Dodd–Frank Act instructs the SEC to implement clawback rules obliging a company to

---

17 Council of Institutional Investors, 'Say on Pay: Identifying Investor Concerns', 2011

confiscate an executive's incentive-based pay in the event that a company issues an accounting restatement because it was not previously compliant with SEC reporting rules. This is a typical instance of regulators tinkering at the margins; neither accounting errors nor outright fraud were alone the cause of the banking crisis.

A more meaningful use of clawbacks would be to use them to tackle the incentives bankers have to swallow tail risks. For example, a proportion of a trader's annual compensation could be held in an interest-earning escrow account which he could only access once he had exited all his positions and left the firm. In the event that the trader lost money for the bank his account would be drained in direct proportion to the loss. The average tenure of a modern CEO is three to five years, so compensation packages which pay out during their term of office encourage short-term decision-making. It's unreasonable to expect stability when volatility increases the value of the instruments held by key decision-makers. Equity-based compensation should therefore be 'locked-in' until they retire from the firm. This is already current practice at Goldman Sachs, where partners are required to defer 75 percent of their share awards until after they leave. Just as the trader's account would suffer the downsides of his risk-taking, the executive's deferred equity could be held as reserve capital, to be called upon to bear losses if the bank ever got into trouble.

There has also been a valuable debate about paying senior managers in contingent convertible securities, known as CoCos, instead of shares or share options. These are debt instruments which automatically convert from bonds to shares following a trigger event signaling the bank's weakness. Because the share price of a bank on the rocks will likely be very low, the value of the CoCos will plummet once it has metamorphosed into equity form. This would mean senior management would see the value of their bonus pool evaporate in the event of a bank failure and in principle the banks could rely on these bonds for capital in a crisis. Managers would also have to confront angry shareholders who will have seen the value of their own holdings diluted. Andrew Haldane argues that the best stress trigger would be a decline in the bank's share price itself, as this was a reliable early warning of financial distress.

We also support the principle of clawing back an executive's cash salary based on a set of pre-agreed criteria. These criteria would be the inverse of the performance targets that determine an executive's pay packet and could include a fall in the share price beyond a certain level, a breach of maximum leverage ratios, or a rise in the yield on the bank's bonds. The important thing would be to make sure that these conditions were set in a way which if they were met would unequivocally signal to the management that the bank was in trouble. This would prevent costly legal wrangling on the part of the CEO. By actually making the payment, the fear of losing the cash would kick in, especially if the cash was already spent. Bankers' families would then act as a further constraint on risk seeking. It would be minimally intrusive but would provide sufficient reassurance to the public that actions have consequences. In the eighteenth century stockbrokers who wished to trade on the London Stock Exchange were required to put up a hefty subscription fee. If any broker was found guilty of financial malpractice their subscription would be seized and distributed to charity. This idea could be resurrected.

The broader problem of shareholder short-termism is harder to deal with. We could make a start, however, by abolishing short-term managerial performance targets based on return on equity. These targets encourage risk-taking and share price volatility, benefiting sophisticated gamblers at the expense of long-term investors, like pension funds.

Reforming the Masculine Culture

Sex also matters in the City. We have argued that the evidence shows that existing policy reinforces differences in gender, which impacts negatively on business. So what would a policy that understands and respects human behavior look like?

Equal Pay

The first area to address is remuneration. Legislation for equal pay is in place in the US, but enforcement requires transparency. Federal government contractors have long been required to conduct pay-equity self-audits. Banks, which also benefit from public funds, should do the same.

Pay audits would strengthen the principle of rewards on merit. We have seen how people have a natural tendency to promote and reward those similar to ourselves. Where women are largely absent this leads to a self-reinforcing culture of male dominance that works against meritocracy.

In a pay audit, the average salary and bonus is published for each grade, broken down by gender. Such transparency itself helps break a biased culture. A clearer, published, framework for bonus awards could help ensure that the level of each bonus would be more dependent on genuine individual performance.

Parental Leave

Another area in need of reform is parental leave. The current system strengthens the bias against women in the workplace. In contrast to virtually every other country in the developed world, the United States does not mandate paid maternity leave for female employees, and only 8 percent of private sector employers voluntarily provide paid leave.[18] Removing this bias will require a cultural shift so that it becomes normal for

18 US Department of Labor, Bureau of Labor Statistics, 2006

either parent to take time out to look after a baby, and so that career breaks are not career-limiting. In the UK we're hoping to encourage this shift by moving to a system of shared parental leave, where the father can share the mother's statutory maternity leave. The argument for more balanced childcare is not to argue for equality for equality's sake. The roles men and women play in having children are conspicuously different; men don't get pregnant, give birth, or breastfeed. But these natural differences in behavior are exacerbated by cultural stereotypes and reinforced by a law that strengthens the bias against women in the workplace.

Women on Boards

These changes aim to get women to the top of finance. The best boards bring a diversity of human behavior and experience, and what bigger determinant of human behavior is there than sex? Yet the male dominated culture of the boardroom holds these improvements back. In the US change has been incremental. In 2006 11 percent of board seats in the S&P 1500 and 14 percent of board seats in S&P 500 companies were filled by women; six years later this had risen to 14 percent for the S&P 1500 and 17 percent for the S&P 500. Today a quarter of S&P 1500 companies have no women directors at all, as do 10 percent of all S&P 500 companies.[19]

How can we best break this deadlock? One of the best ways to make finance more attractive to women is for there to be more women in finance. A study commissioned by the UK Government found that one of the greatest barriers to progress was a lack of women in senior roles to act as mentors and role models for their female colleagues.[20] The research strongly

19 Ernst and Young, 'Getting on Board', 2012
20 Lord Davies of Abersoch CBE, 'Women on Boards', February 2011

indicates that the environment for women in senior roles improves once about a third of leaders at board level are women, and that 30 percent also represents a tipping point at which behavior changes for the better and companies achieve the best financial results.[21]

We need to tackle this without unduly burdening business. But how do we get there? In the US the SEC currently requires listed companies to disclose how they take diversity into consideration when making board selections. Norway, Spain, Finland, and Iceland have already legislated, adopting a quota system where companies are legally obliged to raise the number of women on their boards, or face sanctions. This has certainly yielded results. In Norway, for example, the proportion was only 24 percent in 2005. By 2009 this had risen to 40 percent. Yet as we have seen, legislation can also have unintended consequences. In Norway many companies simply expanded the size of their boards to meet the government's deadline on time. There are also signs that women are being brought in from outside to sit as non-executive directors, rather than being promoted up through the company as executives.

In the UK we have adopted a voluntary, business-led approach, with the aim of changing the culture of business from within. The 30% Club, a group of company chairmen campaigning for 30 percent female board membership, has been particularly effective at making the case for change. Since this work started we have seen a near 50 percent increase in the number of female non-executives in the FTSE 350. Crucially, 38 percent of all recently appointed FTSE 100 directors and 36 percent of all newly appointed FTSE 250 directors have

---

21 See McKinsey & Co., 'Women Matter: Gender Diversity, a Corporate Performance Driver', 2008

been women.[22] The early indications are that the business-led approach works, and a voluntary change in culture will ensure that progress will be sustainable and long term. We would not recommend removing the threat of legislation entirely however, in case progress were to stall.

In this book we have made ambitious policy recommendations that follow from our analysis of the crisis. We have made detailed recommendations about corporate governance, the need for more women in the City and Wall Street, deep changes to the way we use technology to model economies, and the need for regulators willing to use fewer but tougher rules to allow finance to safely thrive.

All of these recommendations should support changing the culture to put morality into business decisions, and recognize the ethical context in which we all work. Only then will we deliver a capitalist system that is fit for the challenges of a globalized world.

---

22 *Parliamentary Debates*, House of Commons, 7 January 2013, col. 54

EPILOGUE

This book is about human behavior. We have tried to bring together insights from a wide variety of fields to understand how people actually behave. Our motivation was to try to understand more deeply why the financial crisis of the early twenty-first century happened, and what we need to change to reverse the trend of increasingly frequent financial crises.

In studying behavior, and applying the lessons to finance, we have been struck by the similarities to other areas of life. Perhaps it should have been obvious that the patterns of behavior behind the banking crisis also lie behind other crises. The context was different, of course, and the details equally unpredictable, but the patterns and dynamics remarkably similar.

Time and again we have seen skewed incentives; optimism bias; short-termism; the herding of the crowd; social norms; loss aversion and the tipping point.

Our conclusions for financial policy are at once broad and humble. Broad, in that the whole culture of finance needs to change to learn the full lessons from the crisis. We are not naively hoping that human nature will change; rather we are asserting that the soft, cultural and social context in which people act is a crucial part of the system. Leadership and strong institutions are required.

It is clear, too, that for many decades the economics profession has proceeded down an increasingly narrow alley of mathematical precision. That direction must be reversed if we are to use effectively the great advances in technical capability and computing power to understand how economies really work. This has started. While understanding individuals' behavior is necessary it is not sufficient: we need also understand the dynamics of group behavior, on which all economies are based.

As well as being broad, our conclusions are also humble. All people are flawed. Everyone behaves, at times, in irrational ways. So we need to design policy to deal with these inevitable flaws, whether in individuals, banks, or the economy as a whole, hence our focus on strong institutions, social norms, stronger governance, meritocracy, and better incentives.

Do not mistake this for a left-wing critique. It is deeply ironic that Occupy Wall Street excoriate the financial services industry as a master symbol of all that is wrong with capitalism. Karl Marx would be proud of the bankers. After all, we're talking about an industry where gains are subsidized by the public and losses socialized by the state, where companies are controlled by workers not owners, and where most of the profits end up in the hands of the former.

It is essentially conservative to argue that capitalism is based on just rewards, not a one-way bet, that free markets need frameworks, both legal and cultural, to prevent an anarchic free-for-all, and that barriers to equal opportunity should be brought down so that the rewards of capitalism can be fairly shared. Crucially, conservatives instinctively understand that regulators are themselves flawed and that the law of unintended consequences is one of the most consistently true laws there is. No amount of financial regulation can change what is constant in human nature. If we try to ban certain types of behavior, or define in detail what level of risk-taking is acceptable, we will always be one step behind the finance industry's amazing capacity for innovation. In short, this is a case for a stronger framework to ensure that a genuinely competitive market can flourish.

It is also essential for conservatives to argue for a capitalism based on just rewards: against rewards for failure. After the crash it is vital to win the argument again against those whose solutions would destroy the prosperity they want to redistribute.

To win that argument, the center-right must be prepared to tackle rewards for failure, and promote a truly competitive market, in which failure is not rewarded by state bailout.

In both the United States and the United Kingdom, real-terms take-home pay has stagnated for many years, even before the crash. Where the actions of finance, by supporting the economy, support real take-home pay for the middle classes, they should be supported. But where the system benefits finance at the expense of the taxpayer or of the wider economy, it is the center-right who must rise to the challenge.

It is a failure, not a success, of capitalism to allow power to be concentrated, subsidies extracted and competition stymied by private monopolies as much as by the state. A truly free market should promote innovative new entrants and allow market leaders to be challenged. Governments in the UK and the US have begun to introduce an understanding of human behavior into their work. Early results are very impressive: understanding how people behave really does help improve policy. But understanding of these issues is not yet embedded or widespread, and application has been in micro-initiatives. A nudge is not enough. Broader understanding of the dynamics of human behavior needs to be applied more widely. Supporters of capitalism must get this right or the destructive solutions of the left or far right will gain ground.

To change the culture in finance, we must change the way big banks are governed so shareholders are more active and better informed. We must be modest, though, about the chances of changing culture through shareholders, and so strengthen boards, and strengthen sanctions for those who behave recklessly.

None of these changes will tackle the problems we face overnight. Nor will they stop bubbles or crises in future, for bubbles and crises are inevitable. But they can help reduce the frequency of crises and help to stop the next crisis being so bad.

It is often said that the next really big crisis happens when the last crisis has just receded from the memory of those who lived through it. That can only be true if we learn the lessons. We hope this book adds to the learning of those lessons, and we hope to be around long enough to warn of them for many decades to come.

BIBLIOGRAPHY

Papers and Speeches

Agarwal, Sumit, Benmelech, Efraim, Bergman, Efraim and Seru, Amit, 'Did the Community Reinvestment Act (CRA) lead to a culture of risky lending?', NBER Working Paper No. 18609, 1 October 2012

Alesina, Alberto and Angeletos, George-Marios: 'Fairness and Redistribution: US versus Europe', MIT, 2002

American Association of University Women, 'The Simple Truth about the Gender Pay Gap, 2012 Edition

Anderson, Cameron and Brion, Sebastian, 'Overconfidence and the Attainment of Status in Groups', Working Paper Series, *Institute for Research on Labor and Employment*, UC Berkeley, April 14, 2010

Andrews, Holly, 'Snakes in Suits: Dealing with Psychopaths in the Workplace and Boardroom', speech to the Institute of Risk Management 19 November 2010, IRM, 2010

Barber, Brad M. and Odean, Terrence 'Boys will be boys: Gender, Overconfidence and Common Stock Investment, *Quarterly Journal of Economics*, Harvard, February 2001

Bebchuk, Lucien, Cohen, Alma and Spamann, Holgar, 'The Wages of Failure: Executive Compensation at Bear Stearns and Lehman 2000–2008', European Corporate Governance Institute Working Paper No. 287, June 2010

Bechara, Antoine, Tranel, Daniel and Damasio, Hanna, 'Characterization of the decision-making deficit of patients with ventromedial prefrontal cortex lesions', *Brain*, vol. 23, issue 11, July 2000

Benabou, R., 'Groupthink: Collective Delusions in Organizations and Markets', NBER Working Paper No. 14764, March 2009

Benartzi, Shlomo and Thaler, Richard, 'Save more tomorrow: Using behavioral economics to increase employee savings', *Journal of Political Economy*, vol. 112, 2004

Black, William K. 'Why nobody went to jail during the credit crisis', speech to Financial Sense Newshour, 14 September 2011

Bordo, M., D., Redish, A. and Rockoff, H., 'Why didn't Canada have a banking crisis in 2008 (or in 1930, or 1907, or ...)?' NBER Working Paper No. 17312, August 2011

Bush, George W., 'George Bush speaks to HUD employees on National Homeownership Month', Washington DC, 18 June 2002

Byrnes, James, Miller, David C. and Schafer, William D., 'Gender differences in risk taking: A meta-analysis', *Psychological Bulletin* 125, 1999

Camerer, Colin, Lowenstein, George and Pralec, Drazen, 'Neuroeconomics: How Neuroscience can Inform Economics' in the *Journal of Economic Literature* vol. 43, March 2005

Carr, Nicholas, 'Is Google Making Us Stupid? What the Internet is doing to our brains', *Atlantic Magazine*, July/August 2008

Catalyst, 'The Bottom Line: Corporate Performance and Women's Representation on Boards', October 2007

Clinton, William J., 'Remarks on the National Homeownership Strategy', White House, 5 June 1995

Coates, John M. and Herbert, Joe, 'Endogenous steroids and financial risk taking on a London trading floor', April 2008

Cobb-Clark, Deborah A., Kassenboehmer Sonja K. and Schurer, Stefanie, 'Healthy Habits: The Connection between Diet, Exercise and the Locus of Control', Melbourne Institute Working Paper No. 15, available at SSRN, August 2012

Cox, Christopher, 'Testimony Concerning the Role of Federal Regulators: Lessons from the Credit Crisis for the Future of Regulation', 23 October 2008

Cranfield University, 'Female FTSE Index and Report 2010'

Cuomo A. M., 'No Rhyme or Reason: the "Heads I Win, Tails You Lose" Bank Bonus Culture', State of New York 2009

Davies of Abersoch, Lord, 'Women on Boards', February 2011

Elson, Charles and Ferrere Craig, 'Executive Superstars, Peer Groups and Over-Compensation – Cause, Effect and Solution', Available at SSRN, 7 August 2010

Engel, Robin S., Corsaro Nicholas and Skubak Tillyer, Marie, 'Evaluation of the Cincinnati Initiative to Reduce Violence (CIRV)', University of Cincinnati Policing Institute, 20 October 2010

Erkens, David, Hung, Mingyi and Matos, Pedro, 'Corporate Governance in the 2007–2008 Financial Crisis: Evidence from Financial Institutions Worldwide', *Journal of Corporate Finance*, vol. 18, January 2012

Fahlenbrach, R. and Stulz, R., 'Bank CEO Incentives and the Credit Crisis', Swiss Finance Institute, Research Paper Series No. 9–27

Favara, Marta, 'The Cost of Acting "Girly": Gender Stereotypes and Educational Choices', *Institute for the Study of Labor Discussion Paper No. 7037*, November 2012

Federal Deposit Insurance Corporation and the Bank of England, 'Resolving Globally Active Systemically Important Financial Institutions', Jointly published paper, 10 December 2012

Ferrary, Michel, 'CAC 40: Les Enteprises feminisées résistent-elles mieux à la crise boursière?', Ceram Business School, 2008

Friedman, Milton 'The Social Responsibility of Business is to Increase its Profits', *New York Times Magazine*, 13 September 1970

Gray, John, 'After Social Democracy: Politics, Capitalism and the Common Life', Demos Paper 1996

Haldane, Andrew, 'Rethinking the Financial Network', speech delivered at the Financial Student Association, Amsterdam, April 2009

– –, 'Small Lessons from a Big Crisis', Remarks at the Federal Reserve Bank of Chicago 45th Annual Conference 'Reforming Financial Regulation', 8 May 2009

– –, 'The $100 Billion Question', Comments given at the Institute of Regulation & Risk, Hong Kong, 30 March 2010, Bank of England, 2010

– –, 'Capital Discipline', speech to the American Economic Institute, Denver, 9 January 2011

– –, 'The Short Long', speech to the 29th Société Universitaire Européene de Recherches Financières Colloquium: New Paradigms in Money and Finance?, Brussels May 2011

– –, 'Control rights (and wrongs)', Wincott Memorial Lecture, Westminster, London, 24 October 2011

– –, 'The Dog and the Frisbee', speech given at the Federal Reserve Bank of Kansas City's 36th economic policy symposium, 'The Changing Policy Landscape', Jackson Hole, Wyoming, 31 August 2012

Huizinga, Harry, and Laeven, Luc, 'Bank Valuation and Regulatory Forbearance during a Financial Crisis', European Banking Center Discussion Paper No. 2009-17, March 2011

Kay, John, 'The Kay Review of UK Equity Markets and Long-Term Decision Making', UK Department for Business, Innovation and Skills, July 2011

Keizer, Kees, Lindenberg, Siegwart and Steg, Linda, 'The Spreading of Disorder', *Science* vol. 322, December 2008

Kirkpatrick, G., 'The Corporate Governance Lessons from the Financial Crisis,' OECD, 11 February 2009

Large, Sir Andrew, 'Financial Stability Oversight – Past and Present', speech to the London School of Economics, January 2004

– –, 'Financial Stability: Managing Liquidity Risk in a Global System', 28 November 2005

Lewis, Michael, 'The Man who Crashed the World', *Vanity Fair*, August 2009

Lucas, Robert, 'Econometric Policy Evaluation: A Critique', in *The Phillips Curve and Labor Markets*, Carnegie-Rochester Conference Series on Public Policy, 1 (New York: American Elsevier, 1976)

MacKenzie, D., 'Long-Term Capital Management and the Sociology of Arbitrage', *Economy and Society*, August 2003

McKinsey & Co, 'Women Matter: Gender Diversity, a Corporate Performance Driver', 2008

Miller, E. K. and Cohen, J. D., 'An integrative theory of prefrontal cortex function', Annual Review of Neuroscience (Stanford, 2001)

Miller, Marcus, Weller, Paul and Zhang, Lei, 'Moral Hazard and the US Stock Market: Analyzing the Greenspan Put', *Royal Economic Society Journal*, vol. 112, 2002

Minsky, Hyman P., 'Financial Instability Revisited: the Economics of Disaster', Prepared for the Board of Governors of the Federal Reserve System, 1964

Mozilo, Angelo R., 'The American Dream of Homeownership: from Cliché to Mission', John T. Dunlop Lecture, 4 February 2003

Morck, Randall, Shliefer, Andrei and Vishny, Robert, 'Alternative Mechanisms for Corporate Control', *American Economic Review*, September 1989

Munro, Geoffrey and Ditto, Peter, 'Biased assimilation, attitude polarization, and affect in reactions to stereotype-relevant scientific information', *Personality and Social Psychology Bulletin*, 1997

NIESR, 'Employment and Earnings in the Finance Sector: a Gender Analysis', 2009

Olsen, Robert, 'Implications of Herding Behavior' *Financial Analysts Journal*, July/August, 1996

Partnoy, Frank and Eisinger, Jesse, 'What's Inside America's Banks?', *Atlantic Magazine*, January/February 2013

Post, Thierry, van den Assem, Martijn J., Baltussen, Guido and Thaler, Richard, 'Deal or No Deal? Decision Making under Risk in a Large-Payoff Game Show', *American Economic Review*, 2008

Rajan, Raghuram, 'Has Financial Development Made the World Riskier?', Kansas City Federal Reserve Annual Symposium, Jackson Hole, Wyoming, August 2005

Rhee, Robert, 'The Decline of Investment Banking: Preliminary Thoughts on the Evolution of the Industry 1996–2008,' *Journal of Business and Technology Law*, 2010, vol. 5, no. 1

Roubini, Nouriel, 'The U.S. and Global Outlook', IMF Seminar Washington, D.C., 7 September 2006

Sapienza, Paolo, Zingales, Luigi and Maestripieri, Dario, 'Gender differences in financial risk aversion and career choices are affected by testosterone', *PNAS*, 24 August, 2009

Searle, A., 'Group Psychology, valuable lessons from our "new-fangled" subject', *Psychology Review*, 1966

Shefrin, Hersh and Statman, Meir, 'Behavioral Finance in the Financial Crisis: Market Efficiency, Minsky, and Keynes', Santa Clara University, November 2011

Soros, George, 'Theory of Reflexivity', MIT, 26 April 1994

Stringham, Edward, 'The Emergence of the London Stock Exchange as a Self-Policing Club', *Journal of Private Enterprise*, vol. 17, no. 2, Spring 2002

Taleb, Nassim Nicholas., 'End Bonuses for Bankers', *New York Times*, 7 November 2011

Treasury Select Committee, ninth report, 2010–11

Treasury Select Committee, tenth report, 2009–10

Tuckett, David, 'Addressing the Psychology of Financial Markets', IPPR, May 2009

Turner, Adair, 'What do Banks do, What should they do and What Public Policies are needed to Ensure Best Results for the Real Economy?' Cass Business School, 17 March 2010

– –, Mansion House Speech, 21 September 2010

Tversky, Amos and Kahneman, Daniel, 'Judgment under Uncertainty: Heuristics and Biases', *Science, New Series*, vol. 185, no. 4157 27, September, 1974

Valukas, Anton R., 'Chapter 11 Case No. 08-13555, re: Lehman Brothers Holdings Inc.' United States Bankruptcy Court Southern District of New York, 11 March 2010

Wilson, Nick and Altanlar, Ali, 'Director Characteristics, Gender Balance and Insolvency Risk: An empirical study', unpublished study, Leeds University Business School, May 2009

Periodicals

Reference was made to various editions of the following newspapers, magazines, journals and official reports:

9/11 Commission Report
Bloomberg News
Atlantic Magazine
The Economist
Financial Crisis Inquiry Commission, 'Final Report of the National Commission on the Causes of the Financial and Economic Crisis in the United States'
Financial Services Authority, 'The Failure of the Royal Bank of Scotland: Financial Services Authority Board Report'
Financial Times
Guardian
Hansard
Independent
New Yorker
New York Times
Daily Telegraph
The Times
Slate Magazine
Sunday Times
Prospect Magazine
Wall Street Journal

Books

Ahamed, Liaquat, *Lords of Finance: 1929, The Great Depression, and the Bankers who Broke the World* (London: Penguin Press, 2010)
Akerlof, George and Shiller, Robert, *Animal Spirits: How Human Psychology Drives the Economy, and Why It Matters for Global Capitalism* (Princeton: Princeton University Press, 2010)
Ariely, Dan *Predictably Irrational: The Hidden Forces that Shape our Decisions* (London: HarperCollins, 2010)

Babiak, Paul and Hare, Robert, *Snakes in Suits: When Psychopaths go to Work* (London: HarperCollins, 2006)

Balen, Malcolm, *A Very English Deceit* (London: Fourth Estate, 2002)

Bernstein, Peter, *Against the Gods: The Remarkable Story of Risk* (New York: John Wiley & Sons, 1998)

Bootle, Roger, *The Trouble with Markets: Saving Capitalism from Itself* (London: Nicholas Brealey Publishing, 2009)

de Botton, Alain, *Status Anxiety* (London: Hamish Hamilton, 2004)

Brooks, David, *The Social Animal* (New York: Random House, 2011)

Carter, Graydon (ed.), *The Great Hangover: 21 Tales of the New Recession* (New York: Harper Perennial, 2010)

Chapman, Meyrick, *Don't Be Fooled Again* (Gosport: Pearson Education Limited, 2010)

Coates, John, *The Hour Between Dog and Wolf: Risk-Taking, Gut Feelings and the Biology of Boom and Bust* (London: Fourth Estate, 2012)

Darley, John and Latané, Bibb, *Bystander Intervention in Emergencies: diffusion of Responsibility* (New York: Columbia University Press, 1968)

Eichengreen, B., *Golden Fetters* (Oxford: Oxford University Press, 1996)

The Epicurean Dealmaker, www.epicureandealmaker.blogspot.com

Faber, David, *And then the Roof Caved In: How Wall Street's Greed and Stupidity Brought Capitalism to its Knees* (New York: John Wiley & Sons, 2009)

Ferguson, Niall, *The Ascent of Money* (London: Penguin Press, 2008)

Galbraith, John K., *The Great Crash 1929* (London: Hamish Hamilton, 1955)

Gray, John, *Gray's Anatomy* (London: Allen Lane, 2009)

Harford, Tim, *Adapt: Why Success Always Starts With Failure* (London: Little, Brown, 2011)

Kahneman, Daniel, *Thinking Fast and Slow* (London: Allen Lane, 2011)

Keynes, John M., *The General Theory of Money, Interest and Employment* (London: Macmillan & Co., 1936)

King, Stephen D, *Losing Control: The Emerging Threats to Western Prosperity* (New Haven: Yale University Press, 2011)

Knight, Frank H., *Risk, Uncertainty and Profit* (Boston: Houghton Mifflin Co., 1921)

Leeson, Nick, *Rogue Trader* (London: Little, Brown, 1996)

Lo, Andrew, 'Fear Greed and the Financial Crisis', in the *Handbook on Systemic Risk* (Cambridge University Press, 2011)

Lodge, Guy and Seldon, Anthony, *Brown at 10* (London: Biteback Publishing, 2010)

McDonald, Lawrence, *A Colossal Failure of Common Sense: The Incredible Inside Story of the Collapse of Lehman Brothers* (New York: Crown Business, 2010)

Mackay, Charles, *Extraordinary Popular Delusions and The Madness of Crowds* (1841)

McLean, Bethany, and Nocera, Joe, *All the Devils are Here: The Hidden History of the Financial Crisis* (London: Portfolio Hardcover, 2010)

McNeill, William, *Keeping Together in Time: Dance and Drill in Human History* (Harvard: Harvard University Press, 1995)

McRaney, David, *You are not so Smart: Why Your Memory is Mostly Fiction, Why You Have Too Many Friends on Facebook, and 46 Other Ways You're Deluding Yourself* (Oxford: Oneworld Publications, 2012)

Mason, Paul, *Meltdown* (London: Verso, 2009)

Norberg, Johan, *Financial Fiasco: How America's Infatuation with Home Ownership and Easy Money Created the Economic Crisis* (Washington DC: Cato Institute, 2010)

Oakeshott, Michael, *Rationalism in Politics and Other Essays* (London: Methuen, 1962)

Parker, David and Stacey, Ralph, *Chaos, Management and Economics* (London: IEA, 1994)

Peston, Robert, *Brown's Britain* (London: Short Books, 2005)

Pinker, Steven, *The Blank Slate: The Modern Denial of Human Nature* (London: Viking, 2002)

Plato, *Republic*

Prechter, Robert, *The Wave Principle of Human Social Behavior* (Gainesville, Georgia: New Classics Library, 1999)

Rajan, R. G., *Fault Lines: How Hidden Fractures Still Threaten the World Economy* (Princeton: Princeton University Press, 2010)

Reinhart, Carmen and Rogoff, Kenneth S., *This Time is Different – Eight Centuries of Financial Folly* (Princeton: Princeton University Press, 2009)

Roth, Louise M., *Selling Women Short: Gender Inequality on Wall Street* (Princeton: Princeton University Press, 2006)

Schelling, Thomas C., *Micromotives and Macrobehavior: Fels Lectures on Public Policy Analysis* (New York: W. W. Norton, 1978)

Shakespeare, William, *King Lear*

Skidelsky, Robert, *Keynes: The Return of the Master* (London: Penguin Press, 2010)

Smith, Adam, *The Theory of Moral Sentiments* (London: Penguin Classics, 2010)

Sorkin, Andrew R., *Too Big to Fail: Inside the Battle to Save Wall Street* (London: Penguin Press, 2010)

Tett, Gillian, *Fool's Gold* (London: Little, Brown, 2009)

Thompson, Venetia, *Gross Misconduct* (London: Simon & Schuster, 2010)

Wight, Robin, *The Day the Pigs Refused to Be Driven to Market: Advertising and the Consumer Revolution* (London: Random House, 1974)

Wolmar, Christian, *Fire and Steam: A New History of the Railways in Britain* (London: Atlantic Books, 2008)

Polling for this book was conducted by YouGov

INDEX